Commedia dell'Arte

A companion to John Rudlin's best-selling *Commedia dell'Arte: An Actor's Handbook*, this book covers both the history and professional practice of commedia dell'arte companies from 1568 to the present day. Indispensable for both the beginner and the professional, it contains historical and contemporary company case histories, details on company organisation, and tips on practical stagecraft.

It enables the reader to understand how successful commedia dell'arte companies function, and how we can learn from past and current practice to create a lively and dynamic form of theatre.

The many practical resources on offer include tips on:

- writing a scenario
- mask making
- building a stage
- designing a touring backdrop
- costume
- music

and much, much more.

John Rudlin is a freelance theatre director, playwright and author. His books include *Jacques Copeau* (1986), *Copeau: Texts on Theatre* (1990), and *Commedia dell'Arte: An Actor's Handbook* (1994).

Olly Crick is a drama lecturer at Hereford College of Art and Design. He has performed Commedia dell'Arte with 'Unfortunati' and is an associate of The Mask Studio and Ce----

Commedia dell'Arte

A Handbook for Troupes

John Rudlin and Olly Crick

London and New York

First published 2001
by Routledge
11 New Fetter Lane, London EC4P 4EE

Simultaneously published in the USA and Canada
by Routledge
29 West 35th Street, New York, NY 10001

Routledge is an imprint of the Taylor & Francis Group

© 2001 John Rudlin and Olly Crick

Designed and typeset in Avant Garde and Palatino by
Florence Production Ltd, Stoodleigh, Devon
Printed and bound in Great Britain by
Biddles Ltd, Guildford and King's Lynn

British Library Cataloguing in Publication Data
A catalogue record for this book is available from the British Library

Library of Congress Cataloging in Publication Data
Rudlin, John.
  Commedia dell'arte: a handbook for troupes/John Rudlin
  and Olly Crick.
     p.   cm.
  Includes bibliographical references and index.
  1. Commedia dell'arte—History and criticism.   2. Improvisation
  (Acting).   I. Crick, Olly, 1960- .   II. Title.
  PQ4155.R828 2001
  792.2'3'09—dc21   00-046017

ISBN 0-415-20408-9 (hbk)
ISBN 0-415-20409-7 (pbk)

For
Pernille, Holly, Daisy, Taran,
Kaïa and Rose

■ Contents

Illustrations

▪ Preface

This book is intended as a companion to my *Commedia dell'Arte, an Actor's Handbook*. The intention of that book was to help 'give *commedia dell'arte* back to the actor in the hope that it may again provide one of the base languages of a theatrical lingua franca.' It was also founded on a personal conviction that 'if there is to be a regeneration of the theatrical medium in the next century, it must come via the re-empowering of the performer rather than the continued hegemony of the playwright and director.' We are now into that century, and the signs are encouraging: sufficient young, and some not so young, performers have been (literally) acting on the advice given in that book to tempt the publishers into allowing the indulgence of a sequel. This new volume was inspired by a review of the first one in *Theatre Research International* (Vol. 20, no. 2, p. 165) which chastised me for not going far enough, wanting to know more about the interaction of the Masks, not just their individual actions:

> The vital interest of the *commedia* lies in the rhythms of each mask and in its rhythmical relationship to others. These rhythms have repercussions for the use of the playing space and help create interesting and meaningful choreography on stage. . . . Rudlin offers this book as an introduction to the individual and group study of *commedia*. It is to be hoped the main course arrives soon.

For my part I hope that appetite has not been dulled during the seven subsequent years of culinary preparation. There has been much research and experimentation necessary in order to respond to the reviewer's demand. This work has been undertaken mainly at Centre Sélavy in rural France, where up to three workshops have been run annually for the past seven years with a teaching staff comprising Amanda Speed, Olly Crick and myself. Collaborating with Olly has been particularly valuable since he comes from the Carlo Boso school of training, which I perhaps undervalued in *An Actor's Handbook*. He also trained and performed with Barry Grantham in England

and has connections with many practising or recently disbanded Commedia companies, as well as with active individual practitioners, which stem from his backgound as a performer. It is to be hoped that the reader will find that his experience complements mine (as playwright, director and former academic). Part 3 of this book, 'Forming, Training and Performing', results from our workshop collaboration, Part 2, 'Commedia Now' is the product of his primary research, and Part 1, *Commedia dell'arte all'improvviso*, was put together by me from secondary sources in the Sélavy library.

Our working titles for these sections were 'how', 'now' and 'then'. The intention, as with *An Actor's Handbook*, has been to attempt to link the original Commedia of the street performers and the 'golden age' troupes which followed, with recent contemporary practice – without passing through the sentimental excesses of the Baroque and Rococo periods, the peculiarities of Pantomime, and the distortions of the Grotesque. Our focus, as the title implies, has been the itinerant troupe at work, and in Part 3 we attempt to put together the experience of past and present in a way that is directly assimilable by new groups, whether in educational, amateur, semi-professional or professional environments.

What we have done in the first two parts is first of all to piece together the records of the internationally renowned troupes leading up to the turn of the sixteenth century and beyond to try to give a coherent glimpse of what their lives were like, not because they were internationally renowned, but simply because theirs are the only records we have. Nobody wrote about the little people, and most of the time we don't even have their requests for licence to perform, since their offerings were not 'legit'. We don't even know the names of the companies (if they had one), let alone those of the actors that performed in them. The present historical is something we have been able to address, though, and our trawl through the small companies of the present day and the, sometimes painful, notation of their struggles to survive, should at least stand the scholars of the future in better stead. Our selection of troupes is just that and no more: to track down the information we have included has been exhausting, but we know it is not exhaustive.

Ideally a second edition of *An Actor's Handbook* would have coincided with the publication of the present volume, but such luxuries are rare in the world of modern-day publishing. Such a revision would have allowed a lot more information to be offered on individual Masks – for example, the division of the Lovers into younger and older pairings, the distinction of the role of Franceschina from that of the Courtesan on the one hand and Colombina on the other, further separation of Pantalone from Il Magnifico, clarification of the difference between the masked and the white-faced Pedrolino, and discussion of the whole issue of the 'Southern' Masks,

Pulcinella, Coviello, Cola, etc. There is also material in that book which now properly belongs in this – the monographs on the San Francisco Mime Troupe and TNT, for example. In their place an entry on the work of Rheinhardt would have made the picture of early twentieth-century directorial attempts at the resurrection of Commedia more complete.

Some conventions are carried forward from *An Actor's Handbook* which need to be restated: the use of *'commedia dell'arte'* as Italian, and 'Commedia' (as a species of comedy) as English; 'scenario' as being received into English, but not *'canovaccio'*; *'lazzi'* left as Italian; 'Mask' when referring to a Commedia character (whether masked or not), 'mask' when referring to the physical object; 'Zanni' when referring to the Mask, *'zanni'* when meaning the type. Further, all the Masks are referred to by their original Italian names, not their French or English equivalents, thus 'Arlecchino', not 'Arlequin' or 'Harlequin' and, in particular 'Colombina', not 'Colombine' or 'Columbine', and certainly not 'Columbina' – who never existed anywhere. The Masks are not italicised, however, since that attribute becomes wearing in a long work. Words printed in bold, for example *'capocomico'*, signify that there is a full entry under that name to be found elsewhere in that part of the book.

John Rudlin

■ Acknowledgements

We would like to thank the following for permission to reproduce the various photographs used: Sylvie Châtillon, David Corio, Michael Rothman, Pierre Ruaud.

Our thanks are also due to Tony Addison, John Achorn, John Apicella, Catt Avery, John Ballenger, Geoff Beale, John Beedell, Roberto Bifferini, Paul Bongiovanni, Steve Bueschner, John Broadbent, Mike Casey, Mike Chase, Judith Chaffee, Anna Cottis, Andy Crooks, Howard Gayton, John and Angela Glennard, Barry Grantham, Richard Hitchcock, Didi Hopkins, Aaron Johnson, Peter Jordan, Ninian Kinnear-Wilson, Jim and Marilyn Letchworth, Frank Lotito, James MacDonald, Beth McMillan, Ernesto Maldonaldo, 'Newman', Alex Newman, 'Nito', Joan Schirle, Michele Schultz, Toby Sedgewick, Ritchie Smith, Colleen Sollars, Amanda Speed, Todd and Allison, Donna Yarborough, and the Yahoo Commedia Club, for information supplied.

We are also continually appreciative of the work done by our students, both in England and France – without them many of the ideas in this book could not have been researched.

Finally we would like to extend our gratitude to anyone who ever taught us anything about *commedia dell'arte* but whose influence, as with all the best teaching, has been forgotten.

Part One

Commedia dell'arte all'improvviso

This section is composed of monographs on the leading Italian *commedia dell'arte* companies from 1568 (the earliest mention of any of them) to 1622 (when Richelieu became a cardinal and royal requests for the presence of itinerant Italian troupes in France came to an end). This period can be considered as the golden one of improvisation before Commedia became increasingly text-based. As well as Italy and France, Spain is also taken into account, but not other countries where Commedia is known to have had an occasional presence, including Bavaria, England, Russia, etc. One must beware, though, of assuming that the names of European countries indicated the same territories, or even nationalities, that they do today. Italy, after the 1559 Treaty of Cateau Cambrésis between France and Spain brought to an end sixty years of attempted French domination, was composed of three republics – Venice, Genoa and Lucca; the Papal State – which extended all the way from Rome up to Bologna; Milan, Naples and Sicily – which were ruled directly by the Austro-Spanish Empire of the Habsburgs; Ferrara and Tuscany – which were more or less Habsburg protectorates, and Parma and Mantua – which were protected by the French. Savoy, under the bright young star Emmanuel Phillibert, who had recently humiliated the French at the battle of St Quentin – was for a while able to do its own thing. France meanwhile was torn apart by repeated religious civil wars and held together by string in the form of the machinations of the Queen Mother, the Florentine Catherine de' Medici, while her three

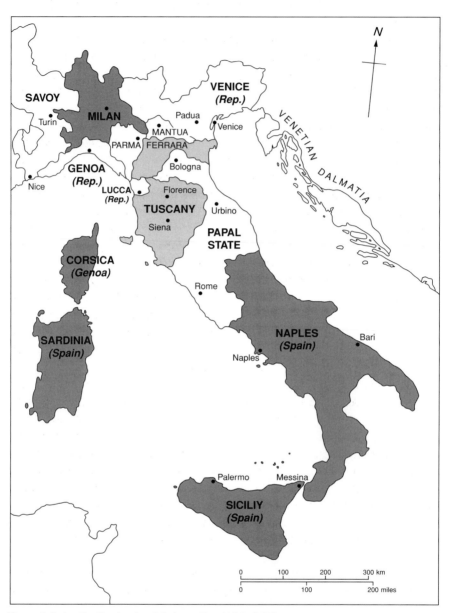

Figure 1 Italy after the treaty of Cateau Cambrésis (1559)

hapless sons, Francis II, Charles IX and Henri III, bungled the kingship job one after another.

Commedia dell'arte evolved from its humble origins into being *the* entertainment form of its epoch within the twenty years prior to the period under consideration. Suddenly it was able to pass over existing religious and cultural borders, as well as the Alps and the Pyrenees, in the way that Renaissance and Mannerist painters had done before. The same right of passage was also afforded to musicians, with wandering Flemish composers, for example, much in evidence in Italy. Culture contact was thus not limited as to Muse or to direction: this was, above all, the time of the itinerant virtuoso, in whatever art form, and such individuals were able to transcend even the ravages of war as they went from one court to another, or one artistic centre to another, regardless of their national or class origins. The problem with Commedia though, as always with theatre, was that one virtuoso was not enough to perform a play: how could several band together in a way that enhanced rather than limited their renown – and thus their earning potential?

Improvisation lies at the heart of the answer. *Commedia dell'arte all' improvviso* was not an isolated curiosity in sixteenth-century Italy: *cantatore improvviso* was also, for example, an accepted profession. Professional performers discovered that the craft which bound them together was the ability to improvise collectively in public. As for amateurs, since the nobility were excluded from the public platforms of both theatre and politics, they found consolation in attending closed literary academies, of which there were nearly 700. There they would compare classical manuscripts, suggest new readings or interpretations, decipher inscriptions on medals and coins, and sit in judgement on Latin odes or debate the propriety of a phrase. Unfortunately they also 'tended to bestow on an unprofitable pedantry the honours of real learning'.[1] To enliven their dull and pretentious proceedings they also turned to the excitements of improvisation and invited poets to deliver impromptu Petrachan-style odes and sonnets; other *all' improvisso* games included contests in mock oratory on unprepared topics – speeches which must have borne some resemblance to the sonorous *sproloquio* of Il Dottore.

As well as being used by the new generation of *comici dell'arte* to legitimise the hitherto street art of improvising, the literary academies are of further interest to the study of Commedia because many of the major troupes emulated them when choosing their names. Most academies opted for an appellation with, as they saw it, deliberate Socratic irony, for example the Lunatici of Naples. Other preferred cryptic bathos, such as the most famous of them, the Accademia della Cruca, (The Academy of Bran), which took a sieve as its motif – meaning that learning, after they had sifted it, was as pure as it could be. The names of Commedia troupes such as the Gelosi, the Confidenti, the Accessi, the Dediosi, the Fedeli, the Uniti, the Affezionati, the Constanti, all emulated the nomenclature of these learned societies, thus indicating, they hoped, a communality of cultural purpose between the world of academe and the *arte* of the professional comedian. There also grew up an elitist rivalry between troupes similar to that which existed between the literary organisations, a more or less friendly struggle to be *primus inter pares*. This concept of 'first among equals' extended to the status of individuals within the troupes; of particular note is that the academies afforded equality to their female members, and actresses were similarly accepted into *commedia dell'arte* companies. Isabella Andreini, for example, was not only a leading member of the Gelosi, but was also elected to the academy of the **Intenti** in her home town of Padua. She also published two books of poems, and a pastoral, *La Mirtilla*. Tasso wrote sonnets to her. Other companies, such as the early **Confidenti** and the **Dediosi**, had a woman as *capocomico*.

In most troupes, as we shall see, there was, further, a desire to emulate the internal democracy by which such *belles lettres* societies were run. However, actors tend to be second only to chickens in their desire to establish a pecking order – as Orazio Nobili said of Domenico Bruni, the leader of the later **Confidenti**, 'he holds the position of best among betters'.[2] Nevertheless, the co-operative intention, at least, of the *comici* should not be doubted, and the requirement for brotherly love was written into the earliest extant mutual contract (Padua 1546), which determined that ` . . . in order such a company shall survive in fraternal love', it would ` . . . without any hatred, rancour and dissolution, make and observe with love, as is customary among good and faithful companions, all articles written hereunder . . .'[3]

If it was necessary to legislate for such fraternalism, however, it may be that experience had already shown that it was not that easy to sustain when faced with the rigours of touring. Sisterly love, as the first actresses made their appearance on stage in the last quarter of the *cinquecento*, seems to have been an even rarer quality as prima and seconda donnas vied for recognition. In the audience, too, women had to struggle for their place, but not with each other. When necessary, royalty solved the problem of the propriety of women attending Commedia by commanding separate ladies only performances in private chambers. For the *hoi polloi* the answer was often segregation: for example, public theatres in Spain had places set aside exclusively for women – a gallery called a *cazuela*, a *jaula de las mugeres*, or a *corredor de las mugeres*. They had their own doorkeeper, but the doors were not always kept successfully shut. A typical complaint comes from Seville in 1627 'that women occupied seats in the

Figure 2 Isabella Andreini. Frontispiece to her *La Mirtilla*, Verona, 1588.

first and second rows of the *sillas* and *bancos* among the men, and likewise in other parts of the theatre, from which great scandal resulted.'[4] An *alguacil* (peace-officer) was always stationed in the *cazuela* (a.k.a. a round stew pan with close-fitting lid intended to steam food slowly) to keep the women within bounds since otherwise 'they pelted the actors with fruit, orange-peel, cucumbers, or anything found at hand, to show their disapproval, and generally came provided with rattles, whistles or keys, which they used unsparingly.'[5]

In France, ladies can hardly be said to have visited the only public theatre, the Hôtel de Bourgogne until Richelieu began to take an active interest in theatre in around 1635. Women did go to the theatre but c'était surtout des femmes perdues. . . . Les honnêtes femmes n'allaient point à l'Hôtel de Bourgogne et n'y pouvaient aller, affrayées par les insolens et par l'immoralité des spectacles; mais leur abstention même était un mal et laissait le champ libre à l'immoralité comme aux insolences. (It was above all women who had lost their reputation who went to the Hôtel de Bourgogne . . . honest women didn't go there because of the impropriety and immorality of the shows; but their very absence left the door open to immorality and impropriety.)[6]

Commedia needs lost souls (of both sexes), as well as honest ones: in it the refined is defined by contact with the unrefined, and the indelicate becomes delectable as a relief from the delicate. The top companies, to whom we now turn, were the ones that were able to keep their feet in the *piazza* whilst their heads were in the *palazzo*.

■ ■ ■

Zan Ganassa
(1568-1610)

Whilst, as we have seen, some 'golden age' Commedia troupes sought to create a company image by adopting a collective cognomen, other performers remained happy to receive their share of the take from a boss whose name and fame stood for them all. As far as is ascertainable, Alberto Naseli, known usually only by his stage name Zan Ganassa, was the first such *capocomico* to take a Commedia troupe to Paris. Of his previous work in Italy, little is known, except that he probably came from Bergamo itself, thus having more right than most to call himself 'Zan' (a diminutive of 'Zanni', unless one argues that 'Zanni' is a diminutive of 'Zan' . . .). On stage he certainly spoke in Bergamese dialect. His Magnifico was Stefanello Bottarga and his first *innamorata* Vincenza Armani. Tomasso Garzoni wrote of her that:

> Of the learned Vicenza I cannot speak, but by imitating the eloquent style of Cicero, she has placed the comic art in competition with oratory . . . [and] in part by her admirable beauty, in part by her indescribable grace, has built an increased following for herself.[7]

Together (one assumes, though only Ganassa is mentioned) they played at Mantua in 1568. Vincenza then left the company and shortly after took the wearing of her role as a lover to the extreme by taking poison. A funeral oratory written by her lover, **Adriano Valerini**, praises her cooking, embroidery, Latin, musicianship, composition and singing of madrigals, sculpture in wax and, of course, her acting – in three different styles: comedy, tragedy and pastoral. She can be credited as being the first of the refined, educated female lovers.

Ganassa next appears as part of the festivities in honour of the marriage of Lucrezia d'Este in Ferrara in 1570. It is this performance that must have prompted Charles IX to invite Ganassa and his *compagnons italiens* to Paris in 1571 as part of the celebrations for his royal entry into the city with his bride. After playing for their royal patron, the company began giving public

Figure 3 Stefanello Bottarga as Pantalone, from the 'Recueil Fossard', a collection of images of *commedia dell'arte* put together by a musician at the court of Louis XIV. Clearly his Panatalone was a 'Magnifico', evidence that the terms were interchangeable in the sixteenth century.

performances in August, probably at the only public theatre in Paris, the Hôtel de Bourgogone.

Exporting *commedia dell'arte* was not, however, to prove that simple. On 15 September, the Parlement de Paris issued an *arrêt* forbidding the Italians to play again in public on pain of 'prison and corporal punishment'. The fact that the actors had letters patent from the king and personal permission from the *prévôt de marchandes* was to be ignored. The *prévôt* was told to give no more such permissions in future, and residents of Paris were forbidden to attend performances or face a ten *livre* fine. A second *arrêt* was issued a month later, which would seem to indicate that performances had not completely stopped. Ganassa and his troupe probably over-wintered in

France, but without performing. Parlement's prohibitions were not a case of censorship following on scandal – Ganassa was known for his sense of decorum and being 'prolific only in absurd and tasteful witticisms, and so modest that every modest spectator could be much delighted by him and truly hold him in affection'.[8] He was actually praised, albeit posthumously, by Father Giovanni Domenico Ottonelli in his *Della Christiana Moderatione del Teatro*[9] for providing performances 'free of all obscenity'. It was rather that, being the first Italians to play in Paris, Ganassa and his well-disciplined company had not only stumbled unwittingly into a power struggle between king and Parlement, but also trodden on the toes of a vested interest. It was claimed they were charging three to six *sols* for tickets, 'an excessive sum never before levied for such purpose and an imposition on the poor',[10] but is doubtful that the Parlement was acting solely out of consideration for its less affluent citizens, rather responding to the complaints of the Confrèrie de la Passion. This once religious brotherhood, no longer able to function as the society in charge of the now suppressed mystery plays, had been granted, in 1548, the sole privilege of theatrical performance in Paris 'under its name and to its profit'. Since the Hôtel de Bourgogne was the only public theatre, and the Confrèrie owned it, this normally afforded them a monopoly. The 'Brothers' set the price of admission, took the box office and had total say over the programme. The Italians, thinking themselves 'secure in their royal protection, refused to submit to these conditions, and were thus subjected to the rulings of the Parlement'.[11] A more sinister rumour is that that the Queen Mother, Catherine de' Medici, and her second son Henri, were at this time plotting the massacre of leading Huguenots and had only invited the Italian actors over as a diversion to cover their activities. Charles IX, who had had a Protestant nurse, and whose chief advisor, Admiral Coligny, was a Huguenot, and who was currently arranging for his sister Marguerite de Valois to marry the Huguenot Henri de Navarre, was suitably distracted.

Zan Ganassa clearly learnt a lot from this experience, if not as an actor, then as a manager and entrepreneur. Having been the first to take *commedia dell'arte* to Paris, he now put French politics behind him and transplanted his troupe to Madrid. There he avoided falling foul of the Cofradiás[12] by contributing 600 *reales* to building his own theatre in the Corral de la Pachecha in 1574. Spanish actors, up to this time, owned their own staging which they set up for each performance. Ganassa's was a permanent stage with a tiled roof. He agreed to be paid back ten *reales* for each of sixty performances and to give two benefits for the local Cofrades. Ticket prices were half a *real* to get in, plus one for a seat, or a quarter for a place on a bench. One can estimate the value of a *real* at this time from the fact that

Ganassa paid his two Spanish musicians two *reales* a day. He repeated this kind of investment in 1582 when he helped the Cofrades in the building of the second of Madrid's two permanent theatres, the Corral del Principe, with a gift of twenty-five *escudos* plus a considerable loan.

Ganassa's season in Seville in 1575 drew such crowds to the Corral de Don Juan that there were petitions for the prohibition of his performances. It was reported that people were slipping away from their work, as a result of which the Audiencia ordered Ganassa only to perform on public holidays. By now he was used to such bans, and was careful to let the dust settle before performing again in Seville in 1578.

His shows were not always crowded out, however: there is a record (27 August 1579) of his refusing to play to a small house in Madrid, and returning ticket money to such spectators as had turned up. Otherwise, with the exception of a few days at Corpus Christi, when he was performing to King Philip II in Toledo, he played twice or three times a week in Madrid, in the Corrals of the Puenta and the Pachecha, from June of that year until the middle of the following February. In March he appeared in Valladolid, and continued there until September. Then the municipal authorities, after much debate, ordered him to leave 'as he was causing idleness among the population and was taking too much money away from the city.'[13]

From 30 November 1581, with the exception of two sets of performances, one 'en casa del Comisario general' and the other, as we shall see, at Guadalajara, he acted almost daily in the Teatro del la Cruz until the end of February 1582. But, on the 27th of that month, records there are interrupted by the entry 'No represento Ganasa a causa de su prison'. For someone used to treading the fine line of acceptability in foreign lands, such loss of liberty must have come as something of a shock. His offence is not known, but it may have been debt – he himself was currently owed over 3,200 *scudi* by Pietro de' Medici and may have had to borrow in turn to keep himself from a cash-flow crisis. It is believed that after this hiccup he sensibly spent some time touring in Portugal.

Apart from that one *faux pas*, Juan Ganasa (as he was known) became so popular in Spain as to enable him to settle in semi-permanent exile. He did not only perform *commedie dell'arte*:

> On several occasions he and his company acted religious plays *(autos)* on Corpus Christi Day and for these productions Ganassa may have drawn upon his knowledge of Italian stage machinery. It is likely that he had acquired some experience of religious drama before coming to Spain, for in Italy mystery plays and pageants were staged with even more splendour than their equivalents in Spain.[14]

At his command performance before the king and queen, Ganassa met another Italian actor, Vincenzo Botanelli (Curzio), and by 1581 they had joined forces. Also in the company were Cesare de Nobile (later with the **Dediosi**), a Giovan Pietro Paquarelo (or Pasquariello if that was his stage name and, as some people think, he invented the role), Scipone Graseli, Giulio Villanti (or Vigliante), Giacomo Portalupi and Carlo de Masi – all Italians. Stefanello Bottarga's name does not appear, though he is known to have been in Valencia in 1583 and was in charge of an *auto* in Seville in 1584. Lope de Vega, however, mentions in a letter having seen Juan Ganasa making fun of his master 'Estefanelo' during a performance in Madrid.[15] It seems likely, therefore, that Botarga was initially part of Ganassa's Spanish troupe, but then broke away. Whether Ganassa returned to Italy from time to time to recruit, or whether others like Botanelli joined him in Spain, is not known. What is certain is that he maintained the Italian-ness of the troupe and its repertoire, whilst making some concessions to Spanish for the sake of comprehensibility:

> . . . although in the beginning neither he nor his companions were much understood . . . , nonetheless he tried with gestures and the occasional word to please and provoke laughter until, having become proficient in the language, he managed to mix some Spanish words with his own Bergamese dialect so that he could always be understood.[16]

In January 1582 the company took time out to play at Guadalajara, for the festivities for the marriage of Don Rodrigo and Anne de Mendoza. Their first performance, on a Saturday night, was on a platform stage erected in a banqueting hall. As was the custom, benches were also placed on the stage for the grandees. So many of these turned up that there was no room for the actors to act, but they got through the performance somehow, and to great applause. On the Sunday night Ganassa presented another indoor show and on Monday afternoon staged a play in the courtyard 'before a great concourse of people who had come from all over Spain for these festivities. The following day he presented another play, which lasted until eight o'clock in the evening.'[17]

The troupe gave another command performance for Philip II in Toledo later in the year, and plans were made then for future work on the king's behalf. He granted Ganassa a royal licence allowing him to perform two working days a week, as well as on public holidays, thus resolving the problems he had earlier encountered with local authorities – though reducing his income somewhat. Philip, however, shortly switched his attention from

Figure 4 Possibly a representation of Zan Ganassa as 'Arlequin' with 'Zany Cornetto'. Other attributions for the series of engravings of which this is part are that the company represented is the Gelosi, the Confidenti or the Raccolti. From the 'Recueil Fossard'.

comedias to the preparation of a punitive expedition by sea, and here the light dims on Ganassa's fame – although he is known to have performed again in Seville at Corpus Christi 1583, in Madrid in December and again there in February 1584. There is a mention of his still being active in Spain in 1610.

His legacy to Spanish theatre was considerable: apart from the regularisation of theatre buildings already mentioned, and his paving the way for other Italian actors and companies (such as the **Confidenti**) to play in Spain,[18] the impact of *commedia dell'arte* on written drama was extensive. Even carnival was enlivened by the introduction of *ganasas* and *botargas*, competing masked figures on horseback. *Botargas* still exist to this day.

One last question remains not to be resolved: was Ganassa the first Arlecchino? Tradition says yes, but there is little hard evidence to support his claim against that of Tristano Martinelli. On the one hand it would have been just like Martinelli to have stolen Ganassa's idea after their paths crossed in Paris in 1571. If Arlecchino was Zan Ganassa's stage persona, then he may well be the seemingly slender figure in the *Recueil Froissard* engravings which date from that period. If it was him that first played Arlequin in

Paris, on the other hand, then Ganassa must have eaten well in Spain, for there he was renowned for his gargantuan girth and standing on his hands may have become difficult.

The Gelosi
(1568–1604)

They were one of the first, if not the first, company to assume an emblematic name like those of the literary academies, instead of simply appearing under that of the troupe's leading actor. Their name is taken from their motto: 'Virtú, Fama ed Honor ne fêr Gelosi' ('Virtue, honour and renown are only for the jealous'), implying perhaps that those qualities are for those who guard them jealously. A further interpretation, involving a less current gloss on the word, would be that as actors they were zealous to please.[19] Furthermore, like a modern production company, they also furnished themselves with a logo. Such an emblem was then known as an *impresa* – and here again the Gelosi were copying the practice of the academies. Their chosen image depicts a two-headed Janus: perhaps indicating the dual identity of the actor – or the necessity of looking in all directions in order to protect one's good name as a performer. Certainly the two leading players whose reputation became almost synonymous with the company's good name, Francesco and Isabella Andreini, were renowned for leading virtuous and honourable lives, though some of their fellow actors got into scrapes from which they may have been glad to look the other way.

The most recorded instances of Gelosi performances come from Milan, but that may simply reflect the fact that records were better kept there, or that they have been more readily uncovered. First recorded as playing during carnival in Milan 1568, the Gelosi are known to have performed in all the major towns of Northern Italy, and appear to have consciously rejected the safety net favoured by most other fashionable companies of having a single patron/protector. The Duke of Mantua, for example, seems to have attempted several times to adopt them, both severally and individually, and eventually turned to the **Accessi** instead. The Duke of Ferrara was also a constant supporter, but the Gelosi were clever enough (and good enough) to be able to avoid sole sponsorship. Retaining autonomy was clearly an astute managerial move, since it allowed them a freedom of movement which meant, for example, that they were able to visit France more frequently than any other company. The fact that they were in a position to afford such independence reflects the quality of their work and its earning power – they were as at home playing in front of crowned heads as less exalted troupes were in front of the butcher, the baker and the candlestick maker.

The Gelosi occasionally performed written plays as well as *commedie dell'arte all'improvviso*. It might almost have been to them that Shakespeare had Polonius refer when he spoke of 'the best actors in the world, either for tragedy, comedy, history, pastoral, pastoral-comical, [etc.]'. The composition of the troupe seems to have been reasonably stable compared to that of some other companies, but there were inevitable comings and goings over such an extended period, only some of which can be traced. Sometimes, also, the troupe seems to have divided, perhaps to get through a lean patch until the next 'big one' – or perhaps (in a company where everyone was a star), they simply needed time apart. At other times there were periods of collaboration with other famous troupes such as the **Uniti**. The basis of the Gelosi, however, was always what was called 'the usual ten': two *vecchi* (old men), four *innamorati* (two male and two female lovers), two *zanni*, a captain and a *servetta* (serving maid). In writing his *Bravure* (effectively his memoirs), Francesco Andreini recalls the company at its height as having included:

Pantalone	Giulio Pasquati (from Padua)
Il Dottore Graziano	Lodovico de Bianchi (from Bologna)
Zanni	Simone Basilea (from Bologna)
Francatrippe	Gabriele (?delle Haste) (from Bologna)
Innamorati	Orazio de Nobili (from Padua) and
	Adriano Valerini (from Verona)
Prima donna	Isabella Andreini
Seconda donna	Prudenzia (from Verona)
Franceschina	Silvia Roncagli (from Bergamo)

with himself playing *Capitano Spavento di Vall' Inferna*. Then, as if to prove that there is nothing usual about *commedia dell'arte*, he mentions an eleventh player, a third *vecchio*, *Zanobio*[20] – Giorlano Salimbeni (from Florence). So Andreini is certainly not giving us a company list for a specific date – no scenario would accommodate three old men – but making a conglomerate of his own best choices. One performer he does not mention, for example, is the first known leader of *i comici Gelosi*, Vittoria Piissimi, their first *prima donna*, who came and went, or rather went and occasionally came back (she was also with the **Confidenti**) after 1579. This was hardly a lapse, since, as we shall see, there was not room in the company for two prima donnas: Vittoria and Andreini's wife, Isabella.

The Gelosi's first visit to France was in 1571, probably at the invitation of Louis de Gonzaga, Duke of Nevers, in whose house in Paris they played before guests including Charles IV, Duke of Lorraine. A special performance was given at a *fête* for the English Ambassador Extraordinary, Lord Buckhurst, who allowed that 'for good mirth and handling thereof (they) deserved singular commendacion.'[21] Next they created an entertainment for the baptism of Charles-Henri de Clermont at the château of the de Brezé family in Nogent-le-Roi (130 kilometres from Paris on the other side of Chartres). There they played in front of King Charles IX, the Queen and the Queen Mother, Catherine de' Medici. It was after this that one of those temporary alliances between troupes may have taken place; **Zan Ganassa** was in Paris and the Gelosi may have returned there to join him and been subjected to the same prohibitions by Parlement against the acting in public of all 'players of farces and such like common amusements' not properly authorised, i.e. not protected by the monopoly afforded to the *Confrérie de la Passion*. The Gelosi thus found themselves on their way home, despite holding letters from the king describing them as 'les comédiens du Roi', and are most likely the Italian company which is recorded as having played with distinction in Lyon in December, prior to a chilly journey back over the Alps.

By March 1572 they were back in Milan, and remained that summer in Italy, thus avoiding one of the most unpleasant episodes in French history: the St Bartholomew's Day Massacre in Paris on 24 August. This was instigated by Catherine de' Medici and her son Henri (later to become Henri III), and was followed by similar attacks on Huguenots all over France – one tenth of the French population were Protestants at the time, and one third of the nobility. Three to four thousand Huguenots were murdered in Paris alone. The Gelosi spent the late summer and autumn in Genoa.

In 1573, the first record of them is of a collaboration in autumn with amateur *dilettanti* to give the first performance of Torquato Tasso's pastoral *Aminta* on the island of Belvedere – on the Po, near Ferrara – at a Villa belonging to the Estensi. They played before Philip II of Spain and his train, but were rewarded by 'little gain and many insults'.[22] They over-wintered in Venice from where, in February 1574 Rinaldo Petignoni (Fortunio) as *capocomico* sent an apology to the Duke of Mantua for the company not being able to visit during carnival – they were contracted to remain in Venice. In July they found themselves in Milan again for the festivities for the victory of Lepanto. From there they were summoned back to Venice at the request of Henri III, the new, as yet un-crowned, king of France, then passing through Italy on his way home from Poland.[23]

For the twenty-three-year-old Henri, the Gelosi performed *La Tragedia* by Cornelio Frangipani (which is more of a *cantata* than a tragedy) and two *commedie all'improvviso*, with interludes. Simone Basilea (di Bologna) was at the height of his powers as Zanni, playing him as 'Zan Panza de Pergora': an eye witness described his performance as the 'Bergomask porter' as 'rare', finding him 'even rarer in his arguments and in his spirited inventions.'[24] Henri is not mentioned as being amused by him, however, but he was particularly taken by Vittoria Piissimi (Prima Donna) and Giulio Pasquati (Il Magnifico) who the same observer described as having 'grace and sharpness, full of caprices mingled with sententiousness'. Henri must have indicated his wish to see them in France, but it was to be nearly four years before his invitation could be taken up. Between 1562 and 1587 there were eight religious civil wars in France, and the country became so unstable that a takeover by Spain seemed on the cards. In the circumstances it is remarkable that Italian companies managed to find any propitious times for visiting.

In spring 1575, therefore, the Gelosi remained safely in Milan, and spent the winter in Florence. There they were arguably hardly any safer than they would have been in France: Francesco de' Medici had begun his reign in 1574 and there were 164 assassinations during the first eighteen months. His sister Isabella was strangled in her nuptial bed by her husband who suspected her of betrayal, and his brother, Piero, did the same to his wife, Eleonara di Toledo. Those suspected of plotting against Francesco himself were followed by Francesco's agents as they fled abroad and murdered in France and England. Meanwhile, Isabella Andreini was pregnant and gave birth to her first son, Giovan Battista, on 9 February 1576. Sometime this year the Andreinis also married privately, although they underwent a public ceremony two years later. Exactly at what point they joined the Gelosi will probably never be known, but it cannot have been any earlier than spring 1576.

Henri III, it has to be said, was the kind of king that gives theatre a bad name. He was a man of keen intelligence and cultivated taste, but given to cross-dressing, collecting little dogs and hiding in the cellar during thunderstorms. He similarly hid from the responsibilities of government and France remained torn with civil war while he indulged himself with, for example, his taste for Italian comedy. On 25 June 1576 'the worst ruler of the worst dynasty that ever governed'[25] wrote to his ambassador in Venice charging him to send the Gelosi to France. The ambassador replied that he could not immediately pay them travelling expenses as requested because Giulio Pasquati from Padua was away at the emperor's court in Vienna with some of the company. The king would have to wait until the Magnifico returned. . . . Meanwhile, in November, the Gelosi fulfilled an engagement in Florence. Finally, in January 1577, a caravan consisting of a considerable number of coaches, organised by the Venetian Republic, crossed the Alps in the dead of winter. They paused at Lyon. There is no record of the Gelosi performing there, but it would seem that they must have done, given later evidence of their popularity in that city. Pushing on towards the king's residence at Blois in the Loire valley, the entire company were captured by the Huguenots and put to ransom at La-Charité-sur-Loire (halfway between Clermont-Ferrand and Paris). Henri de Navarre, who had become leader of the Huguenots in 1575, may have had something to do with this kidnapping. Later, however, he protected his brother-in-law Henri III from the Duke of Guise and the Catholic League, and was appointed by him as successor to the throne on his deathbed in 1589. As Henri IV, he in turn was to invite the Italian players to France, having perhaps got to know them during their imprisonment. There was nothing friendly about that, though: the ransom note indicated that if the king wanted to see more than the heads of his beloved actors, he had better release all Huguenots currently imprisoned and pay 10,000 gold florins and 50,000 silver. Henri III complied. To show their gratitude, the Gelosi performed before him the very same evening that they arrived in Blois. Henri then charged admission of 'un demi-teston de tous ceux qui les viendraient voir jouer'[26] for further performances given in the Salle des Etats, which enabled him to recoup at least some of his ransom money.

In May the company moved to Paris and began performing in the hall of the Petit-Bourbon where 'they levied four sous a head (twice the normal price) from every French person that wanted to see them play; nevertheless there was such a demand and such a congregation of people that the four best preachers in Paris put together did not attract as many.'[27] Such popularity was bound to lead to trouble with the moral minority. The hall was hired from the Confrérie de la Passion at an 'ecu tournois' per performance. The Gelosi's biggest success was *La Princesse qui a perdu l'esprit*, complete with music, machinery and a naval battle. However, on 26 June:

> The court assembly . . . forbade the Gelosi . . . to continue acting their plays, since certain councillors of the said assembly had advised that all such plays (especially when performed before the youngest members of society, who were the most likely to be influenced, cuckoldry being rife at present), taught nothing but debauchery and adultery, and were nothing more than a school for bawdry for the young of both sexes in the town of Paris.
>
> In fact it was true that there were great excesses amongst certain tutees, principally ladies and young women, who seemed to have taken their cue from the soldiers of the time, who displayed their gold-braided chests when they put on their parades, because they showed

off their breasts in the same manner, with exposed bosoms and other pectoral regions in perpetual motion, so that these good women went about like a pair of compasses or the pendulum of a clock, or to put it better, like a blacksmith's bellows.[28]

It should be noted that the first regular French actress (Marie Venier) was not born until 1590, and did not appear on the stage until 1610.[29] It was, therefore, relatively easy for the Italian *donne* to have not only a *succès*, but also a *succès de scandale*. The Gelosi again pleaded immunity, based on royal letters, but Parlement rejected them once more and warned the actors that if they came waving them again they would have to pay 10,000 *livres* into the poor box.

In September, however, performances were able to be resumed on royal command: 'I desire that it be done so and that there be no mistake ... for I have pleasure in hearing them and have never heard more perfect' wrote Henri. It is possible the Gelosi then stayed in France until the following April. All we know is that Battista Amorevoli de Trevi, the Franceschina of the troupe (it was presumably not he who started the breast-baring fashion), published a short poem in Paris during that time entitled *Desio d'honore et zelo d'amicitia*, and it seems unlikely that the Gelosi left him behind in order to pursue a literary career.

In 1578 they were back in Florence. Vittoria Piissimi left, Isabella Andreini performed for the first time and other company changes were made. In 1579 they played Venice in January, Ferrara in February, and then Mantua from whence, on 5 May, by decree of the Duke, were exiled 'from the City and State of Mantua the comedians called the Gelosi who lodge at the sign of the Bissone, and also Signor Simone, who plays the part of the bergamask, and Signor Orazio and Signor Adriano, who play the parts *amantiorum*, and Gabriele called delle Haste, their friend.'[30] No reason was given, though it is notable that the Andreinis are not mentioned, so some kind of scandalous behaviour may be presumed. One commentator suggests that the machinations of Vittoria Piissimi may have had something to do with it, since she was now the star of the Duke's favoured company, the **Confidenti**. The Gelosi went straight to Milan, where they played in June before going on to Genoa where they played before Prince Ferdinand of Bavaria who called them 'die best Gesellschaft so in gantz Italia von Comedianten.'[31] In November they headed south again, to Ferrara.

In 1580, between May and September, they were in Milan where they managed to achieve the goodwill of the Archbishop, Carlo Borromeo – who modified his recent prohibition on public plays so that they were allowed to perform such pieces as had been approved by an Episcopal commission. It is possible that it was during this time that they went back to their roots in Bergamo, teaming up with the **Uniti** for a few days.[32] They are next heard of in 1582 at the Venice carnival. Then, in July of the same year, having ventured to return to Mantua, in an extraordinary episode – even for a Commedia troupe – some of the actors were sentenced to be hanged:

> The Duke desired to see a comedy by the Gelosi that was altogether ridiculous and farcical. So the players obliged him by staging a very absurd and ridiculous one in which all the performers were hunchbacks. His Highness laughed enormously at it, and was altogether delighted by it. When the entertainment was over, he summoned the leading players and asked which of them devised it. *Zanni* said, I did, I did; the *Magnifico* claimed that he had; and *Gratiano* too sought the palm; each assumed that would get a rich reward. But the Duke had the three arrested, and they were condemned to be hanged. All the gentlewomen of Mantua banded together and begged for the players to be pardoned, but without success. The most they obtained was permission to make the ropes in their own fashion. These ropes were made of such rotten cord that all three players fell to the ground and the city cried out, pardon, pardon. But although the poor wretches were taken to prison half naked, and were shaven and bloody, nevertheless the Duke was still determined they should be hanged once more.[33]

This sounds like a huge practical joke, but a most uncomfortable one for the victims. Supposedly they were then imprisoned and tortured. It should be noted, however, that is only hearsay, quoted in a letter from Rome, not Mantua. Moreover, such behaviour would seem bizarre in a duke who was otherwise constantly well-disposed to *comici* and sufficiently knowledgeable about *commedia dell'arte all'improvviso* not to go looking for authorship in a literary sense. The story does have the ring of truth, however, with individual actors each looking out for number one in a mutually contracted situation: often a company's contract would be drawn up as much to protect the players from each other as from outside forces. The earliest one extant, for example, prohibits the members from playing cards together, or any other game: the signatories agree they will only sit down together to eat! Nonetheless, Vincenzo Gonzaga's punishment was so totally out of proportion to the actors' crime that one wonders whether the whole affair may not have been some kind of stunt. It is again notable that Andreinis were not involved. From the description of the performance we may assume that it was a Pulchinella play, showing a Neapolitan influence which would be unusual at this date. The attempted hanging of Mr Punch has a long tradition.

The Gelosi actors seem, anyway, to have escaped a second punishment and made their way to Milan and then to Venice in spring 1583. From there Francesco Andreini wrote refusing a tempting personal offer from Vincenzo Gonzaga to become a member of his new company since he was engaged to the 'most famous S. Alvese Michiele, manager of the hall at Venice.' This *Teatroni di Baldracca* was in fact a customs hall which boasted a secret passage through to the Uffizi Palace, presumably originally for 'duty free', but now also used by the nobility in order to attend performances *incognito*. Such respect for its manager gives us a clue as to how the Gelosi were able to remain independent, if their income from performing in such places was sufficient to enable them to turn down ducal offers. Or perhaps Andreini did not wish to risk being hanged – in jest or otherwise.

The year 1584 was spent on the coast in Genoa and in nearby Savona. In the latter town, a serious antagonism was provoked between two rival factions, one supporting Isabella Andreini, the other Gabriella Chiabrera, presumably the *seconda donna*. For the next few years, records are sparse: they probably played Bologna in autumn 1585, and Mantua, Milan and Turin in 1586. Between January and April of 1587 they were in Florence. From Venice in July of that year comes the earliest extant letter from Isabella Andreini – to the Duke of Mantua, extolling him as a god on earth and offering thanks for taking her daughter Lavinia into his service. Although the rest of the troupe had their ups and down with the Gonzagas, the Andreinis obviously remained in favour.

In 1588 they played Mantua again, then Milan. On 10 December, Duchartre places the Gelosi in Paris again, but subject to yet another parliamentary injunction prohibiting 'all actors, both Italian and French from playing comedies . . . on pain of arbitrary fines and corporal punishment.'[34] This is hardly surprising since in May the populace had taken to the barricades in protest against the dissoluteness of Henri III and in support of Henri de Guise. The Gelosi (or another Italian company, if it was not them) are reported as having left at once – a wise move since on 23 December the king's private bodyguard murdered the Duke of Guise at Blois. This was clearly not a time for comedy.

By May 1589 the Gelosi were back in Florence, in attendance for the wedding of the new Grand Duke, Ferdinando de' Medici, and the Princess Christine de Lorraine. The major Commedia companies were often required at royal weddings, and none were more lavish than this one. In 1587, Francesco de' Medici and his consort, Bianca Capello, had been murdered in a Medici villa. Ferdinando, Francesco's younger brother, was prime suspect, but there was no proof. The Spanish ambassador in Florence at the time reported 'The Medici have now become little Ottomans, assassinating one another in the Turkish manner.' Whatever the circumstances, Ferdinando came into the title and immediately set about finding himself a suitable bride to secure the family succession. Royal marriages were political actions, just as much as royal assassinations. Since the Medici were at the time seeking an alliance with France in order to strengthen their position *vis-à-vis* Spain, Ferdinando decided on Christine de Lorraine, a granddaughter of Catherine de' Medici.

In 1588, in Blois, agents of the bride and groom (who had never set eyes on each other) signed a marriage contract. In 1589 Christine met her fiancé for the first time in Poggia a Caiano in mid-April. The future Grand Duchess entered Florence on 30 April. The Medici had always celebrated their dynasty with legendary festivities. Ferdinando now went so far as to stage a realistic recreation of a naval battle in the interior court of the Palazzo Pitti. But the high point of the festivities was *La Pellegrina*, a piece of what might now be called total theatre including dance, poetry and a drama by Girolamo Bargagli with a series of six *intermedios* with music by Cuilio Cacchini, Emelio de' Cavalieri, Cristofano Malvezzi, Marenzio and Jacopo Peri performed between the acts. The scenery was lavish and animated by complex stage machinery which had taken eight months to build.

So, for once, the Gelosi were not the main attraction, but as well as playing in their usual customs hall, the company were this time invited into the Uffizi Palace to perform in the grand *sala delle comedie*. A much publicised row broke out between the two *prime donne*, Vittoria di Piissimi and Isabella Andreini over whether the command performance should be of *La Zingana* (with Vittoria in the lead) or *La Pazzia d'Isabella* (Isabella's speciality). This may have been partly a cunning ploy to double their income: eventually the former piece was given on Sunday the 6th and the latter, a week later. The altercation also presumably had the effect of ensuring that they were not playing in an atmosphere of anti climax after the main feature of *La Pellegrina*. The Gelosi then went on to Mantua, probably followed by a stay in Milan during autumn and winter.

Little is known of their activities in the early 1590s – they may have played in Mantua in October 1590, certainly it was them in Milan in November of that year. The same time the following year they were in Florence and then there is no trace of them until, in January 1584, when there is evidence of the company beginning to be able to draw on a second generation of players: one evening a fourteen-year-old boy in a jerkin through which his arms protruded covered in a pair of hose – presumably to conceal the fact that he had no shirt – set out from Bologna on the road to Florence in search of his father who was reported to have returned from Sicily and Naples and to be serving the Gelosi. This was Domenico Bruni, who later told the tale of how in the excitement of his arrival he embraced the innkeeper and embarrassed the good man with his wife by hailing him as his father. Francesco Andreini took the boy under his protection, fitted him out with a cloth jacket, and set him to learn a prologue.

The gap in performance records continues throughout the decade (apart from a sighting in Genoa in 1596, and another possible one in Bologna) until, in 1599, Smith has the Gelosi making another visit to Paris.[35] Again, it seems, there was no problem in performing at court but the company were 'restrained' for charging for public plays at the Hôtel de Bourgogne. A week later a permit was granted, for which they may have had to pay a

Figure 5 Francesco Andreini, frontispiece from his *Le Bravure di Capitano Spavento*, 1607.

considerable sum. In 1603 they made their final journey to France. In August they acted first in Paris, again at the Hôtel de Bourgogne, and then at Fontainebleau, staying at the French court until the following April. Henri IV then supplied a personal note of safe conduct for 'Isabella commediante' and her company, and for their 'hardes, armes, bagages, bagues, joyaux';[36] they also carried with them a letter of recommendation from the Queen to the Duchess of Mantua. On the journey home, on 11 June 1604, Isabella Andreini miscarried and died in Lyon at the age of forty-two. She left behind seven children, five of whom took holy orders. One of her sons was godchild to the Duke of Mantua. Her husband Francesco never acted again and the Gelosi disbanded. After a state funeral a medallion was struck in her honour; on the verso she is depicted as an eternal goddess, with the inscription ÆTERNA FAMA.

Pedrolino
(1576–?)

By the end of the sixteenth century it was unusual to find a company still touring under the name of its principal Mask, but such was Giovanni Pellesini's fame as Pedrolino that he continued to do so. He himself often played solo at banquets and the like. His company are first heard of touring Tuscany in July 1576. They spent the winter in Florence before going to Pisa, then to Lucca, whence they would have gone back to Pisa in July had not a letter from *commissario* Capponi informed the Grand Duke 'that the notable scandals of the love affairs of the actresses made it advisable to forbid their return'.[37] In April 1580 Pedrolino's performances met with success, both in the private rooms of the Duchess of Ferrara and below *in banchi*, i.e. on the trestle stages in the street. Pellesini and his Pantalone also played the Fool. A table was set at a banquet with:

> . . . a hole in the middle big enough for a man to get through; it was covered by a large, empty pie which had a hole in the bottom to correspond with the hole in the table. A cover was set on the pie, but this could be raised. *Pedrolino* the actor was concealed under the table. No-one knew he was there except Her Highness, the Duchess. When they had all taken their seats . . . *Pantalone* came into the hall, indicating that he was looking for *Pedrolino*, since he was a greedy fellow, in the dining-hall, and called out for him. *Pedrolino* then raised only his head out of the pie, so that none of his body was seen, and replied that by misfortune his greed had driven him into the kitchen, where the cooks had made him into a pie.[38]

The Duchess next recommended Pedrolino's troupe to her brother, the Duke of Mantua, a Commedia buff if ever there was one. The Duke proposed uniting Pedrolino's company with that of another, known to him as 'Vittoria's', but to us as the **Confidenti**. To ensure that this company stayed together, he arranged a marriage between the two *capocomici*, Giovanni Pellesini and Vittoria Piissimi. This arrangement, however, rather backfired

Figure 6 Woodcut from the title page of Guilio Cesare Croce's *La Gran Vittoria di Pedrolino* (*The Great Victory of Pedrolino against Doctor Gratiano Scatolone, for love of the beautiful Franceschina*), Bologna, 1621. Pedrolino, masked and seemingly bearded, is generally accepted to be Pellesini.

when Pedrolino refused to leave Venice to attend the 1581 carnival in Mantua. Vittoria wrote to the Duke:

> I have seen what your Highness has written to Pedrolino, and, though as your humble servant I ought to acquiesce in what I know to be your will, . . . I beg you by the Bowels of Jesus Christ not to be the cause of my ruin . . . begging you again to grant to me and Pedrolino the life of my honour and of body which consists in the remaining of Pedrolino yea grace my Lord grace for the love of God I beg you on my bended knees . . .

In other words, Pedrolino must have cited his own honeymoon as the reason for not going to Mantua and left it to his wife to try to make the peace with the Duke. Clearly it had turned into something more than an arranged marriage! Two months later Vittoria wrote again that she had:

> been told by many that Pedrolino and I have forfeited your Highness' grace through not being able to serve you this Carnival . . . I live the most miserable woman in the world, and I return to beg you at your feet to take me back into your favour, and the same I say of Pedrolino since he has run into error because of me.

The story does, however, become less poignant when one discovers that the real reason for Pedrolino's dereliction of duty was that the new company, the **Confidenti**, were actually performing in Venice (presumably a more prestigious and better paid gig). The Duke of Mantua did relent in time, however, for the **Confidenti** to play at his wedding later that year.

Pellesini is undoubtedly the Pedrolino of the Flaminio Scala scenarios, and if Lea is right that Scala edited them retrospectively with an 'all star cast' in mind, a sort of 'dream team' without regard to the composition of the company at any one particular time, then the importance of Pedrolino as first *zanni* cannot be overestimated. He appears in all but one of the fifty scenarios, usually taking the sort of prominent role later associated with Arlecchino. Pellesini last appeared in Paris at the age of 87 in 1613-14 with Martinelli and the **Accessi**. 'Gay spirits and sharp wits are needed in the theatre and one hardly finds these in bodies as old as theirs, wrote Malherbe,[39] but in Duchartre's opinion he still played 'with spirit and a high sense of comedy'.[40]

Adriano Valerini

There is only one recorded instance of Valerini leading his own troupe and, strictly speaking, we do not know enough about it for the company to qualify for inclusion here. He is, however, an interesting example of the way in which Commedia began to claim social, and even clerical acceptance in the last quarter of the sixteenth century. A nobleman by birth from Verona, Valerini was a Doctor of Philosophy, a playwright, a poet of some accomplishment in the vernacular as well Latin and Greek and, as we have seen, the bereaved lover of Vicenza, as well as the father of Diana Ponti of the **Dediosi**. Although he played Aurelia, the distinction between his own name and that of his role was stronger than in many cases.

After **Ganassa** he joined the **Gelosi**, but left by 1585 when he played with his own troupe in Milan. Jacomo Braga (later of the **Uniti**) was his Pantalone and Pellesini his Pedrolino, so the troupe may have been the one otherwise referred to as '**Pedrolino**'s', but on this occasion it was definitely Valerini who was *capocomico*. They had only given a few performances when the Governor of Milan refused permission for them to continue. Valerini protested, but the Governor insisted that he feared he might be committing a mortal sin by permitting such acts. He addressed the matter to archbishop Borromeo, who sent for Valerini and gave him permission to reopen, provided that all scenarios were submitted to him for approval. Those he approved, he sanctified with his signature. When Valerini died, Diana inherited a puzzlingly large number of scenarios signed 'Carlo Borromeo'.

Valerini's unexpected success with the Archbishop reminds us that persecution by the church and civil authorities had as much to do with keeping the *comici dell'arte* players on the move as the quest for the best pitch to play at any given season.

Figure 7 Adriano Valerini. Frontispiece from his tragedy *Afrodite*, Verona, 1578.

The Dediosi
(1581-99)

Diana Ponti, 'Lavinia', was the *capocomico*, and the company was also known by her name, sometimes as the Diana Comica Dediosa. There is no complete company list extant, but the ubiquitous Tristano Martinelli played Arlecchino for a time. Montaigne saw them in Pisa in 1581 during his Italian travels and records that Zanni was called Fargnocola. He visited the actresses backstage and sent them presents of fish [sic].[41] Ponti was probably not with them at the time, not because Montaigne does not mention her, but because she is known to have appeared with the **Confidenti** shortly after. She was certainly back in charge when the Dediosi played in Mantua 1585 and Genoa in 1586 and 1588. In that year the Pope banned female performers from the Papal State as part of the Counter-Reformation, with the result that the Dediosi could only obtain a licence to perform in Rome as a 'men only' company – and so presumably went there without Ponti. Women were, however, allowed to watch their performances, except the courtesans who had been banished. Whether some of them went off to join the second oldest profession and become *comici dell'arte* remains a matter of speculation. The Dediosi were back in Rome in 1590, and Mantua in 1593, possibly Ferrara in 1594, Milan and Cremona 1595, Mantua and Bologna 1596, Genoa, May 1587. In that year Flaminio Scala (Flavio) seems to have taken over as *capocomico*. The last definite record of them is in Verona in August 1599.

The Confidenti

I Comici Confidenti announced by their name that they were 'confident of pleasing' their audience, thus comparing themselves with the already established **Gelosi**, and, perhaps also implying that they could do better than being merely 'zealous' – thereby taking over the first position among equals. This they certainly did, but not until the **Gelosi** disbanded. There may, in effect, have been two different companies playing under the Confidenti name since there is no continuity of records between those of 1574–99, when they were led initially by Vittoria Piissimi under the patronage of the Duke of Mantua, and those of 1611–39, when they were managed by Flaminio Scala under the patronage of Don Giovanni de' Medici, the member of the Medici family charged with running the Uffizi Palace.

1574–99

Duchartre asserts that a company of this name went to France in 1571 'after playing throughout Italy', but the earliest official record is a petition dated 8 June 1574, in which the Confidenti ask for a renewal of their licence to play in Milan. However, a letter dated the 25th of that month mentions them playing earlier in the year in Cremona and Pavia, where their Zanni, one Battista Vannino da Riminio, was arrested for helping a frightened child escape from the officers of the law(!). *Capocomico* Vittoria Piissimi was considered an excellent ballerina: Giovan Battista Mamiano, in a memoire of 1620, spoke of her as 'the dancing actress'.[42] **Adriano Valerini** said her figure was so fine that in a page's clothes she deceived everyone.[43] For Tomasso Garzoni she was a paradigm:

> Without doubt she deserves to be ranked as an embodiment of the arts, for her gestures are proportionate, her movements harmonious and co-ordinated, her actions disciplined and pleasing, her language sweet and affable, her sighs measured and stealing, her laughter suave and

delicious, her deportment noble and generous, and her whole person has the perfect decorum that belongs to an actress.[44]

They played the following June in Milan again, but then nothing is known for four years until they appeared in 1579 in Massa. In spring 1580 they were at Mantua, from where they wanted to go on to Verona and Padua, but it is not known whether the permissions they sought were granted. In the same year they played in Ferrara and Bologna and were in Venice by December, where they remained for the entire carnival season; thence to Mantua for the marriage of Vincenzo de Gonzaga to Margherita Farnese, and from there to Bologna once more. They were in Bologna again the following year, 1582, and left at the end of July or the beginning of August for Genoa: a supplication on their behalf to the Genovese Senate for permission to 'exercise their customary very honest comedies' was presented and received a partial licence for three months on 6 August.

Whilst in Bologna they had fobbed off the emissary of the Duke of Mantua in early July with the excuse that they could not attend the Duke since they were awaiting the arrival of two of the company, Signora Diana (Ponti) and Gratiano from Florence. If they did go to Mantua, then they must have done so very quickly before playing Genoa. Whether they did or not, the troupe was obviously split at this point and waiting to regroup before going on – or perhaps waiting for replacements for defecting members.

The company certainly did split in 1583. A letter from Vincenzo de Gonzaga, dated 2 April, makes certain the presence of the Confidenti in Mantua that same month, but other incontestable documents place the **Uniti**-Confidenti in Genoa. This means that some of the Confidenti must have left and joined the **Uniti** in name as well as in person. Those of the Confidenti that remained under its banner included Fabrizio de Fornaris (Capitano Coccodrillo), Bernardino Lombardi (Dottore Lanternone) and an unspecified Celia. Fornaris was another nobleman turned player and playwright – his *L'Angelica* was published in Paris in 1568. In it he gives a glimpse of himself in performance as 'Il Capitan don Alonso Coccodrillo, hijo d'el Colonel don Calderon de Berdexa, hermano d'el Alferez Hernandico Mandrico de strico de Lara de Castilla la vieja, cavallero de Sevilla, hijo d'Algo verdardero, trinchador de tres cuchillos, . . .' (etc., etc.).

This troupe played the carnival season of 1584 in Turin and Milan, and then left for Paris where they performed at the Hôtel de Cluny. They are known still to have been playing in French provincial towns in 1585. Returning to Italy, they played Genoa again in April 1586, then left for two years in Spain, 1587-88, where they were known as Los Confidentes Italianos, led by the brothers Tristano and Drusiano Martinelli. It is not certain what

Figure 8 Fabrizio de Fornaris as Capitano Coccodrillo, with Francatrippa (probably Gabriele Panzanini) doing a handspring over him. From the 'Recueil Fossard'.

Mask Drusiano played, perhaps his role was principally managerial, as the husband of his wife Angela. To confuse matters, Tristano was also married to an Angela, Angela Salomoni. Whereas there is no record of Zan Ganassa having any female members in his Spanish troupe, Los Confidentes petitioned the king for a licence to permit their women to perform the essential roles of lovers. This was granted 'inasmuch as the women in the company are married women and their husbands are with them'. It was especially provided, however, that they should not be allowed to appear in the habit or dress of men, and that 'henceforth no boy be allowed to act attired as a woman'.[45] That cross-dressing should suddenly have seemed so shocking to the Spanish is odd since, although women performed regularly in carnival as women, boys had had to do the job so far on the 'legitimate' stage – as they continued to do in England until the Restoration. To add to the confusion, the authorities did not seem certain whether the part of Franceschina was being taken by a man or a woman (in fact it was Silvia Roncagli) and added their permission just in case.

By September 1589 the Confidenti were back in Italy, performing at Parma and then in Genoa in the following months. They were in Ferrara in 1599 for carnival, but after that the name seems to have lain dormant until 1610, though one chronicler places them in Genoa and Lucca in 1606.[46]

1611–39

Flaminio Scala, (1547–c.1620) a scholar and a gentleman, is known himself to have played the lover under the name of Flavio; though possibly retired by the time he managed the Confidenti, he still used the name as a *nom de plume*. It is, in fact for his authorship that he is most remembered. He was the first to publish a collection of scenarios, *Il Teatro delle favole rappresentative*, literally 'the theatre of enacted fables', published in Venice in 1611. Some suggest that the fifty 'days' of performances assembled therein represent the repertoire of the **Gelosi**, for whom he is thought to have performed. Were it that simple. First of all the fables have been worked up in a literary manner, with a preliminary 'argument' for each, telling the story prior to the commencement of the action in a much more prolix and ornate manner than any company would require. Secondly, as Katherine Lea says,

> . . . no doubt it is right to see in the *Capitano Spavento, Isabella, Aurelio, Oratio, Vittoria*, and *Pedrolino* of the scenari, the Andreini, Valerini, Nobile, the Piissimi and Pellesini of real life [. . .] But to be consistent we must continue the process and identify *Arlecchino* with Martinelli,

Flaminia with Orsola Cecchini, *Flavia* with Margharita Garavini, *Cinthio* with Jacopo Fidenzi, *Cassandro* with G. B. Zecca, *Nespola* with the wife of Marcello de' Secchi, players who belonged variously to the *Accessi, Fedeli, and Confidenti*.[47]

She concludes that Scala obviously had in mind the chief actors of his day without regard to the composition of a company at any particular period. He was writing up ideal scenarios for an ideal troupe 'with such an all-star cast as the Duke of Mantua and the King of France had dreamed of but rarely achieved'. There is no hard evidence that Scala ever, in fact, played with the **Gelosi**: what we do know is that he was friendly with Francesco Andreini, who wrote the preface for the *Teatro delle favole rappresentative*, and may have supplied him with **Gelosi** material. Unless Scala had supplied it to the **Gelosi** in the first place ... we will probably never know. What it is important to recognise is that modern concepts of authorship are not applicable to early *commedia dell'arte* – in fact what Scala was doing in publishing such a work was raising the literary profile of the genre. His readership seems to have been intended to be the literary academies, whose members were certainly numerous enough to offer his tome a substantial market. Whether he intended them to read or to act out each 'day' is not clear. Neither is it clear whether, when he took over the running of the Confidenti in 1611, he furnished the troupe with some, or even all, of their scenarios.

Somewhere around 1612–13, both manager and company came under the protection of Don Giovanni de' Medici and records become more precise and numerous. The *capocomico* was Domenico Bruni, the erstwhile protégé of Francesco Andreini. A foreign traveller reports seeing them in Bologna at the beginning of November 1615:

This is perhaps the best company that is now on tour: they are always engaged from one carnival to the next, and from there they go to Venice, where they earn what they please. Now as for the personnages, first there are two Zanni, the sly one who does the plotting is called *Scappino*, and the other who is so witty that you could never hear his like is *Mezzetino*. There are four women, first *Lavinia*, who is the prettiest, the youngest and acts the best, the second *Valeria*, and the other two who take the part of maidservants are *Nespola*, and *Spinetta* the wife of *Scappino*. There are two lovers, *Fulvio*, the first, speaks the better, and as I am told once acted at Pesaro in the house of Signor Federigo, and this one is the brother of *Valeria*, who is no chicken. The second is *Ortensio*, husband of Lavinia: a *Pantalone*, a Bergomask *Beltramo*, a *Spanish Captain*, an Italianate Frenchman called *Claudione* complete the troupe. Fulvio, however, also takes the part of a *Romanguolo*, and also of a *Graziano*, and so all play two parts when occasion demands.[48]

Scapino was played by Francesco Gabrielli	
Mezzetino	Ottavio Onorati
Lavinia	Maria Antonazzoni
Valeria	Valeria Austoni, sister to Francesco Antonazzoni
Nespola	the wife of Marcello di Secchi
Spinetta	the wife of Francesco Gabrielli
Fulvio	Domenico Bruni
Ortensio	Francesco Antonazzoni
Pantalone	Marcantonio Romagnese
Beltramo	Niccolo Barbieri

Claudione only appeared in the 1615 season. Bruni also played Il Dottore when required.

The composition of the company reflects the new sensibility of the new century – the 'ur' Bergamese figures of Zanni and Brighella have been replaced by the more sophisticated Mezzetino and Scapino and Il Dottore only appears occasionally.

This troupe remained substantially together until 1620. That they did so was thanks to exhaustive smoothing over of internal disputes by 'Flavio'. He was not always with the troupe and his letters and their replies, together with individual actor's complaints to Don Giovanni (who also seems to have had the patience of Job) and the correspondence between patron and manager together give us a unique picture of the internal squabbling, back-biting and politicking that made up the supposed 'ensemble'. As seems to have been practically *de rigeur* in such a company, the two leading actresses were for ever quarrelling, and this threw the rest into two sharply opposing camps. Valeria was the wife of Giovan Battista Austoni who acted occa-sionally as Battistino and also functioned as a kind of road manager. He was a stirrer, if there ever was one. On 12 August 1615, Francesco Gabbrielli felt constrained to write to Don Giovanni that he was:

> . . . innocent of all that I am taxed with [. . .]. I have not erred (as all the company will testify for me) [. . .] your Excellency's kindness to me has passed the extreme of benevolence; I know how blameworthy I should be were I to abuse this grace, particularly at a time when your excellency is writing to the company to congratulate us on our union. [. . .] Concerning my acting my worst, I do not do it because it would

be an injury to myself and an affront to others. But since my desire is only to make your Excellency aware that I desire to serve you alone, I am annoyed at the wrong done me by Messer Battistino in writing these lies to Signor Flavio.[49]

Meanwhile Valeria, as well as provoking her husband to tittle tattle, strengthened her power base by enticing Domenico Bruni into becoming her 'admirer'. The next to take up the cudgels was Marcantonio Romagnesi who fell out with the Austoni in Genoa, in the summer of 1616. Battista Austoni took advantage of Romagnesi insulting Valeria to bring up an old grievance, complaining that he was not allowed an equal voice in company meetings. This backfired on him and Don Giovanni advised his dismissal. This, however, entailed the loss of Valeria – no bad thing, except for the gap left in the artistic balance of the troupe. Francesco Antonazzoni wrote that Spinetta would do as much as she could, moving up from second *servetta* to second *innamorata*, but she was not 'strong'. The company also considered the wife of Leandro (who had been sent for to replace Bruni), but she was untrained; they were against someone whose stage name was Isabella because she could not read, against the daughter of Virginia for fear of her mother . . . and so finally decided to invite a certain Violina 'who is experienced in comedy, learns verses, and sings, provided she will leave her good-for-nothing husband behind'.[50] Presumably Violina refused because in September 1616 the leading members of the company wrote to Don Giovanni to say that, on the advice of Signor Flavio, they had reinstated Valeria, but that 'Messer Battistino, her husband, will remain [. . .] out of the company, nor will he be admitted in any respect, even for the smallest job.'[51]

The **Confidenti** were at Lucca and Florence in 1616, at Bologna in 1617, at Ferrara, Mantua, Venice, Genoa, Lucca and Florence in 1618. There the enmity between Lavinia and Valeria came to a head once more as a result of the former's outstanding success in *La Pazzia di Lavinia*. Lavinia's husband, Francesco Antonazzoni, sided with her but the effectiveness of his support was undermined when she accused him of carrying on yet again with Nespola. On 4 March, Francesco Antonazzoni wrote to Don Giovanni that he knew:

> . . . by more than one sign that Signor Fulvio [Domenico Bruni] was my enemy . . . I don't know the cause, unless it be because of my wife and my sister – and finding that it was impossible in any way to obviate this ill-will of his, I proceeded to have recourse to Signor Flavio. . . .
> I begged him to get me separated from my brother-in-law [Battista Austoni]. . . . All this last year Signor Fulvio has done nothing else but

say he doesn't want me to be where he is and that he doesn't want to act where my wife was prima donna. Knowing I am the least of the company and he the chief, [and that] he would have shown me the door – [I] proceeded to think of my own affairs – my wife, my debts, my sister in a nunnery, all on my shoulders.

And he put in a good word for his wife:

I come to beg you that my wife should have the grace of your Excellency to be placed in the chief parts, or at any rate, turn and turn about, but not along with my sister; I should say also, without Signor Fulvio; but as you wish him to be with us, I shall accept, [though he] has said a thousand times that if he is forced by your Excellency to remain in the company it will give him signal annoyance, and he will act his worst. So you can see what can be expected from a mind determined on evil. My wife makes a thousand protestations to me, saying she doesn't want to be where Nespola is, even if I kill her. I beg your Excellency to see that Signor Flavio writes to her in your name and comes to pacify her on the matter, because I shouldn't like to go on living in one continual inferno.

But on the previous day, perhaps without her husband's knowledge, Lavinia had herself written to Don Giovanni that she had:

. . . ever had a loathing for Nespola because of her previous relations with my husband, but have ever sought to deal with her as well as I could, hoping, however, that in time I should find a means of escape. Now I am forced to beg your excellency to grant me this first favour, that I, your humble and devoted servant, demand of you – namely that Nespola should not be where I am, nor I be where the said Nespola is. [. . .] Since I see that my husband turns a deaf ear to this matter, I hasten to say that during the coming year I will not set foot on the stage to play if this woman is in the company – I'd rather eat roots and beg to keep alive.[52]

Then there is a long silence before they are last heard of in Milan in 1639 with a promise of going to France. The lack of evidence does not mean, necessarily, that the squabbling died down, only that Scala died, perhaps worn down by his attempts to keep the peace and maintain patronage by presenting things in the best possible light in his letters to the Duke. Even when dissension was at its worst he was able to report that 'Unione, Unione' was all the company desired. There is a characteristic flicker of humour through his despair as he ends one report on the usual *imbroglio* by remarking that 'all these accidents are designed for the great tribulation of the poor Flavio, for I can think of nothing but how to maintain a unity, and if you could see me it would remind you of Moses keeping up the hopes of the Hebrew people.'

The Uniti
(1578–1640)

The Union were led by Bernardino Lombardi, who payed Il Dottore. The exact date of their formation is uncertain, but a troupe called the 'Uniti Comici' certainly played in Ferrara in 1578 in the private rooms of the Duchess of Urbino, who was, presumably *en visite*. Ferrara had a history of support for Humanist theatre under the Este family during the Renaissance, but relations with itinerant *commedia dell'arte* troupes were less certain – companies seemed to prefer to avoid direct patronage by the Estenses and played at Ferrara for short periods at a commercial rate. The Uniti, for example, turned instead to the Duke of Mantua (Vincenzo Gonzaga), replacing the **Confidenti** in his affections, and were in fact alternatively known as 'The Company of the Most Serene Duke of Mantua'. Some say that the Duke's casting couch proclivities finally caught him out, since he later married the *seconda donna innamorata*, Aurelia, who originally wrote to him 'to advance herself in the profession'.

The Uniti associated with the **Gelosi** in 1580 in Bergamo. After that they played the usual circuit of Northern Italian cities, for example Genoa in the summer of 1581, but there is no record of them having gone abroad. This may be because the company was even less fixed in its membership than most, with 'name' performers only picking up with them when more prestigious work was not on offer elsewhere. Despite the flux in personnel (or perhaps because of it), and compared, for example, to the **Confidenti**, they seem to have been remarkably united in their internal relations. In 1581 **Adriano Valerini** left the **Gelosi** and joined them soon after. Some say he was rejoining, having been the originator of the company before leaving for the **Gelosi** in the first place. In 1583 the company also included

Francatrippa	Gabriele Panzanini
Piombino	Girolamo Salimbeni
Innamorata	Vittoria Piissimi

This company appears to have joined forces with a **Confidenti** breakaway group in Mantua in 1583, becoming known for a short period as the Uniti-**Confidenti**. One outcome of this temporary union is that Pedrolino seems to have changed companies afterwards, leaving the Confidenti and becoming the leader of the 'Comici Uniti'. On 3 April they wrote to Vincenzo, and since the entire co-operative signed the letter, for the most part in the names of their Masks, it gives us a chance to see how extensive the new operation was: Pedrolino, Bertolino, Magnifico, Gratiano, Lulio, Capitano Cardone, Flaminio, Battista de Bertolino, Franceschina, Madame Giulia Brolo, Isabella, Gio, Donato, Grillo. They were in Ferrara, Reggio Emila and Mantua in 1584, and were invited back there the following year by the Prince, Vincenzo Gonzaga. Once in Mantua, however, Vincenzo's father, the Duke, sent them all away since they had not taken the trouble to obtain the necessary permits for performing! But, as we have noted, when Vincenzo succeeded his father he took them under his wing and, seven years later, wrote recommending them to the Podesta of Verona, but the latter wrote back that they were opposed to entertainment of any sort.

In following the trail of the Uniti one has to be careful since any disparate grouping of *comici* were likely to describe themselves adjectivally as 'uniti'! We can, however, be certain that it was them that played in Florence at the end of 1592, Genoa in 1593 and Milan in October 1594, in honour of the marriage of the Count of Aro. In December of the same year they were in Florence, in 1595 and 1596 in Milan, in Genoa twice in 1599. In 1601 they appeared in Mantua, Milan and Pavia. We know they were in Florence again in 1604, but then there is a gap in the records until 1613 in Milan; they were in Genoa in 1614. A company list for that year gives:

Pantalone	Jacomo Braga (from Ferrara)
Curzio	Domenico de Negri (also from Ferrara)
Capitano Matamoros	Sylvio Fiorillo (from Naples)
Scaramouche	Giovan Battista Fiorillo (his son)
Trivellino	Andrea Fraiacomi (from Bologna)
Cortelazzo	Ippoloito Mendeni (from Mirandola)
Adriano	Andrea Mangii (from Genoa)
Graziano	Michel Zanardi (from Ferrara)
Franceschina	Ottavio Bernardino (from Rome, the city that had barred actresses – in the one female role that continued to be regularly cross-dressed elsewhere).

The Accessi
(1590-1628)

Their name signifies 'the inflamed'. According to Paul Castagno,'words derived from cavalier literature such as *Gelosi*, *Confidenti* and *Accessi* signified a sense of enterprise, daring and a spirit of adventure.'[53] Such titles also 'express an ideal of singularity and originality in contrast with the classical attitude with its aspiration to the norm, universal and measured.'[54] The *capocomico* was Pier Maria Cecchini who developed the role of Fritellino, and other company members included:

Flaminia	Orsola Cecchini
Capitano Rinoceronte	Gerolamo Garavini
Arlecchino	Drusiano and Tristano Martinelli

Vincenzo Gonzaga, the Duke of Mantua, recommended a company of this name to the rectors of Brescia in 1590, and they responded that such a licence was not in their gift but would have to come from Venice. There is no other record of a company of that name until they spent three months in Genoa in 1597 and were two years later at Mantua for carnival. They intended to leave for Ferrara after Easter, but were pre-empted by the **Confidenti** and went to Bologna instead. In March 1600, they left from Mantua for France, in response to a personal invitation to Tristano Martinelli from Henri IV, ending 'Priant Dieu, Arlequin, qu'il vous ait en sa sainte garde. De Paris le 21 décembre 1599. Henri.' (It was quite unprecedented at that time for a crowned monarch to write personally to an actor.) They also had a warm recommendation from Gonzaga to the Duke of Aiguillon and Nevers. They travelled by way of Bologna, Milan and Savoy, preceded by Drusiano Martinelli to Lyon. When the King arrived there in July, the company were still in Turin, retained by Charles Emmanuel of Savoy, but Drusiano managed to fetch them by early August. Wars then broke out with Savoy, preventing Henri from enjoying their performance until autumn and delaying his marriage to Maria de' Medici (at which they played) until the 17 December. The Accessi were the star attraction at the festivities and Martinelli presented the king with his *Compositions de rhétorique de M. Don Arlequin*, including, curiously, fifty-nine blank pages and dedicated to:

> the magnanimous gentleman, Henri de Bourbon, first bourgeois of Paris, chief of all gentlemen of Lyon . . . admiral of the sea of Marseille, master of one-half of the bridge at Avignon and good friend of the master of the other half, . . . secret secretary of the most secret cabinet of Madame Maria di Medici, high treasurer of the Italian actors.[55]

The Accessi followed the court to Paris in January 1601 and stayed there until the end of October. By this time Arlequin was practically the king's licensed fool. One day he seated himself in the chair which Henri had just vacated and addressed him as 'Arlequin', promising him continued favours and a pension. The king did not object, and let the role-reversal continue until finally replying 'Holà, you have played my part long enough, let me now play it for myself.'[56]

Returning finally to Italy, the Accessi seem to have gone straight to Rome, then dog legged back up to Turin in January 1602. There is then a gap in the records until in November 1606 when Henri IV wrote to his cousin, Ferdinando de Gonzaga, asking him to use his influence with the Duchess of Mantua, who had promised to send the troupe back to France. They did finally go in 1610, when Henri and Maria acted as godparents to one of Martinelli's sons. Eventually Martinelli siblings acquired so many royal godparents that Arlequin considered them to have been shared round like a litter of kittens.

According to Lea the history of the Accessi and **Fedeli** are so inter-twined that they need to be followed together, with the bare bones of notices illuminated by:

> . . . the flare of correspondence struck out by the friction between Cecchini, Andreini, their wives and admirers. When the flint and steel of these two families fail, the little world is set alight by the sly negotiations of Martinelli who continues to wander in and out of the two companies, making them indefatigably and breaking them recklessly, a man spoiled by patrons and dreaded by his companions.[57]

In 1612 the company journeyed to Linz and thence Vienna to play before the Emperor Matthias. Here Arlequin, without having to resort to pointed role reversal, was awarded a piece of paper which admitted him into the aristocracy. He is said to have 'returned home jauntily with the patent of ennoblement of which he was so proud'.[58]

The Accessi were in Paris again in 1613, after stopping at Lyon like the **Gelosi** before them. They played Fontainebleau, then went back to Paris to perform alternately at the Hôtel de Bourgogne and for the court at the Louvre. The company at this point, other than Arlequin and Fritellino, was as follows:

Pantalone	Federico Ricci
Pedrolino	Giovanni Pellesini
Graziano	Bartolomeo Bongiovanni
Capitano Rinoceronte	Girolamo Gavarini
Leandro	Ricci (Federico's son)
Lelio	Giovanni Battista Andreini/Baldo Rotari
Florinda	Virginia Andreini/Lidia Rotari

The Accessi returned to France again in 1620/21 and played the Hôtel de Bourgogne, as usual, then Fontainebleau. The last falling out with the **Fedeli** was in Cremona in 1626.

The Fedeli
(1601–52)

The Fedeli were founded by Isabella Andreini's first son, Giovan Battista, in 1601, three years before her death. Although his father, Francisco, hung up his Capitano's boots at that time, the rump of his company, the **Gelosi** immediately joined the Fedeli. Giovan Battista's first wife was Virginia Ramponi, an outstanding singer and dancer who took the role of Florinda opposite his Lelio, and who seems to have been more instrumental in running the company than her husband. One of the **Gelosi** actors to join them was the ubiquitous Tristano Martinelli. Other regular performers were:

Lidia	Virginia Rotari
Pedrolino	Giovanni Pellesini
Pantalone	Federigo Ricci
Cinzio	Jacopo Antonio Fidenzi
Aurelia	Brigida Bianchi

In 1606 they joined forces with the **Accessi** to give a series of performances in Milan, but serious disputes between the two *capocomici*, G. B. Andreini and Pier Maria Cecchini (Fritellino) soon put a stop to further collaboration. They are next heard of in 1608 performing in Mantua for the marriage of Francesco de Gonzaga and Marguerite de Savoie. Virginia also took over the lead role in the Rinuccini-Monteverdi opera *Arianna* at short notice. The following year, after playing Genoa in June, union with the **Accessi** was again attempted, this time in Turin, but conflict broke out once more and the companies went their separate ways.

Records are then extant of them playing variously in Venice, Genoa, Mantua, Bologna, Ferrara and Milan before heading for Paris in 1613 at the request of Marie de' Medici. That sounds simple enough, but the plain record belies the tortuous preparations that preceded the visit. First it needs to be understood why it was Marie that sent the invitation to the Italian players and not, as previously, her husband Henri IV.

On the eve of war against Spain and Austria in 1610, Henri had planned

Figure 9 Giovan Battista Andreini, Isabella Andreini's first son, frontispiece from his *Lo Schiavetto* (The Slave Boy), Venice, 1620.

to join his troops at Chalons. He appointed Marie as regent during his absence (she was the niece of his old ally, the Duke of Tuscany and he had married her after separation from his first wife, Marguerite de Valois). In order to secure her position, Marie had for a long time wanted to be properly crowned Queen of France and now insisted on the ceremony taking place prior to her assumption of the regency. Henri finally agreed to postpone his departure – and the opening of the campaign – for three weeks. On the 13 May the queen was crowned in splendour at St Denis. The next day the king's carriage was blocked by two carts. As it stopped, one François Ravaillac, a bankrupt schoolmaster and failed Benedictine novice, leaped on to one of the back wheels and stabbed the king twice in the chest. He died instantly.

In September 1611, after a barely decent interval of mourning – it had only been a marriage of convenience, after all – and with the political climate in France seeming stable again, Marie, now the widow of Henri IV, regent and mother of the new king, Louis XIII, wrote to her favourite actor, Tristano Martinelli, who she invariably addressed as Arlequin. She had seen him perform with the Accessi in Lyon (at her marriage with Henri IV in 1600) and Paris in 1601. She now requested him to put together a good company and come to the French court as soon as possible. Two years of bickering ensued as Martinelli tried to gather together his own company. Virginia Ramponi eventually insisted that since the Fedeli, led by G. B. Andreini and herself, was the best company, and since Martinelli was part of it, they had better all go. Arlequin wrote to his protectress accordingly and she replied:

> Arlequin, I see from the letter which you wrote me about the company of comedians that they have finally come to a decision to begin the journey hither, albeit they have waited a long while, and I had almost lost the hope of seeing them. They will, however be well received, and each, I trust will enjoy the journey. This will suffice to serve you as a passport . . . Hasten then, as quickly as you may on this my assurance and dispose yourselves to maintain the high reputation of Arlequin and his troupe, together with the other good roles which you have recently added to it. The King, my son, and I await the pleasure and diversion that you always provide.[59]

Martinelli, despite his boasting to her that 'il faut les attirer comme grenouilles au bon morceau' (you have to catch them like frogs – with a tasty morsel) never did manage to collect a company of actors together. In replying to Marie's letters he addressed her as 'la Reine, ma commère', and she called him 'Arlequin, mon compère' in return:

> For your private ear, Arlequin . . . You may be assured of the King's good graces. My son and I remember what you desire for the baptism of the child your wife is about to bear, and shall have ready the golden chain which has been promised you. I wish to give it to you with my own hands without trusting any of my subordinates, for I know how ill-disposed you are toward any intermediaries. The sooner you set forth, the greater will be your welcome. Come, then, with all speed. . . . At Fontainebleau, this twenty-sixth day of May, 1613.[60]

Although the Andreinis may have thought they were going to France as the **Fideli**, Marie continued to insist that they were 'Arlequin et ses compagnons' and had them paid as such. They arrived in Paris at the beginning of September (after the usual *en route* stops to play Turin and Lyon) and remained until the end of July 1614, playing the Louvre and the Hôtel de Bourgogne, occasionally following the court to Fontainebleau or to St Germain. Marie leased the Hôtel de Bourgogne for them and paid the Confrèrie de la Passion their rake-off of one *ecu* per day. The Confrèrie still retained the revenue from nine of the twelve boxes, however, and Marie was obliged to make up the Fedeli income with a subsidy of 600 *livres* a month.

There are subsequent records of them performing in Italy in Mirandola and Venice (1616), Mantua (1617), Venice (twice) and Brescia (1619), Milan (1620).

Louis XIII was ten years old when his father was murdered, but became just as fond of *commedia dell'arte* as his father had been – and his mother too. In 1620 it was Louis who asserted his kingship by inviting the Italian funny man and his *compagnons* to his court, not his regent mother (whom he had exiled in 1617). On receiving his letter the devious Martinelli now tried to strike up an alliance with G. B. Andreini's old rival Cecchini, who in turn corresponded at length with the Duke of Mantua over which actors to employ. At the last minute, however, Cecchini pulled out. Once again Andreini accepted the role of *capocomico* and it was the Fedeli who set off again for Paris. Their journey was interrupted, as usual, by the Duke of Savoy, who insisted that they play Turin, and in Chambéry by the death of the actor playing the second male lover. They arrived in the French capital in early January 1621; the young king is then known to have attended a staggering twenty-three performances in January and February. By this time Martinelli, who as we have seen was never particularly *fidèle*, had had enough of his *compagnons*. He begged leave of the king and left clandes-tinely at the beginning of July, taking two others with him. Nevertheless, at Louis' express request, the remaining Fedeli stayed in Paris through carnival of 1622, following the court to Fontainebleau and then back to Paris. The king was away from the end of April 1621 to the end of January 1622, but when he returned he immediately asked for an Italian play. And he saw fifteen more between the end of January and 20 March, when he left Paris again. In Lyon, in December of that year, he bestowed a cardinal's red hat on the head of the Duc de Richelieu, who was shortly to become his principal advisor. Ironically, young Louis then celebrated by attending an Italian play. It may have been his last since Richelieu was both a nationalist and a neo-classicist. His drive to promote an indigenous French theatre was to create a lacuna for Italian companies playing in France until 1644. (Richelieu died in 1642, Louis in 1643.)

So, in 1623, it was back to Italy for the Fedeli – Venice, then Turin, although one might have expected it to be the other way round. We know they played Brescia and Cremona in 1626, Venice again in 1627, Prague and Vienna (before the Emperor Ferdinand II) in 1627–8. In that year Giovan Battista got married for a second time – to Virginia Rotardi (Lydia), his long-time mistress, whose husband had just died. Records then become progressively more scarce: Vicenza and Venice in 1633, Mantua 1634, then a gap until Andreini is known to have been back in France 1643–7, but not necessarily with a company. The last record of the Fedeli by name is in 1652, when they performed a play written by Andreini, *La Maddalena lascive e penitente*, in Milan. The fact that it was a scripted piece offers a suitable stopping point for these records, not only of the Fedeli, but of a kind of Commedia, the *commedia dell'arte all'improvviso*.

Part Two

Commedia now

In this section we present a series of case studies of groups of the last quarter of the twentieth century (and beyond) playing Commedia in the English language. We are primarily concerned with those performers who have chosen to attempt to earn a living out of this once popular genre, for whatever reason and in whatever circumstance. It is specifically their insights and observations on how they run their affairs and what the particular consequences are, that may help 'those who come after' to both perform, succeed and popularise the form again. The companies often have an entirely unique history, situated somewhere on a line between the participants' often highly romanticised interpretations of what the original *commedia dell'arte* companies were like, and the artistic graft and business skills implicit in running a successful theatre troupe. Some of this history is still in the making as methods are reinterpreted and reapplied. We have thus included examples of both successes and failures, as well as attempting to abstract more contemporary trends associated with performing and (and subsisting) as a *commedia dell'arte* troupe.

This section can be read either simply as a series of monographs on some modern troupes, or, with one finger in part three of this book 'Forming, Performing and Training', as affording sometimes exempla, sometimes cautionary tales. In that section we offer our selection of the best working practices we have come across so far. In this section you can follow some of the events after which it was relatively easy for us to be wise. Our criteria for inclusion reflect a fairly rigid definition of what *commedia dell'arte* actually looks and sounds like on stage. Companies represented either adhere to a performance methodology very closely linked with the traditional Masks and their story lines, believe in actor-led theatre, make at least a percentage of their living as Commedia performers, and are viable touring units, or they represent a unique contemporary distillation of one or more aspects of historical *commedia dell'arte*.

We chose not to include here amateur confederations, companies who are starting up (or have been in the process of starting up for several years), academic vanity troupes, physical theatre, mask or clown companies who list *commedia dell'arte* as one of their myriad training or performance influences, or groups still financially apron-stringed to their place of training. These, for the most, must find room for themselves in some other publication. Some we do mention under 'Other Troupes', however, as they may indicate a route as to how a company might be developed, or reveal possible other directions to be followed. In taking this position we realise that many companies that the reader might expect to find here, such as Trestle Theatre or Théâtre de Complicité, are not included.

We do not disagree with people who say that historical *commedia dell'arte* is dead. We would like, though, to point out that, historically speaking, Aristophanes, Molière, Goldoni, Shakespeare, to name but a few, are also dead. Old texts have been shown to need new forms, so consequently perhaps old forms need new texts? Either way, live theatre cannot solely feed on the justification of historical accuracy. Today when a Commedia Mask is alive on stage it only exists in the here and now, albeit dressed in ancient regalia, and can only succeed in entertaining by making a direct emotional link with its audience. This section offers a reportage on the discoveries (and rediscoveries) made by contemporary performers of this ancient style, and attempts an articulation of how they feel it works today. Despite the autisms of performance art and multimedia events, the footings of the founders of western theatre and comedy are still very much with us, and actors, artists and performers still dig and delve to unearth the fundamental principals of their profession. We are reporting on those who look to the past to improve what they do for a living now – and not on those who are merely curious. The intention is to reveal how elements from the past of Commedia have been chosen, adapted, even ultimately rejected in the practice of the last twenty-five years or so, not as theories to be debated in research papers, but in performance.

■ ■ ■

The sister arts

How does one obtain a training in the arte of which Commedia is composed? Mainly, as we shall see, a drama school, Stanislavski derived, psychological approach to character can be a hindrance rather than a help in playing the Masks. It is not surprising, then, that our first three examples of modern troupes were led by latter-day capocomici who served their apprenticeships in, respectively, dance, three-dimensional art and classical music.

The Intenti (1984-?)

Barry Grantham has combined a career as a dancer and an eccentric comic. His father was an actor and assistant director at one time to Alfred Hitchcock, and also played the role of 'Pierrot Noir' in Houseman's *Love in a Dutch Garden*. He wrote a Pierrot scenario for his son, then aged twelve, and produced him in the role for professional performances. By the age of fourteen Barry was performing a solo comedy-character act in the English northern club circuit, and was sent to dancing lessons, so that he could end his act with a comedy dance. The lessons took over and he learnt to dance properly; he soon found himself engaged to dance in films such as Powell and Pressburger's *The Red Shoes* and *The Tales of Hoffman*, in which he was featured respectively as the 'Baby Puppet' and a Debureau-type Pierrot, before finally becoming part of the Monte Carlo Ballet. Here he became for a time the protégé of Stanislas Idzicowski, himself the technical successor to Nijinski in that company. Noting Grantham's penchant for comedy, Idzicowski showed him the traditional forms of the *commedia dell'arte*. In particular he coached Barry in the role of Harlequin, which he in turn had learnt from the Italian ballet master, Enrico Cecchetti.

Grantham worked as a dancer, comedian and choreographer up till the 1950s when he saw the Georgio Strehler production of *The Servant of Two Masters*, with Marcello Moretti as Truffaldino, as part of an International

Festival of Theatre in London. The performance made a profound impression on him. West End theatre at that stage was in the process of transforming itself from being entirely fourth wall proscenium arch based to a more open form of performance. Barry Grantham saw Strehler's version of *commedia dell'arte* as definitely helping this process of change along. From then on, although earning a living as a teacher and choreographer, he was inspired to spend a considerable amount of his spare time researching traditional Commedia. Although bitten with the bug of the enthusiast, he still maintained that he was interested in the form 'as a source point, rather than as an end in itself'.[1]

In 1984 he produced a large workshop *commedia dell'arte* production at the Oval House Theatre in South London with an international cast, and out of this developed one of the many short-lived companies that Barry formed with fellow minded individuals he met whilst teaching or performing. The name, taken from the academy of which Isabella Andreini was a member, was to be the Intenti: a company of comedians with the intention of providing amusement.

Although this troupe performed for a week at the Bear Gardens [2] museum in Southwark to some critical acclaim, near the site of the modern Globe Theatre, lack of money and factionalism lead to its swift demise. All members of the company had other work priorities which, along with several different competing methodologies, created severe tensions, and this incornation of the Intenti was swiftly put to bed.

Barry then created a solo lecture demonstration about *commedia dell'arte* which toured for several months, combining quick changes with period music and slides to cover the gaps. Periodically, for commissions and special occasions, the Intenti have been resurrected with various personnel changes. Despite the short lives of these companies, Barry is very upbeat about all of them, enjoying working in a style he loves and in the company of other enthusiasts in sunshine or in rain. He maintains that there are only two ways of forming a Commedia company: the first is that of a small collective who share the same ideals and aspirations, who will work together until the money comes in, the second being a troupe run by someone rich enough to pay the wages until the work and rewards start to emerge. So far neither the right individuals have coalesced around him for long enough for the former, nor has he achieved a sufficient pot of money from which to pay wages until artistic success has ensured financial security. Barry Grantham is currently working on a book about performing comedy.

The Unfortunati (1982–7)

The troupe that eventually became the Unfortunati was started by a group of friends including Ninian Kinnear-Wilson, John Glennard and John Broadbent. This company went through many changes of personnel and direction, and encapsulates many of the problems and solutions faced by any company attempting to perform Commedia: namely defining a public profile, its own performing style and methodology, as well as earning a living by so doing.

While training as a sculptor at Art College in Liverpool in 1976, Kinnear-Wilson became interested in how created objects might have an artistic function within society. Discovering *commedia dell'arte* via Giacomo Oreglia's book, he used it as the basis for his final practical assessment at college, utilising a carefully made sedan chair and vacuum formed masks. This show was performed first, on New Year's Eve 1976, as part of an Elizabethan banquet at his parents' Tudor farmhouse. He and the rest of the members of the group now saw within the archetypes of the *commedia dell'arte* the potential to upset the social complacency that they perceived as surrounding them: the anarchy, vitality and earthiness they found within it were a perfect antidote to inertia and apathy.

A key feature of the early Unfortunati was that the members consciously worked from the mind set of a trained artist, rather than a trained actor. The ensuing work method carried on to varying degrees throughout the company's history, seeming perhaps to some actors completely revolutionary. It allowed the group members to view their own company, during its existence, as an experiment. Even when shows didn't work for an audience, or only partially succeeded, these events still had great value, much in the way experimental drawings, or sketches would have to a designer or illustrator. In reinventing or creating a piece of art, one must accept that it will not often be made perfect the first time round, or even the second or the third. Experimental versions are not necessarily mistakes and learning from them can be a *via positiva*.

The lack of any official theatrical or drama school training was certainly a benefit at this early stage. Surviving Unfortunati members all have commented that most performers from such backgrounds, having being trained to deliver one version of set text or movement as their major performance skill, had the greatest difficulty in obtaining the fluidity and continual reinvention of one's Mask in the on-stage moment – these being skills that characterise a good Commedia performer. Drama school training, in relation to *commedia dell'arte*, appeared too often to demand a negation of a necessary vital personal creativity. Commedia needs creators, not interpreters.

Kinnear-Wilson and Broadbent were also part of the Sealed Knot (The English Civil War Society), a national organisation dedicated to the recreation of the English Civil War period, including its politics, clothing and above all, battles. Members all shared a fascination with period authenticity. Costumes and accessories were, (and still are) researched in great depth, and then handmade and used by individual members at battles and social events. Such crafts stood Wilson and Broadbent in good stead for their theatrical future: part of the impact of the early Unfortunati was the quality of its costumes, masks, props and staging.

Having bloodied themselves on the fantasy battlefield, the group now blooded themselves as performers, and set themselves the task of developing a brand of comedy that could respect historical authenticity whilst providing contemporary entertainment. In 1979 they put on shows at Sealed Knot events and period banquets, succeeding in a field not unlike American Renaissance Fairs. At this stage all were earning their living by other means, joining together at weekends to research, rehearse and carouse.

The following year the company's masks were still made of papier mâché, but in February 1981 Broadbent and Kinnear-Wilson attended a course in *commedia dell'arte* at the St George's Theatre in London, run by director, performer and teacher Carlo Boso, and mask maker Stephano Perrocco of the Sartori Studio. They were profoundly influenced by their experiences at this workshop both in terms of performance, and also learnt how to make leather Commedia masks. Boso, both overawed and inspired them. In John Broadbent's words:

> Carlo Boso went back to the roots of Commedia, the early comedy of the streets, balancing it against the later period classical approach of the Piccolo Theatre of Milan, keeping alive a spirit of true comedy. He managed to put all the historical research and quest for authenticity (we had) into a theatrical context, as well as make the workshop extremely enjoyable for all participants.

Thanks to their art-school training they picked up the techniques of leather mask making much more quickly than other participants, with Kinnear-Wilson creating several mask blocks during the course of the workshop.

The latter was invited by Carlo Boso to Paris that summer. There he took part in a *commedia dell'arte* workshop out of doors with actors from all over Europe, the final performance being on trestle stages by the banks of the Seine outside Notre Dame. At both these workshops the continental team that Boso had assembled to help him were also teaching, and the skills passed on later found their way into the work of the Unfortunati. As well

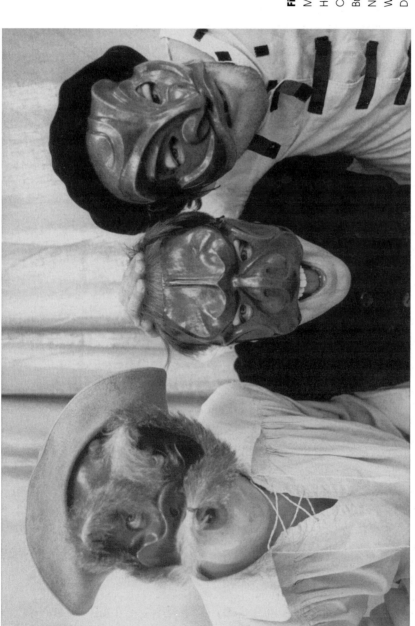

Figure 10
Masks for
Harlequin, Il
Capitano and
Brighella by
Ninian Kinnier-
Wilson. Photo:
David Corio.

as Perocco (mask making), the team consisted of Adriano Iuressevitch (singing and music), Nelly Quette (dance), Pavel Rouba (acrobatics and mime), and Bob Roboth (stage fighting and unarmed combat).

Kinnear-Wilson returned from this experience fired up and enthused the other members of the group, acting as a conduit for the newly learnt performance skills. The group slowly began to build up a collective confidence and increased their performance experience, presenting several shows per day at the Littlecote House seventeenth-century living history week. This frequency of performance was noted as one of the reasons for the growing enthusiasm and confidence of the group as, without long rehearsal periods between shows, the performers developed a closer performance rapport and allowed themselves to enjoy themselves on stage. In the summer of 1982 Kinnear-Wilson and John Broadbent were invited on another Carlo Boso workshop, again with the same teaching staff, but this time the workshops were to be a central feature of the official International Festival at Avignon. Also participating was Didi Hopkins, founder of the **Andrenalinis**. This workshop was to produce two bespoke pieces of Commedia for performance at the festival: *The Dentist* and *The Tragedy of the Queen of England*, both based on Flaminio Scala scenarios. The latter was later recycled by the Unfortunati and reworked as *The Keys to the Kingdom*.

Having studied a model for Commedia in *The Servant of Two Masters* workshop at the St George's Theatre, and then having seen that model put into practice at the Avignon Festival, Kinnear-Wilson's attitude to the Unfortunati as both a research and a performance process became more focused. Observing that the plots and Masks of Commedia functioned as a 'theatrical ecosystem', he felt that the way forward was 'not to change anything until you understand why something works as it is, and is placed like it is'. As a model of baroque *commedia dell'arte*, *The Servant of Two Masters* allows the student to see the relationships between mask, motivation and plot structure. Goldoni himself provided a written script for an already existing and successful scenario and luckily preserved it. Strehler perfected it and Boso took it as a model to develop further and this was the 'ecosystem' that he taught from.

By 1982 a core of performers from the Sealed Knot performance group were ready to go public. A trestle stage, built by the company, was already in existence, as were a basic set of masks and essential stage properties. Those members who did not want or were unable for personal reasons to go professional formed themselves into an amateur organisation called the **Gobbi Players**, to carry on battle and banquet work.

The Unfortunati[3] then rehearsed and wrote three shows for their first tour. These were originally set down in scenario form (on the model of Flaminia Scala), allowing for dialogue and business to be developed in rehearsal and performance. One of the shows created then, *Punch's Progress*, remained in repertoire until 1985, when it was finally given the *coup de gras*. The company worked all the summer of 1983, but not all of the work was paid, and some gigs were shared with the **Gobbi Players**. It is quite clear from their touring schedules from this time that the Unfortunati concentrated on specifically non-theatrical venues: open air fêtes, country displays and the like. There was a definite commitment to venues where audiences could either take or leave what was being offered them, significantly allowing the company to develop a style uncompromised by the fads and fashions of the current cultural 'alternative' theatre ethos. Kinnear-Wilson and Broadbent remember well the number of performances interrupted by parachute displays. However there were also a couple of successes in arts centres and they began to be noticed by other performers.

A week of performances for Alternative Arts in Covent Garden introduced the company to London. Of their three shows, *Punch's Progress*[4] attracted the largest crowd from the Piazza's peripatetic audience. As a result of seeing the variety of training facilities they previously had limited access to, such as acrobatics, juggling and acting classes, the Unfortunati decided to move from their rural Oxfordshire base to London.

One of the difficulties that beset the Unfortunati during their professional existence from this point on was that of retaining members who were good performers, and also committed to the ideals of *commedia dell'arte* as espoused by the founders. London did not only provide a richer recruitment area for new performers, but created many potential distractions. There is always the potential for difficulty when self-motivated performers, perceiving themselves to be equals in all artistic and policy aspects, join an already established company with very firm aims and established methods. The Unfortunati were never in a position to pay a regular wage, always working on a profit-share basis, and the result was that new performers often expected to be considered as equal with the founder members. The latter found that training new performers into the ways of the Unfortunati was often awkward and led to tension within the company. Although Broadbent and Kinnear-Wilson considered they knew more about the modus operandi of both the Unfortunati and *commedia dell'arte*, they felt themselves unable to run the company as owner-managers without being in a position to pay wages. There was no question, therefore, of telling people what to do and how to do it. This led to internal tensions between the founders as they saw things happening they felt perhaps shouldn't, but were unable or unwilling to prevent, or to guide in another direction. This tension allowed other members' agendas slowly to creep in, which in retrospect was sometimes beneficial to the life of the company and sometimes not.

The problem was partly addressed at this stage by deciding to increase the company to five. This number would, hopefully, allow the pressure to be off any one individual when on tour, and stop any 'company scapegoat' syndrome developing. There would also be enough performers to avoid having to double up roles in performance, whilst still remaining a sufficiently small unit to be financially viable.

Another issue that arose was that of pragmatic decisions being given precedence over artistic ones, due to limited rehearsal time. The early exploratory and experimental instinct that had brought the Unfortunati into existence was being curtailed by practical considerations: the need in rehearsal to finish a certain scene by a certain time. Broadbent felt that the independent lives of the characters they were creating were not being given enough development time. Consequently the contrast within a show, the balance between the joyful anarchy of some Masks and the gravitas and tragic potential of others, was not being given enough respect. The older scenarios had been written as a series of connecting *lazzi* – Broadbent's developing sensibilities as to character driven plots and the potential breadth of Commedia were running contrary to the company's old working method.

Although the Unfortunati's shows were always scripted, there was a constant attraction to the idea of being able to improvise performances – something that was certainly an unattainable ideal at this stage of the company's development. It was unclear how improvisation was going to fit into the current tightly plotted and verbally rhythmic repertoire. Despite some training in Theatre Machine style impro, neither was an adequate synthesis of these seemingly opposing styles yet forthcoming, nor was there a collective agreement as to how things should proceed. The notion of characters improvising through a plot was still a long way off for the Unfortunati, and there still existed in rehearsals a tension between the training and exploratory sessions, and those spent 'fixing' sections of the show.

A new style show *Zanni's Playtime* was tried out in performance at an English Civil War battle and didn't seem to work as well as previous Unfortunati shows. Having had a reasonable response to the *lazzi* elements in their previous shows, it had seemed a viable proposition to create a show simply based around the comic servants and their pranks. It now became apparent that business and gags on their own were not sufficient to keep an audience's attention for the length of a performance: a story that the audience became emotionally involved in was required in order that the *lazzi* could be seen to stem from character or narrative impetus. This realisation was to prove common in the work of many contemporary *commedia dell'arte* troupes. Consequently a new model for an Unfortunati show was decided upon, one that involved developing the motivations of the traditional characters into parables of modern life, giving the audience both characters and situations with which they could identify. *Zanni's Playtime* was dropped and the company focused on writing and rehearsing a new show, *Splitter Splits*, containing both *lazzi* and story line. As a further result of that summer's performances, a decision was made that for future shows the company should try to devise plots requiring one character per performer. All performers felt, and rightly too, that worrying about costume and mask changes was a major distraction both in developing one's own *commedia dell'arte* performance persona and in creating the necessary rapport and emotional link with the audience.

Despite the major breakthroughs in terms of performance practice that the company made that summer, both Martine Simone and Debbie Joseph left the company. As both Kinnear-Wilson and Broadbent were committed to carrying on, auditions were held again. Although by now the Unfortunati was secure in its philosophy and working method, in order to integrate and train new members it was considered important once again to return to the common grounding of Carlo Boso's work. Consequently, when Suzy Newman and Amanda Wiltshire arrived, the company all went to Paris to participate in a two-week *commedia dell'arte* workshop.

Despite this common grounding, however, on their return it became apparent that there was a major difference of opinion between the old and the new members of the company. A strong move was made by the newcomers to change the company's direction to an overtly political form of theatre. Unfortunately this went against, not only the older company view that Commedia celebrated and mocked all of society, commenting on the whole human condition, rather than taking one political line, but also the hard won results of their own performance experiments. The fact that two newcomers wanted to dictate company policy was not acceptable. Kinnear-Wilson did not believe that they yet knew enough about Commedia to jettison what the company had learnt about its history and subject matter and replace its parables with politics. It is possible to combine politics with *commedia dell'arte* performance, as the work of the **Dell'Arte Players** and the San Francisco Mime Troupe indicates, but only on a truly collective and co-operative basis. Unable to achieve a favourable resolution, the two women left, and were replaced by three former students of John Wright, who proved enthusiastic for the old ideals, and the company settled down to write two new shows, *Pistachio Nuts* and *Fowl Play* – and to rework yet again *Punch's Progress*.

When any changeover in personnel occurs in a *commedia dell'arte* troupe it becomes imperative that all share (or agree to share) certain fundamental principles, and those principles have to be restated and revisited before being modified if necessary. Modification can only properly take place when all have reached equal knowledge and awareness of the company's work. Thus the Unfortunati, at this stage, quite rightly introduced the idea of a trial or apprentice period when new members arrived, during which they would agree to learn and be shown the ropes, before taking on the responsibility of full company membership.

The new line-up stayed together throughout 1985, performing regularly, and attended another Carlo Boso workshop, this time at the Cardiff Laboratory Theatre where they performed as well as studied. Then, yet again, the two women in the company, Anna Campo and Theresa Rodriguez decided to leave, having decided that the life of small-scale touring was not for them. The men, meanwhile, sat down and had another long talk as to why people, particularly women, kept leaving, and in the light of these difficulties, how to move the company onwards. Financial overheads were also causing problems and there were discussions at this point over whether or not to wind up the company. However, the administrator suggested that they might as well give it one more go, as he had obtained prestigious bookings for the company at both the Northern Mime Festival and the London Mime Festival, which would hopefully function as showcases for the company's work. The decision was to carry on and honour these bookings, using performers they had met at the Carlo Boso workshop in Cardiff. It soon became apparent that having other Boso trained performers on board made life easier in the short term, as they shared a common stage vocabulary; however it made decision-making slower as there were now more relevant voices to be heard. For a period of time the newcomers' enthusiasm balanced out the disadvantage of having the decision-making process taken out of the hands of the most experienced members.

A new programme for the London International Mime Festival was created: *Punch's Progress* was temporarily revived and a new piece agreed. To avoid internal arguments Sally Brookes (also at the Carlo Boso Cardiff workshop) was asked to provide a draft scenario from which the company would create a show. This became *A Plague on You*[5]. It was envisaged as a parable of greed and exploitation with an eventual happy ending. The core of the plot was how easy it is for those in power to cover up their own misdemeanours.

The company now numbered seven, with additional input from a scenario writer and an administrator. In the quest for true *commedia dell'arte*, the shows which followed constituted a very instructive blind alley. It is within every actor's capabilities, whether Commedia trained or not, if presented with a play in scenario form, to be able to work through it enough times to produce dialogue, and thence finally create a finished product. This

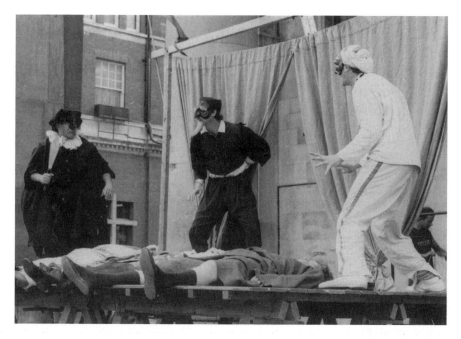

Figure 11 The Unfortunati in *A Plague on You*. Il Dottore, Olly Crick; Pantalone, John Broadbent; Brighella, Mike Chase. Dead Bodies: Peter Jordan, Jane Pycraft, Jenny Bloom.

is what the Unfortunati did to produce *A Plague on You*. However this process missed out the stage which should have preceded the scenario writing, that of spending as much time as possible improvising around as many different scenarios as possible without a view to public performance. Such a process reveals the 'x factor' in any given company: namely the knowledge of who works well with whom and under what dramatic situations. Unfortunately this stage was also missing from both versions of the next show, *Punch's Parliament*.

The Unfortunati now also decided to tackle one of the problems implicit in reviving Commedia: that of the inbuilt sexism of the Masks and the traditional plots. It was decided that the role of the second actress or *jeune première* (played by Jenny Bloom) should be constructed so that she became one of the major plot motivators, rather than merely a victim of circumstance. The character's forthrightness clashed beautifully with the nervous inanities of Peter Jordan's second actor. Similarly Jane Pycraft was given space to develop a strong female character that existed in stage space somewhere between the independence of the first actress and the malevolence of Carlo Boso's witch,[6] and she came up with a character similar in mental attitude to Joyce Grenfell, but capable of being as scary as they come. This was Olivia, the

Doctor's sister. *A Plague on You* was performed to great applause at both the London and the Northern Mime Festivals.

Unfortunately, at this juncture the company lost its administrator, and it became hard to follow up on the success of the two Mime Festivals. The Unfortunati nearly sank through inaction. Nevertheless some work was carried out during the rest of the year: an experiment in improvised Commedia that went disastrously wrong, and two versions of *Punch's Parliament* which were written, rehearsed and tried out. At one specific booking a request was made that some additional input be made into a community event on the day following the performance. With some dissenting voices it was agreed to do a parade, a cabaret and eventually a short show based upon the opening of the new community venue. The first problem was co-ordinating the preparation for this event, since the company's collective decision making policy couldn't come up with a unified method of approach.

The parade went well but the cabaret and improvised show, greatly under-rehearsed, did not: differing views on Commedia and improvisation within the company destroyed any chances of performance success. Although the result was an unpleasant and untheatrical compromise, the lesson learnt from this debacle was very important – namely that the historical methods of improvising round a scenario were valid, but that this present-day company simply did not have the collective experience or mutual trust to make them happen. This experience effectively ended Unfortunati experiments in improvising from a scenario.

The level of confusion involved was also indicative of the personal agendas of the various company members at that time: the personal challenge of attempting an improvised show in front of a live and paying audience polarised opinion within the company and it became clear that some were planning on leaving, whilst a smaller core were still committed to performing and researching into *commedia dell'arte*. With the benefit of hindsight it is obvious that the levels of trust and mutual respect within the company were not sufficient at this stage for a performance activity involving so much risk. The question of politics and *commedia dell' arte* continued to vex the company. Some members were prepared to play antisocial and reactionary stage characters, necessary for a rounded dramatic storyline, but others were appalled even at the thought of considering what they termed 'the enemy' in a favourable light. This may be one of those problems that are with us for all time: during a much later workshop, one actor's experiment in creating a South African racist *Il Capitano* figure managed to polarise opinion, being either considered very funny, or extremely offensive.

Before the crucial booking the company had decided to replace *Punch's Progress*, with another Neapolitan-style scenario, experimenting with the more direct Southern Italian version of *commedia dell'arte*. The previous show, located in the never-never land of a rather un-merrie England, included masked Pulchinellas in traditional white costume, slapsticks and conical hats. In the new show, it was decided that Pulchinella had to be recreated as a contemporary Englishman. There were many unforeseen consequences of this update.

Working again with writer and mask maker Sally Brookes, some important decisions were taken: Mr and Mrs Punch were to live in an industrial skip in the East End of London. They were to be continually visited by a social worker (over wife beating, obviously), at the same time as a vital ministerial box containing a key to the country's nuclear deterrent went missing. The resulting characters, due to the far more localised nature of the dramatic action, had become more time and place specific. As *Punch's Parliament* was rehearsed, characterisation became easier for the actors, as they were able to slip into shallow social stereotypes, rather than Commedia Masks – archetypes capable of existing equally in different scenarios and situations.

From the first Unfortunati Punch show the company sought to retain a satirical edge, as well as Mr Punch's eventual termination of anyone unlucky enough to have come near him, but developed a different (with the exception of Mrs Punch) set of supporting characters. Two shows were developed with this in mind; both, whilst having some good moments, proved in performance to be unsatisfactory for audience and performers. On the first outing the company noticed that the character of Punch did not achieve such a direct rapport with the audience as he had done before, whilst at the same time the storyline had mushroomed into a sprawling epic.

They debated the reasons for their dissatisfaction with the show, and realised that Mr Punch does not like being made contemporary. His antics communicate well enough from the never-never land of puppet booth or old-world village, so why should he change? His inhabiting of the booth or distant unspecified period in our past gives the audience a necessary distance from the action so as not to believe he could actually get them. He is, on one level, the epitome of domestic violence and is rightly to be feared. The audience, therefore, needs to stand some distance from him to feel safe enough to laugh, otherwise his comedy of violence becomes a direct threat. Spectators who are purely 'out for entertainment' react badly to anything that reminds them of the miseries and dangers of real life. The learning point the company reached, and perhaps also the key to playing Punch today, is to keep the audience at a distance from danger, and hence to place the action in some archetypal never-never land.

However the last performance of *Punch's Parliament 1*, out of doors in the old market in Monmouth, went extremely well: in the knowledge that this was the last show, the actors relaxed and stopped being precious about their roles or technique, stopped trying to force meaning onto poor old Mr Punch and performed the show as pure entertainment. It was an energetic and gutsy performance greatly appreciated by the local audience. The show was still consigned to the dustbin afterwards – and the lesson about direct audience contact and enjoyment in performance was therefore not taken to heart as much as it could have been.

Punch's Parliament (2) was an attempt to use Mr Punch as an expression of disgust at present-day politics. However the plot became far more complex than envisaged as the genre of the piece became decidedly unclear. The scene was set in a country (whichever) in the grip of martial law as a corrupt government minister attempted a coup, and all the Masks got caught up in the action. The aim was to parody the extreme views of both left and right, creating a dramatic situation to match. It became a very hard piece to balance dramatically whilst coping with the competing demands for stage time of the Masks and actors involved. The option of returning to a linear adventure where the action revolved solely around Mr Punch, much as it does with Ubu in Jarry's Ubu plays, was not taken up and the company struggled to find the core of the piece whilst the multistrand story took the audience away from Punch's dramatic primacy. The tension that is normally built up with his near-continual presence on stage had got lost as the plot kept him off for much of the action. The rolling momentum and simplicity of action associated with the booth puppet (whose audience always knows what Mr Punch will do next) got lost. Spectators want to see Mr Punch murdering his way up the social ladder, gleeful and conscience free.

In 1987 a new administrator emerged and the Unfortunati performed in Europe for the first time, in Holland. Here they were received very well and consequently were invited back the following year; it became obvious that a street theatre company who had managed to merely survive in England stood a very good chance of thriving on the continent.

In order to find replacements who were more than simply keen, new actors were now replaced after extensive workshops, in this case after a short performance run at the Bridge Lane Theatre in London whilst performing *Punch's Parliament (2)* and *A Plague on You*. New company members were trained for specific roles in a *A Plague on You*, which was to be kept in repertoire. This was an important new way of operating, as it allowed for the vital period of training time, as the new members learnt their parts and developed a sense of collective performance.

Working from Boso's Avignon storyline, Broadbent, with some help from new member Mark Abbott, also produced a scenario for a tragic Commedia, around which the company then improvised. The result was premièred at the Bath International Festival and was the closest the company ever got to putting its ideals into practice successfully. The Unfortunati were still attracting enough summer street-theatre bookings to keep afloat financially, though the winter season only managed to produce a handful of work. However, at the end of this summer there was a serious difference of opinion among members that eventually led to the demise of the Unfortunati and the creation of the **Fortunati**.

A company meeting took place to discuss the fact that they had not obtained any bookings for the winter of 1986/87. Some preferred that the Unfortunati should go dark over the winter, but others wished to carry on training. Finally a core of four decided to carry on training in Commedia and obtained places on the Harlekin Arts Project and spent the winter in Germany. Harlekin Arts was a pan-European EU funded arts project, in which young Commedia performers from Europe, already in companies, could train and create performances in an artistically supportive environment. On their return they expressed their wish to carry on as a new group, but stayed as part of the Unfortunati for the summer, honouring the work and the commitments they had made. At the end of 1987 the Unfortunati were dissolved.

In retrospect the Unfortunati produced both good and bad theatre, but the initial impetus to discover what the thing called *commedia dell'arte* was, kept it going for a long time. The mistakes that were made and the successes that were achieved were all fully debated and noted. The Unfortunati when it ceased to exist had laid the foundations for the **Fortunati**, who took on most of the lessons learnt by all the various Unfortunati casts, and put them to good use.

Soon after this event, Peter Jordan left to rejoin TAG Teatro, where he played, among other roles, the lover in *The Madness of Isabella* and *Scaramuccia*, both gaining good reviews from an English press when the shows were brought over for the London Mime Festival. Sarah Nixon also departed and the **Fortunati** became a two-person outfit which changed its name to Howitt and Broadbent. They wintered once again at the Harlekin Arts Project, and created *Severed Heads*, being their version of the entire French Revolution. Using their *commedia dell'arte* honed skills, they went on to win the 1989 Covent Garden Street Entertainer of the Year Award at the London Palladium, and subsequently performed in theatres and streets until their financially very successful partnership was dissolved by mutual consent.

Beryl and the Perils (1978-86)

Didi Hopkins, whose work mainly concerns us here, was a cofounder of Beryl and the Perils. She states that they were formed 'out of anger and passion about women's place in the world, the politics and sexuality of gender. In hindsight this produced accessible, popular, challenging, and intelligent theatre.'[7] The stated aims of Beryl and the Perils were to boldly go where no other theatre company had been before. Through Brechtian and Berlin-style cabaret political sketches they reached audiences in performance spaces ranging from theatres, such as the Assembly Rooms in Edinburgh, the ICA, the Royal Court Upstairs, to the front rooms of battered wives' refuges and bingo clubs.

They toured internationally as well and were, like, for example, the **Moving Picture Mime Show**, perceived both at home and abroad as being at the forefront of innovative British theatre. They opened the International Festival of Theatre at the Centre 140 in Brussels, appearing alongside Art Blakey, Pina Bausch, Laurie Anderson, and the Peter Brook company. They were frequently called on to share and workshop the hitherto unseen and innovative working methods which had formed their theatrical working style. This style was new to both performers as well as British theatrical audiences, and was a combination of physical acting and the direct approach to an audience, such as a stand-up comedian would use. It aimed to create small scale political vignettes within a humorous and accessible style. This cartoon style of theatre was taken directly from the character Beryl the Peril featured in *The Dandy* children's comic, who remains today an anarchic feisty female, fighting patriarchy every week. Although all the characters in the show had a similar two-dimensional accessibility, when combined with the everyday perils and dramatic situations provoked by the script, a third dimension would appear. The shows were full of barbed-wire humour and cutting-edge feminist politics, and extremely radical for their time.

There are obvious similarities between such a style and *commedia dell'arte*, in that the fixed nature of the traditional Masks, invariably stereotypes when described on paper, comes to life within the action of a performed scenario. What Beryl and the Perils and Commedia had in common was the use of the two-dimensional to represent the three-dimensional, in terms of fixed class, political and emotional attitudes, rather than fully-rounded Chekhovian characters. The cartoon figures (or Masks) only really come to life in interactive performance. The style of performance (and individual skill to do it) together with the use of archetypes and a desire to explore the foibles of the human condition dramatically and humorously were all present. The only thing not present was the wider scope offered by the greater range of humanity present within the Commedia Masks, and their combination of both women's and men's issues.

That the Perils also succeeded in continental Europe was due, in Hopkins' words, to the fact that if a performer is 'emotionally true, this transcends language',[8] and consequently a show is not limited to performing to its home language base. In addition the company was able, by turns, to be intellectual, entertaining and non-dogmatically political (albeit with a focus on women's issues), and so avoided the trap of bad political theatre. Although its house style had originated specifically in order to dramatise such issues, when Beryl and the Perils folded Didi Hopkins personally sought to explore further the performance discoveries that had been made through investigation of other forms of theatre. In 1981 she had been invited to take part in the Avignon Festival performance workshops led by Carlo Boso. The close connection between Boso's approach to *commedia dell'arte* and the Perilous approach to theatre intrigued her. Finding in Boso not only a great teacher, but also a great director, she began to study directing with him in the spring of 1989.

Whilst teaching Hopkins his approach to Commedia, Boso employed her as an actress within a piece he was directing based on Molière's short play *Le Médecin Volant*, chiefly involving the disguised Scapin's attempts to make it possible for his master to marry his true love. This adaptation was funded by the French government and had a commensurably higher budget than Beryl and the Perils had been used to, including a dramaturg to help the research and writing.

Whilst directing Didi Hopkins as an actress within *Le Médecin Volant*, Boso was constantly feeding her information as how to maintain and pass on performance energy, at the same time as keeping the suspense and tension within the drama alive. This experience crystallised ideas for her as to how the role of a *commedia dell'arte* actor-manager might function within a professional company in England. Boso effected this understanding, both during rehearsal and performance, by excitable and emphatic side coaching, not dissimilar to silent heckling. His aim was to try and make the performer aware at all levels of their responsibilities as part of a comedic ensemble. The model of conductor, which comported with Didi's classical musical training as a timpanist, clarified for her a concept of a theatrical conductor, on-stage with other actors as fellow performers, charged with the responsibility (but not in charge) of maintaining the pace, verve, and direction so vital to *commedia dell'arte* performance. This was a process that she was to follow up in her subsequent work as a trainer and with the companies she started.

Such 'conducting' assigns an easily quantifiable role to the Commedia 'expert' within a group of less experienced people, either forming a new company around an acknowledged master or else as apprentices in a larger troupe. It is the responsibility of the more experienced Masks on stage to keep the others from dying a death during the action. Although Didi Hopkins still believed in the ideal that *commedia dell'arte* is primarily theatre created by actors (as distinct from directors or designers), her experience with Carlo Boso gave her another insight. The role of a contemporary *commedia dell'arte* director is actually that of a trainer. It was not how Boso placed the actors on stage or directed the action which was important to her, but the feel of how it all worked in the moment of performance from the specific view-point of the individual actor. Until a collective of Commedia actors are all equally proficient in their chosen roles, it may be that director/trainers (or 'conductors') like Boso are vital, as they provide the necessary formal back-ground and active provocation to allow novices to develop into actors capable of taking responsibility for their Mask and its actions on stage.

Carlo Boso

For the companies studied so far, the lack of an acting background was clearly not an obstacle to approaching Commedia. At a certain point, though, the need for specialist training becomes obvious, and Carlo Boso's name has already come up several times in that context. Originally trained at the Piccolo Theatre of Milan, he apparently coveted the role of Arlecchino in Georgio Strehler's ongoing production of Goldoni's *The Servant of Two Masters*. On the retirement of Marcello Moretti this role went to Ferruccio Soleri, and Boso struck off on his own. He met with the founder members of TAG Teatro di Venezia and soon became their artistic director. Although familiar with many other models of text-based theatre, the underlying model of Boso's forays into the world of Commedia seems to have been almost exclusively the Piccolo's versions of *Servant of Two Masters*: he was seemingly influenced not only by the highly detailed characterisation and elegant *lazzi*, but also the potential and actual dramatic strength of each scene. It was a production he knew word-for-word and move-for-move. In workshops around Europe and the world he would demonstrate the dynamics of the Commedia family by rigidly drilling participants in the opening scene. This would often run counter to the expectations of the workshop participants who, expecting more freedom and improvisation, regularly struggled with the precision and energy required. All Boso demanded of them, however, was the realisation that it was this level of theatre they ought to be striving towards, and that he was working with the best model he had at his disposal.

Boso's stated aim with *commedia dell'arte* is 'to make theatre for the present with the demons of the past'. For him, Commedia as a theatre form never seeks to change the world politically, but presents all ranks of humanity equally with all their joys, fears and fables. He is very explicit in placing each of the traditional Masks within their social context and exact level of emotional development. From this standpoint each character then becomes a unique spokesperson for their own social rank in society, able to talk directly to members of their own class in the audience, and comment on others' viewpoints – a vital ingredient for most forms of comedy and not just *commedia dell'arte*. Thus Zanni represents all refugee-immigrants, Pantalone all petit-bourgeois financiers, the Doctor all elitist learning and the young lovers all awkward smitten teenagers. Each traditional Mask has a social class and an emotional background, and the conflict between these living symbols creates an ideal framework for contemporary Commedia.

Now exiled from Italy, Boso works with the Théâtre de Mystère Bouffe. His workshops can be very grand affairs with specialists and long-term collaborators brought in to add spice and expertise.

The Adrenalinis (1997)

On her return to England from working with Carlo Boso in 1990, Didi Hopkins sought to adopt the trainer/conductor approach that she had learnt from him. When she was invited to teach a performance project at a performing arts College in Liverpool, she decided to base the term's work on *Le Médecin Volant*. She translated the original text from the French, creating a new version more suitable for a young Liverpudlian cast, *The Flying Doctor*.[9] This college production was seen by Stella Hall, at that time the Director of the Liverpool Festival of Comedy, who immediately bought the show, programming it as part of the festival that year (1990). Didi then offered the cast the chance to work as a professional company might do as part of their course, in other words, rehearsals six days a week, long hours and as many performances as could be squeezed in. To support this project she fundraised extensively, both in money and in kind, so that as the show restarted outside college, rehearsal space, photocopying, lunchtime sandwiches, and storage premises had all been secured. In collaboration with Ninian Kinnear-Wilson and John Broadbent of **Unfortunati**, a further training programme was created to run alongside the rehearsals, dealing with mask making, voice and improvisation, modelled on Carlo Boso's Avignon workshops.

Following on from the idea of internal conducting derived from her training with Boso, she also invited John Broadbent and Chris Howitt (**Unfortunati** and **Fortunati**) to take on roles within the show. *The Flying Doctor* was a great success. It gave the students involved a rare and extraordinary experience of professional theatre. It also engendered the idea of continuing Commedia work in the United Kingdom, which Hopkins was later to do with The Adrenalinis.

The Adrenalinis came about in 1997 because Hopkins had been offered a performance slot at the Glastonbury Festival, but had no company at that time. She was, however, currently a lecturer in performing arts at the

University of Middlesex, and offered a group of leaving drama students, much in the manner of *The Flying Doctor* in Liverpool, the chance to work as professionals.

Didi did not perform herself but trained the young company and adapted Flaminio Scala's scenario *The Dentist* for them. Although this young company performed continuously for most of the summer, concluding in a fortnight of two performances a day outside the Globe Theatre, it did not survive beyond the end of the season. Such a cessation, unfortunately, follows a pattern (see **I Gelati**) whereby members of new, as yet unfunded or properly paid Commedia companies simply will not 'hang in' long enough for their work to make an artistic impact or provide a regular income. One has to want to do *commedia dell'arte* above all else, and be prepared to spend several years achieving that end.

One might speculate that the on-stage commitment and energy of an expert Mask within this particular company might have bonded them together longer and provided the necessary impetus and example to carry on. The role of a *commedia dell'arte* actor-manager, according to Didi Hopkin's model, is not simply one of off-stage trainer, but on-stage leader, performer and inspiration. Zan Ganassa would have understood that.

The Fortunati (1987-8)

The Fortunati grew out of the **Unfortunati**. Whilst some members of the Unfortunati wanted to remain as seasonal professionals, others wanted to carry on all year round and become seasoned professionals. John Broadbent, Peter Jordan, Chris Howitt and Sarah Nixon consequently attended the Harlekin Arts project in Bayreuth during January and February 1987. Whilst at Bayreuth, Fortunati put together their show *Beyond the Mirror*, based on Woody Allen's *The Purple Rose of Cairo*, in which characters emerged from a mirror world. Of all the performances created there it was the one most lauded by the local press. Didier Doumerge, the project director, was equally impressed with the Fortunati offering and expressed a wish to direct them at some point in the future. He was also impressed by the group's cohesion and adaptability in rehearsal.

The interpersonal tensions present in the **Unfortunati**, a major brake on the company's ambitions, were noticeable by their absence in the Fortunati. Neither was there the habitual struggle to finance a rehearsal period (since Harlekin Arts provided rehearsal space, specific Commedia trainers, full bed and board, as well as costumes, custom-built masks and new staging to take away for the companies present). It is rare to come across such munificence in the arts, and at the perfect time: such support certainly helped underpin the development of this new company. The lack of internal and external pressures during rehearsal created an atmosphere in which good ideas could be followed to their natural conclusion, rather than reaching the enforced and unsatisfactory end-stops brought about by a larger decision-making body with very limited resources. Fortunati members realised that in the **Unfortunati** the trait of fixing scenes too early had not served either the company, or any of the individuals within it, well. The joy of more freedom led to a deeper sense of mutual commitment. The group now began to enjoy the process of rehearsal, trusting each other's instincts and sense of humour, to the point where all members seemed happy to still be trying out variations on themes in both public rehearsals and performances. All seemed to be working in the same comedic direction. *Beyond the Mirror* toured successfully throughout the rest of the year and the Fortunati decided to expand its repertoire.

Didier Doumergue, from the Harlekin Arts Project, came over to Britain in September 1987 to direct them in *Arlequin, Poli Par L'Amour*, by Marivaux. This show was only ever given a couple of performances. The **Unfortunati**'s agent came to see it and expressed indifference, stating that it would be a hard show to sell, as it fell between the two stools of outdoor theatre (previously her speciality) and small-scale touring. Without agent approval, the company realised they would not recoup the considerable amount of money they had spent on the show and decided to cut their losses and ditch it. In retrospect, the group state that they enjoyed their own devised shows far more anyway. Perhaps they would have done better to continue trusting their own judgement, rather than that of an outside director, however well intentioned.

A further show was created the next year in Metz, again with the support of Harlekin Arts, a *commedia dell'arte* tragicomedy entitled *Oswaldtwistle*. Later Carlo Boso was invited over to direct *The Triumph of Punch*, a reworking of Molière's *Le Médecin Volant*. Both these shows were very well received on their initial performances, but proved impossible to keep in the repertoire due to unavoidable absences from key company members. Versions of *Beyond the Mirror* were created to fulfil bookings and various deputies were used during this period, all of whom were successful. This strategy cost the company a lot of money as the deputies all had to be paid, rather than being part of the partnership.[10]

Beyond the Mirror toured until November 1988. Its last performance was in Vicenza, Italy, with the Fortunati as guests of the Carrara family. This was a unique experience, as they were the only foreign group daring to present *commedia dell'arte* to an Italian audience in a line-up which also included Boso's company TAG from Venice and the Carraras them-selves.

> They arrive on-stage to the sound of bagpipes and obviously the first thing they concern themselves with doing, is excusing themselves. Even in the game of illusion, the sons of the land of Albion must feel slightly uneasy when on the point of presenting a *commedia dell'arte* show, right there in front of an Italian audience . . . Said and done, this squad of Londoners reveal themselves to be truly delightful, charming and put together a pleasant and witty entertainment, with every little thing in place and kindly enriched with lines in our own language, but also very comprehensible in its original English . . . As is only right when dealing with *commedia dell'arte*, intentions are misconstrued, emotions are confused and become entangled, the mistakes acquire an unstoppable progression and the whole tangled skein is only unravelled at the last moment. The Fortunati put in heart and soul, an effective acting and mime technique, well-timed musical moments, a taste for 'nonsense' and for jokes that do not hesitate to call to account even the august name of 'Shakespeare'. Tender as they are rewarding, they demonstrate a knowledge of our stage tradition that is by no means superficial.[11]

Jacques Lecoq

Lecoq's main aim at his school was to produce theatrical artists capable of reinventing theatre, and his twofold strand of teaching was constructed with this in mind. It combined both a rigorous examination of a developmental progression of physical theatrical styles all of which had distinct subject matters and relationships with the audience, and a regular place where the students would be expected to employ these new-found skills and open them to his critical judgement. The position occupied by *commedia dell' arte* within this pedagogy was of the animal-like drives that exist within us, in their basest and most dynamic form. Emphasis varied over the years, and was sometimes merely the game of making half-masks come alive on stage, sometimes the joyful side of humanity overcoming adversity, and sometimes an introduction to black humour, very close to Bouffon in style. Whatever the emphasis, the focus was never abstract, but always directly aimed at expressing the emotional and sexual driving forces both of individuals and of humanity as a whole, rather than on any fixed historical or theatrical form. The students learnt through the form, not merely about the form itself. The style of performance was both dynamic and exciting, motivated as it was by fear, lust, hunger, jealousy, old age and love.

Lecoq was fond of saying to his students that he was training them for a theatre which did not exist – it was up to them to go out and create it.

I Gelati (1984–6)

I Gelati were a brief-lived *commedia dell'arte* company, all ex-Lecoq students, who worked in the United Kingdom in 1984. We include them as an example of a group of talented performers who adopted *commedia dell'arte* as a meeting point from which to start working, and whose own development as theatrical artists was moved on by the experience. At the start of their work it may have appeared that this style could have encompassed their talents and individual artistic directions, however, this was not to be. A combination of artistic differences, the nature of street theatre in England and the brief period of time working together all combined to make this a short-lived project.

The name, meaning 'ice-creams', was intended as a pun on that of the **Gelosi**. They were founded as a result of James Macdonald (now associate director of the Royal Court Theatre), who at the time was working for Shared Experience[12] being asked if he knew anyone who performed Commedia. He said yes, and promptly formed I Gelati from his classmates at the Lecoq School. The only other addition was Eric Atkinson, not a Lecoq graduate, who played Pantalone, and who had just left the **Unfortunati**.

The company survived in this form for a summer tour, performing fairly successfully at various English outdoor festivals[13] with a show entitled *Lunatics, Love and Lunch*. Various members of the company said that some English audiences were mystified by masked theatre, or even outdoor theatre at all. Some company members, used to the more enthusiastic response by European audiences for most outdoor events, must have been particularly dispirited by the English reaction. Others in the company felt unhappy with the artistic standards the company achieved – and it also became clear that various people in the company did not get on with others. In the words of Andy Crook, a founder member,

> The show was staid and lacked ambition and flair. There was always a problem we felt in taking an English audience along with a mask piece. It seemed to puzzle them rather than entertain them. Sometimes we hit it right, but rarely flew. There was not the energy or generosity within the company to keep it going.[14]

This is perhaps an overly harsh judgement, as some elements of the show certainly worked. There were two extended *lazzi*: one of mistaken identities, and one of everyone falling in love with Colombina, which were very satisfying to watch. These were certainly the strong points of the Lecoq-trained company; whilst developing a meaningful storyline, or adapting their performance energy levels for a more staid English audience certainly proved a challenge. The **Unfortunati** found when taking a show abroad that worked for English audiences how much more generous continental ones could be. For I Gelati it must be said that the reverse is probably true, and the delicacy and subtlety of some of their work was simply not appropriate for John Bull's steadfast brand of indifference.

The lack of a masked theatre tradition in England means that most audiences do not have any inherent cultural information as to how to watch masks. As a consequence, if clues as to how to enjoy watching them are not laid down very firmly in the first few moments of any show, then the audience become understandably confused. I Gelati perhaps took English audiences' knowledge of the Masks and their characteristics for granted, as can be done in continental Europe where Arlecchino and Pantalone still appear in many different carnivals. Bim Mason's company Mummerandada was certainly aware of this discrepancy, and that company's masks were created so that English audiences could be allowed in. Similarly **Ophaboom**'s use of *commedia dell'arte* masks relies heavily on their direct relationship and interaction with the audience. Individual spectators can then directly experience the Masks, rather than watch them distantly from the safety of their own numbers.

The company split after the tour, leaving James Macdonald and Andy Crook in England to carry on with other works. These were a self-devised piece, and a version of Molière's *Le Médicin Malgré Lui* the following year, and, the following year, Brecht's *The Good Person of Setzuan* and Yevgeny Schwartz's *The Dragon*. All were performed with casts entirely composed of Lecoq alumni, with Commedia characterisation and movement at their core. At the end of 1986 the company ceased to exist as the members went on to other projects.

Moving Picture Mime Show (1977-91)

The Moving Picture Mime Show, formed in 1977, were also all graduates of the Lecoq school in Paris. During their existence they were part of the British physical theatre avant-garde, in that they were at the forefront of the movement that introduced to a wider public performance styles, techniques and theories that now seem commonplace. The company, comprising Toby Sedgewick, Paul Filipiak and David Gaines, created many different shows, utilising the techniques they had originally learnt at Lecoq, which they further developed, creating a unique visual product with widespread appeal.[15] Overall their style was an irreverent and joyful blend of *pantomime blanche* and expressive mime, with occasional forays into more serious concerns with the aid of naïve full masks, designed and made by the company. Moving Picture Mime Show toured extensively both nationally and internationally, and disbanded in 1986 on good terms and by mutual consent. They reformed in 1991 to create a new show *Generalissimo*, commissioned by the London Mime Festival, which once again combined all their old skills and poetry of movement.

The company, as befitting their Lecoq training, devised all their material themselves, and created their shows out of both collective and individual improvisations. They used very little spoken text in their performances, as the shows were all movement based, but there was, (except in the mask pieces) usually a live soundtrack of effects provided by the performers, as well as some costume, music, and, occasionally, sets. Their style was very much actor's theatre, with ancillary skills only being introduced by mutual consent and to act as a further stimulus for group creativity.

It is in the light of two particular aspects that Moving Picture Mime Show's foray into the world of *commedia dell'arte* in the show *Passionate Leave* needs to be considered: the company's adherence to the theory and reality of the primacy of the performer, as apart from director or designer, and the particular emphasis that Lecoq as trainer and dramatic theorist placed on *commedia dell'arte*. It was the interaction between these two forces, combined with the urge to develop and extend what they already knew, that created this highly successful show.

Passionate Leave was a combination of Moving Picture Mime Show's *pantomime blanche* house style and sharp half-mask *commedia dell'arte* situations. The show was certainly not a pure Commedia, but used *commedia dell'arte* elements in such a way that the different styles integrated seamlessly, underpinned by an unconventional view as to what the basic drives of humanity might include. Rather than starting with fear as the basis of humanity (as Commedia performers are often taught), they started with the idea that modern office workers are at the end of a serious dehumanising effect, caused by the pressures of modern living, and are incapable of any emotional response to life. The story of *Passionate Leave* is the story of Morris Minor, a small clerk in a faceless corporation, taking a holiday to Italy, meeting a wide selection of emotionally rich characters, and having a genuine experience which changes his lifestyle.

Pantomimes blanche were used to set the scenes, and *commedia dell'arte* to provide the story and characters. In *pantomime blanche*, the Airport, the Roman ruins, the hotel and the opera were all created as interludes in their own right. The half-masked characters emerged out of these locations and the audience was left in no doubt as to where the action was taking place, or the purpose of each new character or Mask.[16] The cast played more than one role each, populating their show with ten characters in all.

Due to the clear stylistic division between the setting of the scene and the bursts of Commedia, both elements were allowed to develop to their full potential in performance. Not only did the company indicate the Roman ruins, but gave us a potted living history of them as well. Similarly the comedic style of the story was allowed to develop to its full potential as various masked *zannis* tried to rob the innocent holidaymaker, simultaneously training each other in how to become better robbers. The dynamic energy of a true *commedia dell'arte* performance was therefore not compromised, merely separated out. The mix of mime and language made it a highly accessible show which toured in the United States, as well as all over the United Kingdom.

Call of the Wild (1987)

When the **Moving Picture Mime Show** disbanded, Toby Sedgewick had already decided what he wanted to do next: to explore further the combination of masks, physicality, comedy and dialogue that *commedia dell'arte* offered with a view to performing a purer form of it. He had met Carlo Boso in 1983 at the Avignon Festival while performing with the **Moving Picture Mime Show** and seen workshop productions directed by him. Subsequently, in 1987, he obtained project funding from the Arts Council of Great Britain, to create and fund a United Kindgom-based *commedia dell'arte* company and tour it.

Sedgewick acquired the services of Carlo Boso as trainer, facilitator and director. However the original performers envisaged for the project were not currently available, and another cast had to be assembled from the ranks of the United Kindom's top avant-garde small-scale touring and physical theatre companies.[17] Sedgewick also acquired the services of Ninian Kinnear-Wilson of the **Unfortunati** and Sally Brookes[18] as mask makers.

The project started with a two-week open workshop run by Carlo Boso; intended as an introduction to the working methods of Commedia; it was also attended by members of the **Unfortunati** and several other individuals. It culminated in two Boso-directed performances in the Piazza at Covent Garden.[19] Supposedly merely as an introduction for the new company to Commedia performance, it has to be said that, in the light of what Call of the Wild later produced, these two shows were the closest they ever got to traditional *commedia dell'arte*.

As soon as rehearsals started, serious differences of opinion emerged, ultimately irreconcilable, which affected the whole process and final product. The actors, coming as they did from auto-didactic creative backgrounds, found they were unable, from both artistic and political points of view, to accept either the precepts of *commedia dell'arte* as a style, or the rigorous training in Commedia performance disciplines that Carlo Boso was attempting to pass on. There was a conflict between their own idea of comedy and Boso's perceived overly traditional outlook. Although all the cast and director agreed on the theme of the performance, that of a satire on advertising, these continuing disagreements meant that the structure of rehearsal broke down, and eventually Carlo Boso left, leaving the company to its own devices.

The resulting show, although toured fairly widely, was not repeated after the original agreed time period. Artistically what emerged was a bold experiment, but one that contained too many different elements to be entirely satisfying to either audience or performers. There was no effective agreement before the work started as to what the company was to do and how it was to function, or even a shared sympathy and willingness to explore *commedia dell'arte*. Consequently this bold experiment did not fulfil its original hopes, as set out by Toby Sedgewick. Unfortunately it has to be counted as another example of a lone enthusiast trying to lead a disparate group of actors in a direction in which they really didn't want to go.

Antonio Fava

Antonio Fava has been a constant source of inspiration and technical know-how to English companies seeking to authenticate their Commedia experiments. His position as regards authenticity or inauthenticity in the recreation of *commedia dell'arte* is very interesting as he manages to side-step the issue completely, by claiming that the historical reason for existence is identical to its reason for existence now: for him it is a theatre form that puts sensuality and emotion above text, and does so as a reaction to the conventional theatre of whatever time it exists in.

> The theatre of improvisation (as it would be more correct to call the *commedia dell'arte*) was born as a <u>sensual</u> reply to 'conceptual' theatre. Not that this 'conceptual' theatre, for all its words and concepts, was totally lacking in sensuality – just the reverse . . . what then is the difference between *commedia dell'arte* and traditional theatre? *Commedia dell'arte* rests entirely on the direct and self contained meaning of the action, on its rapid and unambiguous messages, on its relentless appeal to the senses of the spectators, who are allowed to feel themselves part of the action, but only through the exhilaration arising from their receptive capacities.[20]

Through his company, the Teatro del Vicolo, he continues to offer workshops in Commedia every summer in Reggio Emilia.

The Oxford Stage Company

Founded in 1974, and originally called the Oxford Playhouse Company, the Oxford Stage Company has changed from being primarily repertory and main house production company to middle-scale touring theatre. This change was primarily brought about by the closure of the Oxford Playhouse building in 1987, when the company also changed its name. The artistic policy has consistently mixed classics with new works and has enjoyed both financial stability and some artistic success. It has toured both nationally and globally. Under its former artistic director, John Retallack, an innovative programme of both English and continental works was performed.

In 1992 the company produced Goldoni's *The Venetian Twins*. This production toured nationally, but never quite achieved the recognition it deserved, possibly due to a similar production that year by the Royal Shakespeare Company. Nevertheless the show remained true to the spirit of Goldoni's original, and there was considerable discussion between the translator and the actors about the nature of the translation. In the end it was accepted by all that the translation should be plain and unadorned, as is Goldoni's own style, leaving space for the actors to create *lazzi* and stage business, unhindered by overtly comic rhyming couplets or other authorial devices. In the middle of these discussions Peter Jordan, formerly of the **Fortunati**, the **Unfortunati** and TAG Teatro di Venezia, made the point that the story and situation that Goldoni had created were all that was needed by skilled actors to create good comic theatre. Perhaps it was also the presence and experience of Peter Jordan that alerted John Retallack to the wider possibilities of *commedia dell'arte*.

Retallack resolved on more research and this led him to observe workshops that Antonio Fava ran at Exeter University. Consequently he engaged Antonio Fava to be involved as the linchpin of creating a *commedia dell'arte* piece for the Oxford Stage Company. Fava ran workshops to help choose the actors for the production, as well as to cast them as Masks, and he also undertook to make leather masks for the production.

There was an extended eight-week rehearsal period in which he firstly trained the cast, especially those new to the genre, in the movement, improvisational and comedic skills of the *commedia dell'arte*. The company then worked on the chosen scenario, improvising their way through the situations and characters. Although the final casting was decided upon in advance, for rehearsal purposes the performers did not stick to one role alone. The company rehearsed with the writer present, and she attempted to record the performers' improvisations as closely as she could. She then returned with a preliminary text for each scene, which was tried out by the actors before being collaboratively rewritten.

They decided to adapt a Flaminia Scala scenario *The Lady Believed Dead*, eventually retitled *Love is a Drug*.[21] Responses to the show seem to be divided along the lines of age. Secondary schools were targeted as a particular audience, as part of the funding for the shows was from a Sainsburys' 'Arts For All' grant, and they were the audience group who responded the best and most consistently throughout the tour. Older audience groups were

Figure 12 Capitano Spavento (Jonathan Coyne) in the Oxford Stage Company's *Love is a Drug*. Drawing: Julia Whatley.

uncertain, and the reason may have been something to do with the word 'relentless', as it appeared in Fava's definition of *commedia dell'arte*.

The show was very much joke a minute with the emphasis being on getting as much comic business as possible from the characters, their relationships and the resulting set of relationships with the audience. This the company did with considerable élan and success, and it delighted the younger theatre goers. However in all the comic business the story, the skeleton upon which the action and the characters' relationships ultimately depends, seemed to get lost. The result was that the show was very much played on one level and the audience found themselves having to laugh at everything, because there was nothing much else apparent to respond to. This rendered the performance, although very funny and extremely skilful, quite monotonous to those with slightly more sophisticated theatrical tastes. The possibility of using contrasting dramatic moods to feed sensual appetites in the audience other than amusement was conspicuously absent. This might not have been the intention, but it did seem that all the characters were desperately trying to make us laugh all the time.

Antonio Fava stayed with the production for most of its tour and played on stage as a minor *zanni* and musician, wanting to see how his creation would survive, and to be on hand to direct and tinker. This was not part of the original plan by John Retallack, and appeared from reports, to have kept the actors working to their original blueprint as conceived by Fava, rather than allowing them to develop the show apart from their mentor. As this development never happened, it is mere speculation as to whether the cast would have managed to find other levels on which to perform, and hence give the show more variation.

Another anomaly, as regards Fava's stated intentions, was the presence of a writer in the rehearsal process. Although his aims were very clearly stated in the programme, i.e. to allow the actors to improvise their way to a final working text, this appears to have been interpreted as improvising in rehearsal to create a final text, which was not written by the actors, but by an outside hand. The difference between the two is crucial. To develop an actor capable of responding to the mood of audience with comedy, plot, text and drama, the presence of an external script, the speaking of which requires the additional act of interpretation, acts as another barrier between performers and their ability to respond to an audience. It is also the difference between a comic actor and a *commedia dell'arte* performer.

That the show was a great success amongst certain sections of its audience is undeniable, but whether it achieved anything other than to make them laugh a lot, whilst sailing fairly close, but not quite close enough, to one particular ideal of actor's theatre, is debatable. The show certainly raised the profile of *commedia dell'arte* amongst young theatre goers, but this aspect of the Oxford Stage Company's work did not survive the tour, and neither did the performers feel any need to carry on together under a new banner and perform *commedia dell'arte*. This is perhaps the crux of the issue: if Fava's training had actually given the actors the tools of the *commedia dell'arte* trade as he envisaged them, then such a fully-funded tour in good theatres could certainly have been the beginning of something else. It was perhaps due to the continual niggling compromises between Fava's approach and the financial and artistic strategies of the Oxford Stage Company that this bold and high-profile experiment never gathered momentum and carried on.

Ophaboom (1991-?)

Ophaboom were founded by Geoff Beale and Howard Gayton who met whilst training at the Desmond Jones School of Mime in 1990. Later on that year Beale completed the summer school in *commedia dell'arte* at Reggio

Emilia with Antonio Fava, and on his return met up again with Gayton. In 1991, playing with Commedia style half-masks, they created their first show, *Émigré*. The discovery that the expenditure of energy can be fun, which was to characterise all their later work, led them to want to develop, research and perform a contemporary version of *commedia dell'arte*. They also hoped they might manage to recapture its popular appeal.

That summer they performed another two-hander, *Charlatans*, for the Alternative Arts summer programme of street theatre. This show was loosely based around two *zannis* (named Pedro Muscadet and Mr Spavento), selling all manner of odds and sods to the audience, desperate to earn a few crusts or pence to avoid starvation. Later on that year they were joined by Cathy Jansen to perform the first version of *Richard III*, this time for the Alternative Arts Shakespeare Festival. The idea of *zannis* desperately selling anything and everything for a living and getting out of their depth, was miraculously transferred to *zannis* desperately performing Shakespeare and getting out of their depth. This formula, which survived for several years, became the initial mainstay of their reputation and performance style. Much humour was gleaned in performance from the original story, from the *zannis'* departures from it and their actual excursions into the audience. For the company then, the direct relationship gained from audience contact was just as important, if not more so, than the storyline.

Ophaboom now entered a second phase of Commedia investigation. Under the direction of Gian-Franco Bossari two new shows, *Harlequin in Disguise* and *A Woman's Revenge* were produced. Bossari's contribution was to develop the actors' interest in language and patterns of speech. The company did a lot of research on proverbs for the *zannis*, literary sources for the lovers, and so on. Bossari's approach to the Masks was to make them really live again for a modern audience, making Pantalone, for example, less of a chronically incapable old man and more of fifty-year-old East End Geezer. In the words of Geoff Beale:

> He worked well only with those actors who could ride out his lack of interest in really helping, so as a young company without experience, two of the performers suffered and the whole balance became unstuck. I think that he also did not understand the comedy aspect and the desperate need for the audience to laugh for the actors to keep going with the comedy. I think with hindsight we went too far, too fast and neither he nor I were aware of the group dynamic process.[22]

The actors had discovered that their aim – to survive and enjoy performance through story, character and the constant feedback of laughter – was running contrary to their director's ideas, so Bossari was asked to leave. The company had accepted through intuition, if not yet consciously, the primacy of actors' theatre.

This company performed a version of the Flaminia Scala scenario *The Woman Believed Dead* later that year for the Alternative Arts summer street theatre programme, and also at the Vlissingen Festival in Holland. After Bossari's departure, the company, reduced in numbers, performed its version of *Orpheus in the Underworld* at the Edinburgh Fringe Festival.

The year 1992 saw the formation of the business partnership between Beale and Gayton which was the original foundation of Ophaboom. A four-person version of the company, with Jenny Harris and David George, was invited to join the *Elephant Rouge* tour. This was a significant point in the development of the company, as it was to test what they currently knew of theatre, and to put it into the context of surviving as buskers on mainland Europe. The safe context of performing in one's native language was to be left behind, and theory and good intentions were to be severely tested. They consequently underwent a very steep learning curve: if the show worked, you ate, and if it didn't, you didn't eat. Their show was another version of *Richard III*.

As a consequence of this tour the following criteria were identified by the company as influencing its future work: the realisation that happy accidents in performance are vital to street Commedia; that there is comic and theatrical profit to be made from the number of languages available in continental Europe; that improvisation in performance can work; that fun can be had with masks, and (something both the **Fortunati** and the **Unfortunati** discovered) that there was a lot more approval for what they were doing to be had on the continent than in Britain. The improvisational and audience contact skills of Pedro Muscadet and Mr Spavento were further honed on the tour.

This system, however, meant that for the next few years other company members became the 'straight' characters, whilst the *zannis* stole the show, chatted to the public, larked about and kept the audience on their toes. The other actors were not encouraged to improvise or join the *zannis* in audience contact. Although this company performed successfully over the summer, busking their *Richard III* in Denmark, Germany and at the Aurillac Festival in France, the variations in approach of company members to Commedia began to show up. These were differences which could no longer be ignored, despite there being enough paid work for the company to stop merely busking for survival.

Beale and Gayton resolved that all future company members were to be selected through a workshop-style audition. In such workshops, as well as being able to select suitably talented performers, they hoped to find people who shared the founders' approach to Commedia. Formally trained actors, they discovered (as had the **Unfortunati**) often had difficulty with improvisation in performance and were unable to both be at ease, and to change things 'in the moment', in front of an audience. Thus when, in 1995, David George departed, workshops were run with the idea of finding new members for *Romeo and Juliet*, the proposed new show. Meanwhile the company performed *Richard III* at the Venice Carnival again. In spring the company went for the first time to rehearse at Sélavy, the performance study centre set up in France by John Rudlin and Amanda Speed. From then on the isolation and support afforded by this centre as a rehearsal base has proved invaluable to the company.

The form of *Romeo and Juliet* was similar to that of *Richard III*, in that the *zannis* improvised and enjoyed direct contact with the audience, whilst the straight characters provided plot and the necessary springboard for their antics. This also meant that the plot was broken down into a series of simple scenes defined by action and intention rather than text, each capable of being delivered in several different ways. Pedro Muscadet and Mr Spavento might still have all the best *lazzi* and gag lines, but the foundations were definitely coalescing into something closer to the paradigm of *commedia dell'arte*. The uninterrupted time spent at Sélavy also meant that the company could develop musically, and good vocal harmony and powerful singing has become a feature of all subsequent shows.

Although A-level set-text bookers in England may have been mystified by the Shakespearean pastiche that was Ophaboom's *Romeo and Juliet*, it entertained its United Kindom audiences as well as functioning well on the continent. It was not a busking show, being too long, but an outdoor piece of theatre, and as such represented a move forward by the company. At the Aurillac Festival, *Richard III* was performed to publicise *Romeo and Juliet* at a different venue. This pairing of the two shows worked very well and the company began to discover the differences between the *zanni*-based humour and that of the more complicated plot lines of the *Romeo and Juliet* story. The rest of the company became interested in, rather than resentful of, the primitive survival tactics of Pedro Muscadet and Mr Spavento who now had to seek ways of becoming integrated into a plot that did not always depend on their rude quips and mania.

Beale and Gayton are adamant that the energy required to create *commedia dell'arte* must start out of doors, as that is where the issue of danger in performance is addressed directly. They claim that to be a *commedia* performer, you must start looking, not at the safe indoor clown, but at the manic out of doors clown. In a show the audience's impression (and the

Figure 13 Ophaboom: Mr Spavento (Geoff Beale) and Pedro Muscadet (Howard Gayton) at the Venice Carnival. Photo: Sylvie Châtillon.

performer's reality) must be that anything could happen the next moment, depending on the circumstances. Of course the actor genuinely knows what happens next in the story, but he or she must also be openly willing to take on other possibilities as they open up to them, and be able eventually to get back on track again. An outdoor audience does not stay simply to be consciously amused, but because they are compelled to do so by seeing risks being taken and sense that they might miss something amazing if they left. It is this sensation that must be preserved when a company subsequently performs indoors. When considering this approach it is certainly worth spending time watching clowns or comics whose act is made up of interacting with an audience, to see how far, and with what material, one can go.

The second important conclusion reached that year was that the medieval and renaissance social order as personified in Commedia is still present today, and is still a major force in how theatre connects with an audience. Surprisingly enough this realisation came from a medieval fair at Le Puy-en-Velay, when the ability of the audience to costume itself appropriately reflected their very obvious economic status. Free entry on the last day encouraged the 'could only just afford it' standard of costuming. The company states that with this sliding scale of costumery went a sliding scale of arrogance and indifference to the performances they were giving. The richer the audience were, the more they were concerned with themselves, and not a bunch of scruffy individuals trying to entertain them. The actors experienced a sense of the historical reality of the *zannis'* social standing, as well as 'a sense of something from history working now.' It may be that, playing *zannis* all the time, Beale and Gayton now instinctively take the worm's eye view of society, and hence see the world and its riches towering above them as a matter of course.

Curiously enough this *zannis'* world view was reinforced early in 1996, when through the offices of the Venice Carnival, Ophaboom found themselves performing at a ball at the Doge's Palace on the last evening of Carnival. This was one of the most exclusive events of the Carnival, with foreign guests flying in just for the ball. Once again the Ophaboom *zannis* felt themselves surrounded by wealth, arrogance, indifference and ostentation, feeling what it must have been like for their historical counterparts.

After further workshop auditions, Ophaboom went to Sélavy to rehearse and rework *Romeo and Juliet* and *Richard III* for the new cast. There were subsequently three significant performances that year that convinced the company they were on the right lines. The company played at an academic conference on *commedia dell'arte* at the Wimbledon College of Art, throwing itself into the dragon's mouth of academic opinion. They came away successful, having entertained everyone and subsequently published an article as an official conference paper.[23] At Idstein, in Germany, the company's efforts to make their story genuinely fit the locale, via local references, paid off, demonstrating that one of the potential strengths of this type of performance is that it can, without too much fuss, be made to become at least a temporary part of a local culture.

There were similar good receptions for their outdoor performances in Almagro in Spain which left the company in a very optimistic frame of mind. They had proved to themselves that their way of producing theatre worked, and that they could survive financially on an acceptable touring wage level whilst doing it. The stage was set for Ophaboom to be able to develop artistically, in the knowledge that their product was in demand, on the continent at least. They, however, decided not to put all their eggs into one basket, and rather than deserting Britain for the continent (as some outdoor performance groups have done, such as Nickelodeon and British Events), embarked on a fifteen-date United Kindom autumn tour of *Romeo and Juliet*.

In 1997 the company expanded to six members, and two new shows were created – *Alchemy* and *Don Balderdash*. These shows were intended to be complementary, in order to retain the perceived strengths of the company, whilst developing in new ways. The company also received a grant from the Sport and Arts Foundation that year, which enabled them to buy new musical instruments, a van and to commission a custom-built trestle stage from John Broadbent. All of these contributed to the improved production values.

Don Balderdash was created as an alternative to *Richard III*, putting to new use the style developed from the birth of the company, in that it was a street and busking show, keeping a direct relationship with an audience using as simple a story as possible. There was no major attempt to stick to traditional Commedia Masks, merely to an overall feel, with everyone in the company performing masked. This decision was made for two reasons: the first being a democratic one that, as *Alchemy* was going to be a more traditional Commedia, all cast members should experience wearing the mask in at least one show, and the second being to try to open all company members to the freewheeling performance techniques employed previously only by *zannis* Spavento and Muscadet.

Don Balderdash, however, did not last more than a season, unlike *Romeo and Juliet* and *Richard III*. Although it seemed to work most of the time, it was hard work to perform. Geoff Beale reports that as everyone in the company now had licence to improvise and play with the audience, they very often lost the narrative thread by which all the *lazzi* were connected.

From the founders' point of view this was quite frustrating, in that they knew they could deliver the goods in this style, but since they no longer had the monopoly of fooling in this way, it very often fell to them to try to put the show back on the rails, rather than enhance it by relating to the audience directly. As in the **Unfortunati**'s experience with *Four Zannis* and *Punch's Parliament (2)*, when there is no clear pecking order of masks, the interactions within the performance lose their clarity and direction. The audience also becomes unclear as to whom they should be sympathetic and to whom not.

Alchemy[24], initially inspired by Ben Jonson's *The Alchemist*, had a different focus. After the introduction of the Lovers in *Romeo and Juliet*, the intention was to recreate the relationships between the *zannis* and the *force majeur* of their master, Pantalone. The length of the show, and the new comic pairings (splitting up Mr Spavento and Pedro Muscadet for large parts of the action) created initial difficulties with pacing and rhythm. The company were coming to terms with playing situations and gags that were based on plot development and dramatic tension, rather than solely the energy of actor/*zanni* relations with the audience. Their busking origins had not prepared them for the next stage in the company's development, which was into situation, rather than character and confrontational comedy. They would have to learn to be both alive for the audience and in the plot simultaneously.

The year 1998 started with the company from the previous year still intact, and they performed once again at the Venice Carnival, this time with a truncated version of *Alchemy*. It seemed that this show managed to combine all the long-standing company performance strengths as well as the ability to hold the audience's attention through a dramatic story. The company consequently began to work on a different project with slightly different aims, an adaptation of Chaucer's *The Miller's Tale*. Two pragmatic reasons dictated this choice: they had discovered that classic titles, and adaptations thereof, went down well with both bookers and audience and they wanted to create a show aimed at French medieval festivals, which they enjoyed doing. Some departure from the model of early *commedia dell'arte* was thus inevitable.

Scenario writers were to be used. John Broadbent and Tony Addison, both ex-**Unfortunati**, were asked to help prepare an initial storyline for the company to devise around. Broadbent suggesting specific comic scenes and pairings present in the original that should be kept to, whilst Tony Addison teased out the structure of the piece as well as formalising for the company the personalities of the characters involved. This scenario was treated with a fair amount of freedom by the company when in rehearsal at Sélavy, but Tony Addison reports that the general plot guidelines and order of scenes suggested were kept to. He was especially pleased as, in his words, the company 'captured in physical theatre the pictures beyond the words'.[25] Some Commedia Masks were directly applied: Pantalone as the Old Man and Il Capitano as Alison's self-obsessed would-be lover. In the quest for a pre-commedia, more medieval style of performance, all the other characters also wore half-masks which were provided by The Mask Studio. The rehearsal period at Sélavy also allowed time for the musical and dance skills of the company to be further developed.

It was also decided to allow one actor to play more than one Mask, something formerly regarded as getting in the way of the performer's concentration and relationship with an audience. Previous versions of *Richard III* (and *Romeo and Juliet*) with a large cast generally had Mr Spavento and Pedro Muscadet playing lots of roles as themselves without any attempt at theatrical illusion. *The Miller's Tale* was also the first Ophaboom show not to rely consciously on that duo's good offices.

The company felt that the show had moved to the opposite extreme from *Richard III*, in that it had become overly structured. They felt that there was not enough room for play on stage, as all the actions and scenes were too proscribed, and departing from it 'in the moment' created problems for the overall rhythm and comprehensibility of the piece. This was especially true of the European work, when verbal information given was not always enough to enable the audience to understand and enjoy the action. It was, however, regarded as being a good piece of theatre, as well as the beginning of what Ophaboom now recognise as the third period of their existence.

They have mastered both outdoor *zanni*-based performance, and also outdoor plot/character driven theatre. The way the company may develop in the future appears to be by combining these two separate models. Significantly they have developed into a four-person collective with Beale and Gayton inviting David Bere and Sarah Ratheram to become equal partners. The founders, having worked with these two performers for three years, and seeing that they were still interested and had served their apprenticeship, decided to open up the circle of ideas and responsibilities to them.

The training of the two newer members in collective improvisational skills was considered very important, and time was set aside for this to happen. Ophaboom invited the French *commedia dell'arte* company Athra to join them in this period of training. The company then went on to create a version of *Dr Faustus* simply titled *Faustus*, with the aid once again of Tony Addison as adapter and scenario writer. At the time Geoff Beale wrote:

The Faustus show and pre-show workshops should strengthen the *complicité* between the group, with more genuine chances to improvise because we know each other . . . We wish to push characters more, so we don't really know if we will have *Spavento* and *Pedro*, they are there if we a) need them or b) want them, which is a great release.

Our feeling is that this seems to be what happened historically . . . as the plots become more important the *Innamorati* and *Pantalone* rise in significance and therefore the role of the *Zanni* downsizes, particularly those like *Spavento* who cannot really hold a plot line, hence the later *Zanni* . . . Brighella and Harlequin and others were not stupid. With the *Miller's Tale* we had our first real plot structure that the characters were part of. The plot came indirectly from their desires and motivations, rather than in *Alchemy* or the others the direct intervention of the *Zanni*.

So *Faustus* should hopefully give us a show of plot, intricacy and yet the huge visual devices and stupidity that makes our work so bloody good abroad. Any discussion of us must take this on board, the *Zannis* maybe [initially were] our main contribution, but going abroad was part of the spur: performing as a company in seven languages means we are forced to be simple and direct. With the four of us working together we might be able to mix between a more interior complex show and an outdoor in your face one, this is where we might start coming close to *commedia dell'arte* in our opinion.[26]

Reviews of *Faustus* from the 1999 Edinburgh Festival indicate the extent to which that rapprochement with Commedia is being achieved:

Brilliant! Really, it was. This Commedia dell'Arte-based production of the Faust story is absolutely hilarious. Combining physical theatre, slapstick, witty word play, modern references, audience involvement, puppets (very Punch and Judy!) and a little bit of music, Faustus had the audience in fits of laughter from beginning to end. There was a great deal of interaction with the audience, much obviously scripted but some clearly off-the-cuff. . . . The four performers, in a variety of beautifully made Commedia-style masks, play seven characters with an ease which makes clear their total professionalism. Each character is sharply delineated. The company . . . work in the tradition of the *Commedia dell'Arte*, rather than slavishly following its conventions. They have preserved its spirit whilst developing it into a form which is very much of today.[27]

And in *The Scotsman*'s opinion

> Ophaboom Theatre appear to be a well-kept secret. Using *commedia dell'arte* as a starting point, they have developed an entertaining and inventive mix of music, masque, puppetry and energetic movement. . . . *Faustus* is an as yet largely undiscovered treat. This creative reworking of the epic tale is a fast-paced comedy that is frighteningly funny. The show is full of startling vigour and anarchic playfulness that often finds the performers launching across the seating into the audience. Coming face-to-face with one of these grotesque, half-masked characters is an experience in itself.[28]

Thus the major change in company organisation and direction seems to have been successful. Whereas the dual actor-manager system drew the company away from the historical collective model of company organisation, shared responsibility and dedication to shared aims will take Ophaboom into the millennium in style, and a stronger performance *complicité* will allow them to move into deeper areas of comedy. The company remain very much aware of the historical development of *commedia dell'arte* and part of their development process is to compare what they are doing now with what is known of the development of the performance genre. Geoff Beale again:

> I think our contribution to the Commedia debate is to show:
>
> 1   [That] current audience[s] cannot easily accept the lovers for instance without the cipher of the *Zanni* to realise that they can take the piss out of them. The *Zannis* operate as a bridge for the audience back into a more hierarchical world.
> 2   [That] by breaking the fourth wall, the *Zannis* define their own nature . . . they do not have the necessary intelligence to be actors.
> 3   By enacting they often demonstrate an innocent holy fool wisdom that contradicts their stupidity but creates sympathy.
> 4   In our shows, the contact with the audience and the slapstick meant that if sometimes the show was dipping we could up the tempo with the *Zannis*. Certainly in the case of *Romeo and Juliet*.
> 5   For us specifically, and maybe other companies, with the *Zannis* so pre-eminent and almost running the shows a bizarre imagination and fantasy line can be followed in terms particularly of journeys, costumes and props. The cheapness of the props and their obvious lack of quality can be presented without shame by the *Zannis*.[29]

La Compagnie des Trois Oranges (1998–?)

This company is based in France at the Centre Sélavy, though it is currently working in both England and France. It was originally formed by Amanda Speed and Sylvie Thoraval, not specifically as a *commedia dell'arte* performance group, but as an outlet for exploratory alfresco physical and masked theatre. After touring a *commedia dell'arte* performance for two years, however, it appears that Commedia is now the most fixed element of the company's repertoire.

Having trained with Antonio Fava, worked as his assistant and co-taught several Commedia courses at the company base at the Centre Sélavy, Amanda Speed invited a company in 1998 to join her and perform in a scenario entitled *Le Vétérinaire Extraordinaire*. It was toured locally, with a horse and cart providing suitable ambience, and performed at local village festivals, small-town *soirées* and farmyards over a short but intensive period. The tour was intended as an experiment to see if *commedia dell'arte* would still communicate its old magic to a mainly peasant and farming community.

Half the company members invited to join were former students from various workshops held at Sélavy, together with other enthusiasts encountered along the way. The shared grounding in historical assumptions, and training in a common performance style unified the focus in rehearsals very quickly, which made creating the final show easier than expected. Indeed some of the cast members claimed that the rehearsal period was positively enjoyable. By 1999 the company had changed personnel slightly, but had improved the show and produced a bilingual version which toured both France and Devon. This second tour was financially self-supporting.

Although the company is largely administered by Amanda Speed, all members are deemed equals in decision making during rehearsal and performance. With this agreed the company has so far striven successfully towards an ensemble-based form of *commedia dell'arte*. A successful collective company working method has been achieved, and is strongly supported by the performers. The company consciously models itself on the organisational structures of the historical companies, in that company articles state that everyone is equal both as a performer and financially. That this appears to work is reflected in the good company feeling and the palpable support given both in performance and backstage. This may also have been supported by the fact that the company members are not drawn from a specifically theatrical base, but from a much wider range of national, artistic and philosophical backgrounds.[30] From their differing viewpoints, all have come to accept Commedia as being integral to their lifestyle. Not all members of the group, however, feel that the company has fully evolved, and state that they

Figure 14 La Compagnie des Trois Oranges: Petit Pierre (Fraggle), Octave (Alban Hall), Arlecchino (Juliano Perreira), Colombina (Claire Bullet), and Isabelle (Amanda Speed) in *Le Vétérinaire Extraordinaire* in Angoulême. Photo: Pierre Ruaud.

would like the chance to work with a director or other 'outside eye' at some point, as one possible direction.

From conversations with the performers it seems that all are searching to find out what the essence of *commedia dell'arte* is today, rather than imposing a fixed opinion as to what it ought to be on each other. This personal commitment to exploration from all members made for a critical but supportive company, determined to produce a quality *commedia dell'arte* show, and quite open to the means as to how they arrive there.

The original scenario was written by John Rudlin specially for the company, and then collectively developed without an external director. The rehearsal process was structured very loosely, following the needs of the Masks and scenes as they developed, rather than following an rigid external plan. By the second year of the show, the off-stage musician had become more on-stage and was more integrated into the action: thus all *lazzi* and set pieces of business had appropriate live music to support them.

The particular model of Commedia that the company used is very firmly based on the style developed by Antonio Fava. There is no 'great drama' or complicated plot as is sometimes present in the Flaminia Scala scenarios, but a loosely connected series of scenes, ultimately resolved, developing and showcasing the actors' performance strengths. This works in performance, and allows all actors a great freedom to tailor their performances to each individual audience, and occasionally even individuals within that audience. The scenario of the show was the same both years, with changing emphasis and different scene order as the production evolved. The thematic emphasis was EU bureaucratic interference in local agriculture one year, and genetically-modified food the next. The 'genetically-modified' pantomime cow, Molly, (Arlecchino in disguise) became both an object of ridiculous tragedy and an object of intense amusement for the under sevens.

It is hard to see, at present, how the company can survive together for longer periods than the brief funded tours they undertook in 1999. The difficulty is one of financing eight or nine people at a reasonable level for long enough so that they can ultimately reap the rewards of such a promising beginning.

Carlo Mazzone-Clementi

Turning now to the USA, the influence of a third Italian Commedia maestro needs to be considered. Before emigrating from Europe, Carlo Mazzone-Clementi was friends with Marcello Moretti and Amleto Sartori, worked under Vittorio Gassman, with Dario Fo and Franca Rame, studied under Jean-Louis Barrault and Etienne Decroux, performed with Marcel Marceau, played Brighella at the Piccolo Theatre of Milan under Georgio Strehler, co-taught with Jacques Lecoq and was directed in the first Italian productions of Brecht by Eric Bentley.

Born in Padua, Italy, in 1921, he worked in professional theatre in Italy and France throughout the 1950s. He was following the newly developing paths of physical theatre, mask work and comedy, that were to become the foundation stones of not just his work, but also that of Dario Fo and Jacques Lecoq. With Eric Bentley's patronage, he toured the United States in 1958, conducting workshops in Mime and *commedia dell'arte*, and intro-ducing the Commedia masks of Amleto Sartori to America. He then began teaching for the Carnegie Institute of Technology (now Carnegie-Mellon University) where he remained for three years. Later, he founded the 'Piccolo Mime Workshop on Broadway' with Tony Montanaro and Jewel Walker.

Mazzone-Clementi always described himself as in the 'Gozzi' school of the Commedia tradition: the 'Goldoni' school in his mind referred to attempts to re-create and codify the original forms of *commedia dell'arte*, whereas the Gozzi school supported the ongoing metamorphosis of the art into contemporary forms era by era. In his view *commedia dell'arte* does not stand alone from either the world, the way we see it, or the actor who lives on in this world. His conception of *commedia dell'arte* was that it is as fundamental a part of the actor playing on-stage as is that actor's breathing, moving and living. He claimed to have discovered *commedia dell'arte* for himself whilst in Paris: seeing the enthusiasm for the form in the French people who surrounded him, he was more able to accept the uniqueness of his position as both an Italian, a performer and a human being. Mike Chase of the Mask Studio in the United Kindgom claims that if you asked him about

Commedia, he answered with metaphysics, talking about the whole chain of being and how there is no gap between stage and life – before one acts on stage one must know who one is. Indeed the whole of Mazzone-Clementi's work seems to be concentrating on allowing performers to exist on stage at one with themselves:

> Characterisation must begin at home: in the body. Some of us are not at home in our bodies. We must discover what that means, therefore the main emphasis of my work is physical discovery . . . beginning where you are means really knowing where you are, from your heels up, and not (for the moment at least) avoiding contact with reality through flights of imagination, philosophical excursions into existentialism or even, for the moment, emotional recall.[31]

The Dell'Arte Players (1975/6–?)

The Dell'Arte Players were founded at the same time as the Dell'Arte School, with the intention of practising what the school was aiming to teach. Integral to both was the teaching and performance ethic of their founder, Carlo Mazzone-Clementi, which in turn incorporated the methods of his old friend and collaborator, Jacques Lecoq, plus additional elements taken, in particular, from American popular theatre forms. The staff of the school was initially the same as the Dell'Arte Players, plus Mazzone-Clementi and his wife Jane Hill. Gradually the players have evolved a separate identity, whilst at the same time remaining integral to the school. Their base, Blue Lake in Humboldt County, Northern California, serves both as a training ground for themselves and their students, and as a place of retreat.

As their name suggests, the group regard part of their performance roots as being in traditional *commedia dell'arte*. Mazzone-Clementi's oft repeated statement that 'Commedia is dead, long live Commedia' has been taken to heart by this company. By this he presumably meant that although the social and artistic reasons for the original companies' existence have passed, there is the legacy of masks and techniques which still constitute a basis for live theatre. To survive and prosper at any time, Commedia must reflect the society and audiences of that time, and this, among other things, is what the Dell'Arte Players strive to do. They link their performance activities, via historical precedent, to contemporary issues. Thus although their training background is that of Franco-centric movement theatre, as developed by Copeau, Decroux, Barrault and Lecoq, the realities and necessities of effective economic touring in their own country have affected design, ensemble size and performance methodology. Significantly, they have made a virtue out of these necessities and, for example, have focused on developing, as a skill in its own right, the art of multiple characterisation within one show. This allows a wider dramatic canvas within which to construct plots and effective storylines, and prepares actors for mask, costume and energy changes within a show. So important a technique is this regarded, especially given the economic confines of independent small-scale touring that this is taught as a separate skill in the Dell'Arte School.

Based in the Redwood Forest area of California, they have a perspective on ecology, native American traditions and the place of the artist at the centre of things, that does not rest easily with the American mainstream. Nevertheless they constantly aim to 'make productions accessible to our wide touring audience through theatrical inventiveness and by tackling themes that, while inspired by our area, flow into larger currents in the stream of American life'.[32] Politically their shows reflect and satirise that which surrounds them; they take the political potential of *commedia dell' arte* quite seriously, much in the way the San Francisco Mime troupe did in the 1960s, working effectively to combine content and style. From 1979 to 1991, amongst other work, they created a trilogy of plays (*The Scartissue Mysteries: Intrigue at Ah-Pah* in 1979, *The Road Not Taken* in 1984 and *Fear of Falling* in 1991) concerned directly with their surroundings and the politics of ownership and land use. These shows all utilised the structure of a detective thriller, with a strong female lead detective, Scartissue herself, created out of a union between Sam Spade, Fred Astaire's dancing detective in *Bandwagon* and the experience and artistry of Joan Schirle (the character's creator and performer). The company sums up their philosophy and way of working by calling it 'Theatre of Place'. Where they work affects how they work. They consciously create a synthesis between the imported *commedia dell'arte* traditions, and the native American animal stories:

> The Native Americans of the Pacific coast didn't make theatre as we know it, but they created stories about animals that became part of their oral tradition and mythology. The characters arose from the collective observations of generations for whom animals and plants were part of the fabric of survival, ceremony and enjoyment of life. Animals and humans share qualities like courage, laziness, timidity, sensuality; bear, raven, coyote, and salmon became part of stories that were sometimes serious, sometimes comic, spiritual or bawdy. We are also inspired by the stock characters of the early *commedia dell'arte*. Based on day to day observation of barnyard animals, some, like

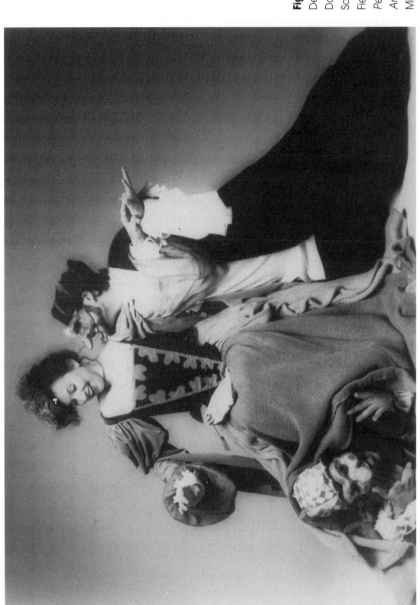

Figure 15 The Dell'Arte Players. Donald Forrest, Joan Schirle and Michael Fields in *Performance Anxiety*. Photo: Michael Rothman.

Pulcinella ('little chick') and *Colombina* ('little dove'), even take their animal's names.[33]

Two shows especially have seen the company take on the Commedia mantle directly, *Performance Anxiety* in 1982 and *Punch* in 1992 and 1993. Playing to the strengths of the different strains of Northern and Southern *commedia dell'arte* these shows focused on bourgeois corruption and the peasant's life within society respectively. Both shows were successes and *Punch* in fact was toured twice, having been earlier workshopped with Dell'Arte School students in 1992.

Homing in on the political and sexist implications within *commedia dell'arte*, *Performance Anxiety* focused on what would happen if one of its scenarios turned out for real. Set in a diner, a leading man and lady are rehearsing a Commedia scenario in which the man's servant, Arlecchino, has to dress up in drag to fool the woman's father. A stage accident results in the actor playing Arlecchino's world flashing by his eyes. He enters a state where he believes he has become a woman and undergoes the miseries of childbirth and persecution by men.

Punch was a more complex show, with no alienation techniques incorporated in it, but an attempt to show the medieval world and the crucial battle between Carnival and Lent, and all that which this entails. Within the context of the Carnival itself (the popular battleground between these two opposing forces) Pulchinella, the artist (a follower of Carnival) runs foul of some of the more Lenten-orientated burghers of the town. The artistic and anarchic Mr Punch cannot be seen to survive by the forces of authority and power.

The company has been touring regularly since 1977, as well as being involved in various solo projects by its members and directing student productions. The Dell'Arte School has also set up a student-based touring company called Second Stage. The Dell'Arte Players themselves are significant not just in their having survived professionally for so long, but in their continual adherence to a set of Commedia principles that do seem to refresh, reinvent and refuel their sense of place and purpose, even when they are not actually performing in *commedia dell'arte* style.

Renaissance Fair companies

Renaissance Fairs in the USA are a natural focus point towards which both professional and semi-professional performers gravitate. They are a weekend and seasonal phenomenon, spread over many different venues over the continent,[34] creating the bustle and hurly-burly of an old fashioned period event, albeit seen through the rose-tinted window of cultural nostalgia. An idealised and mythologised version of European history is created as part interactive environment, part theme park, for a paying public to learn about their European heritage and enjoy themselves. On offer are performers, both dramatic and musical, displays of skills, craft stalls, falconry, archery, etc. Generally the organisers of these events are concerned that the highest level of period dress be kept to. To what extent the emphasis falls on authenticity, education or profit, however, depends very much on the individual fair management.

Whilst most performing participants are paid, the take-home fee is never as large as the actor's union minimum and it is not possible to earn a living wage exclusively from performing *commedia dell'arte* at these events. Hence while some performance groups have a Renaissance Fair show as one part of their repertory, other companies exist solely within this context and with their performers maintaining outside careers, and others use their fair performance experience to try and break out into the wider performance world.

Some Renaissance Fairs have high public profiles, and some not, and the same is true of the *commedia dell'arte* performance companies within them. The companies mentioned here are only representative of those who perform the fair circuit. Some of these troupes are financially independent, and some are contractually tied to the various fairs. All, however, seem to be inhabited by performers who, in an ideal world, would give up their day job if it were at all financially possible. Indeed the story of many of these troupes is that of performers who are continually struggling to make more of a living out of their versions of *commedia dell'arte* than the fairs can afford or allow. With such safe performance niches within these quasi-historical never-never lands, it is certainly a wrench to try and break out into the more unfriendly theatrical present day.

I Arroganti (1996–?)

I Arroganti are a Renaissance fair *commedia dell'arte* troupe, based at the Texas Renaissance Fair, which includes all the founder members of the **Austin Commedia Society**. There was no schism when the latter organisation set up, merely a disagreement with the Texas Fair management. Consequently members of I Arroganti occasionally do turn up in I Megalomani shows (the performance wing of the **Austin Commedia Society**) and close links are maintained both personally and professionally.[35] I Arroganti remains a weekend performance company, and is financially managed by the Texas Renaissance Fair, being a sub-branch of that Fair's performance company.

Their function is twofold, in that they provide, between shows, walkabout characters of Italian actors around the fair, as well as regular *commedia dell'arte* performances. The company history, as delivered by the walkabout actors is as follows:

> The troupe started from the ashes of my father's troupe, I Luminati.
> That troupe was started when my father was banished from Milan
> after the Battle of Pavia when the conquering Spanish took offence at
> the comical Spaniard impressions he was famous for. We had made a
> living doing humorous shows in whatever town the Spanish were not
> in. After six years, the French regained Milan and my father was able
> to return to his shop and be a candle maker again. However, at this
> point, I had spent the last third of my life acting, and decided that
> I liked it enough to form my own troupe. After some hardship,
> I finally formed a troupe with the more amusing scum of Italy, and
> thus I Arroganti was born. We performed for some time in Italy and
> France until two of our more notorious members, Pompe de Bergamo
> (Arlecchino) and Slapappi Chatterini (Lelio) decided to do a spectacle
> juggling act with flaming knives and plague rats. This left half of the
> troupe dead and us on the run from the law. We barely escaped in
> the pirate ship 'Pride of Bedlam' and came escaped to England.
> [A reference to the town of Newmarket, USA, where the Texas
> Renaissance Fair takes place]. We replaced our dead members with
> some locals that first year, but despite that met with enough success to
> make it part of our annual circuit before heading to Lisbon and Cadiz
> for the winter.

They maintain a six-person cast, with four men and two women. Ernesto Maldonaldo is nominally the head of the company, but in rehearsal and in performance he states that they try for an ensemble approach. They tried to work with an external director in the 1999 season, but apparently this was not a success due to differing opinions being held by director and cast, and the experiment is not being repeated. All the company have been trained by the TRF staff in interactive theatre, (the skill of staying in character and improvising with the general public) and believe that they stick close to the Commedia performance model rather than 'falling into the common pitfall of slipping into modern, unstructured improv technique, which sometimes bears as much similarity as sixteenth century improvisation as modern firearms do to those of that era'.[36]

The company has sensible performance rules, given that they are only one part of a larger period environment, such as their 'five second rule' which states that something interesting must happen every five seconds, otherwise the audience will get distracted by something else within the fair. This would not be a bad rule for a professional company either. Their shows are around twenty-five minutes long, and although by the end of a season are known very well by the cast, it appears that their performance slots are too short for the company genuinely to improvise their way through a story. They do, however, make continual adaptations to a scenario throughout the season, depending on circumstances and how the shows have been going. The script and action are self-devised, after a seven-weekend rehearsal period before each season. They stick to a cast of the following masks: Il Capitano, Pantalone, Arlecchino, Colombina and a pair of Lovers. They try to tip the balance in favour of physical humour, rather than purely verbal conceits. The company consider they therefore have a unique approach to *commedia dell'arte*, which has also led to favourable comparisons with other Commedia troupes.

They perform in traditional masks on various wooden trestle stages across the fair. As a recognition of their improved performance quality, they were given a stage of their own in 1999, but due to its location their audiences went down. They have now been invited to perform outside the fair environment on several occasions, but these opportunities have had to be turned down, since the company is scattered across Texas. There are also problems with maintaining regular personnel within the company, but Maldonaldo is an enthusiast, as well as a theatre historian by academic persuasion, and seems happy that he can spread his enthusiasm and fire other people up with the joy of *commedia dell'arte*.

Jim Letchworth (La Famiglia Bologna/ Second Storey/Commedia Tutti Frutti)

Tracking the involvement of Jim Letchworth and his Californian associates in *commedia dell'arte* gives some idea how many troupes there are in the United States working mainly in Renaissance Fairs. In 1977 Letchworth attended acting classes, and became involved in a student production of a *commedia dell'arte* version of *Elizabeth I* by Paul Foster, which toured California that summer. The teacher, Judy Slattum was influenced by the performance style and characterisations of the San Francisco Mime troupe. Letchworth, nowadays also an established mask maker, made his first mask of Pantalone with a gigantic and improbable nose. Six months later, sitting in a restaurant, he claims he saw that same nose on a man at the next table!

In 1979, having moved to San Francisco to study at the American Conservatory Theatre, he was approached by his brother, Drew, to form a *commedia dell'arte* company for the Northern Renaissance Faire in Novato, California.[37] This company was called La Famiglia Bologna and performed a show entitled *The Baker of Bologna*[38] three times a day, thirty minutes per show, as well as moving around the site in character. Letchworth states with conviction that the thirty-minute rule of the fair management taught the actors to be direct, precise and get to the point, and as a consequence their comic timing and playing improved.

The following year he joined the production team of the event and was cast as a walkabout villain, 'The Puritan'. The time commitments of playing this character and running the event made it impossible (in the upper management's eyes anyway) for Letchworth to continue performing with the Commedia troupe, and for that year his role was recast. Understandably upset, the following year Letchworth quit the office job, vowing to concentrate on acting and Commedia, and rejoined the troupe.[39]

In 1981 the company had a difficult time, with competition for work in the Renaissance Fairs, the endemic problem of selling *commedia dell'arte* to a wider public, an unclear administrative and decision-making structure, and clear disagreements on significant issues between the sexes in the company. While Jim Letchworth wanted to stay with *commedia dell'arte*, others wanted to do other broader forms of comedy. The company consequently split up.[40] Letchworth and Marilyn Prince went on to form another group with old friends, called Second Storey,[41] specialising in *commedia dell'arte*. The group performed at a variety of Renaissance Fairs, but was not solely active in them. They made valiant attempts to explore *commedia dell'arte* through the small screen, video and film, but to no commercial avail, and also spent a lot of time researching scenarios by Flaminia Scala, as well as texts by Molière and Machiavelli. They were consciously looking for evidence that the original sixteenth-century Commedia was an all encompassing theatrical tradition, rather than (as currently practised) a loosely defined physical style of period slapstick. During this time Letchworth and Prince, along with Barbara Reinertson (Colombina), worked with the original *Reduced Shakespeare Company* of Daniel Singer, Adam Long and Jess Bravin. They did not, however, accompany them to England. *Second Storey* folded at the end of 1985.

In 1986 Letchworth founded the San Francisco Commedia Company and assembled a new cast. He also acquired a stupendous set, in the shape of a complete (only one careless previous owner) Elizabethan ship, built as one section of a multilevel stage, left over from a Sir Francis Drake son et lumière presentation at the previous year's fair. It seemed that years of patient performing at the fairs had finally produced, in Jim Letchworth's eyes, a dream team of *commedia* performers,[42] three of whom who had worked with another Renaissance Fair company, Commedia Biancolelli. Combining this team and the boat, he created a thirty-minute show entitled *The Tempest* (using, he claims, the same source material as Shakespeare to create an eponymous show), complete with sea demons to cause the shipwreck, and a gang of Pulchinellas, à la Tiepolo, to load it.[43] For another new show *Tutti Frutti d'Amore* (all the fruits of love) Jim managed to obtain a few bookings outside the Renaissance Fair that year, which started the company off on a circuit of performances in wineries and malls, but did not manage to secure them arts funding or long-term financial backing. Although this show was very strong, outside commitments from several members caused yet another personnel change, which yet again created new waves within the company. The company's new Prospero, Bob Taxin, was a clown trained at the Ringling Brothers Circus School. He and Jeanne Thomas (Isabella) had been performing professionally as clowns in northern California and under their guidance this new company began to develop *lazzi*, originally their clown pieces, which became adapted for performance by the Commedia masks. These pieces could exist outside the show, as short entertainments in their own right. The company started to use these elements, instead of the big ship show, during quiet houses, and also as a way of gathering a crowd prior to *Tutti Frutti d'Amore*. As the company developed more and more of these *lazzi*, they were able to sell themselves increasingly outside the Renaissance Fair circuit.

In 1988 a new show was tried called *Comedy of the Ring*, which apparently didn't work as well, as it was too unwieldy and Letchworth was finding his role of both actor and director too demanding. A piece of good fortune resulting from this less successful show was that, in the quieter shows in the mornings, they developed two more alternatives to the big show. The first being what Letchworth calls a return to the 'old ways' of doing *commedia dell'arte*, by which he means improvising from a scenario live in front of an audience. The second being the creation of an audience participation *commedia dell'arte* show by Letchworth and Prince, in which members of the audience were lured up onto stage, had masks put on them, and were then led through a Commedia story.

Despite performing their musical Harlequinade again at Christmas that year,[44] the realisation came about that the company was too large ever to earn a decent individual living, and was consequently slimmed down to six.[45] This smaller number allowed the company to work in greater depth together, and consequently a new more dynamic style began to emerge. In rehearsal the company were encouraged to practise and perfect the *lazzi*, until a good repertoire had been achieved of sufficient standard. These *lazzi* were then linked together by short scenarios, and the results were good enough for the company to abandon the performance of rehearsed shows at the Renaissance Fairs, and to improvise scenarios instead. As all the actors had backgrounds in, and inclinations towards, improvisation, this method worked. The *lazzi* were fixed, the masks were fixed, the story was fixed, but how they moved between them was not. They gave three shows a day, with a repertoire of five or six scenarios to choose from, and as a result of having to listen and respond to each other far more closely than they had been used to, the quality of the acting (which was good to begin with) improved.[46]

The company continued to work the Renaissance Fairs in 1990, and in 1991 undertook a six-week run in a professional theatre in San Francisco's Italianate North Beach area. Originally it was intended as double bill with another *commedia dell'arte* company, but as they pulled out, Letchworth and Prince did the second half with their audience participation two-person show. Although excellent reviews were forthcoming, these came too late and this excursion did not provide the Holy Grail of a living wage for the company.[47] After this none of the company members wanted to risk performing Commedia full time.

In 1999 the company performed as a commedia troupe, musicians and walkabout characters variously for and in, Parades in San Francisco and Palo Alto, the world's most lavish kids' Commedia-themed birthday party in Silicon Valley, several engagements for the Italian-American owned wineries in the Napa Valley and other financially profitable corporate events. The company now exists to provide a good second income for all concerned. Several members concentrate their energies on various Commedia training programmes, passing on their skill and experience to a new generation. In Jim's own words 'One of the themes of Commedia is that the future belongs to the young'.

Commedia Zuppa (1995–?)

Commedia Zuppa are a two-strong company (Alison Williams and Todd Espeland) based in Florida, who successfully earn a living by performing their own two-person version of *commedia dell'arte* at Renaissance Fairs, by training others in its style and techniques and by making and selling masks. Both their teaching and their continually evolving show reflect their ideal and working method of 'actor-as-creator'. Originally entitled The Isabella and Arlecchino Show, they subsequently changed to Commedia Zuppa, due to some inhabitants of Florida having difficulty with the pronunciation and spelling of Arlecchino, and the fact that they were often annoyingly and misleadingly mistaken for a puppet show.

As trainers they teach both mask work and *commedia dell'arte*, and coach and direct shows which contain elements of both. They have worked for several years directing the main stage show at the Kentucky Shakespeare Festival, in Louisville, USA. In 1999 they started work on *The Taming of the Shrew*, beginning with a simple scenario, rather than the historical script, encouraging the actors to develop their own characters and *lazzi*. In doing so they were attempting to overcome a perceived shortcoming in American college actor training (and not just American actor training) in working from scenarios, rather than texts, and in the development of character, character business and character jokes not provided by the original script. Both the style of current actor training and the perceived pathways into the actor's profession make this work doubly hard, but by way of encouragement the answer is always given that one can create a career and a performance style that is out of the ordinary. 'We tell them that we have been full-time professionals (no waiting on tables, no temping) for six years now, and we don't audition, or do movies, or TV, or Broadway.'[48]

As trainers, Commedia Zuppa are brought in as 'hired guns' or guest artists to other theatres to train and direct actors both in the movement and style, but also in the actor-as-creator element of *commedia dell'arte*. Due to their growing reputation, when they are creating theatre either for others or in co-developing performance projects, they say they are no longer dogged by the problems that normally beset young companies of no money, no space and no help. They are, however, creating theatre for others and paid well to do so, and generally with college students. To date none of their students has followed this path and formed their own mask or Commedia company, but it is too early to tell. However, it is refreshing to know that at least some effective alternative to the standard show-business mentality is being taught.

As a double act, Commedia Zuppa perform their variety stunt show *The Daring Devilinis* at Renaissance Fairs around North America. In their own words:

> Our characters are Isabella and Arlecchino, with Isabella being based on the Isabella Andreini 'lover', an older, wiser version of the traditional lover, and Arlecchino a manic child, prone to fits of free association on stage. We eat fire, perform balancing atop a rolling globe, lie on a bed of nails and other circus-type tricks.[49]

Although the chosen characters are based on *commedia dell'arte*, it is clear from this description that they present skills in character, rather than a more traditional scenario-based character or mask interaction within the framework of a story. It is possible, though very hard, to do two-handed Commedia pieces; what they perform (as opposed to teach) is very much variety or circus-skills based. But although their script is very tight, there are frequent improvisations, both of genuinely new material and *lazzi* that are repeated occasionally, such as interaction with video cameras and cell phones.[50] In this they believe they have historical justification:

> We subscribe to the theory that Commedia troupes improvised their script together, based on a scenario, in rehearsal, then had a tight constant show with room for extra *lazzi* if the occasion arose. We do not believe that they went out there and 'made it up' every single show. This belief is based on our work with other performers in improv groups, where patterns of jokes and interactions begin to occur even when the stated aim is to make it all up each time, and in the knowledge that it is very hard to be funny when you are improving every single time.
>
> Over the last six years the one thing that has helped us evolve to a tight, clean, consistently funny show, has been trusting the characters and their drives, rather than the 'tricks' they portray. By trusting the strength of the character that we discovered in our original mask exploration, we've been able to forge a connection that goes beyond the next trick . . . the audience wants to know the character, [and] the trick takes the place of dramatic conflict as a reason to enjoy meeting and experiencing the world of the characters.[51]

The company, therefore, by its own terms, appears to have found a viable and pragmatic system of connecting their Commedia derived theatre training with their vaudeville performance which brings the relationship of character and audience very firmly to the fore. It also appears that this interesting synthesis may be the result of both partners training simultaneously in the theatre arts at college, and helping to pay for that education by being fire eaters and skills performers at night clubs. This side-by-side development of both collegiate dramatic theory, together with direct contact of a thrill-seeking theatrically unsophisticated audience certainly influenced the direction of the nascent company. This combination of dramatic training and affinity with circus skills has also led many others towards *commedia dell'arte*.

Although using the phrase *commedia dell'arte* fairly frequently to describe their work and particular aspects of it, Commedia Zuppa make no claims to be a troupe in the historical sense, and make no sentimental claims to be flag wavers for a new form of people's theatre.

> For us, a big part of Commedia is that it entertains, and a big part of teaching is that students enjoy the work, and even if some of it takes months or years to sink in, there is at least a part that is relevant to where they are as actors now. . . . what we do as the Devilinis is Commedia. We are mass entertainment and our focus is character driven, and about getting the audience to like the character and them wanting to return to see them again. The show is about character in situation. We are not masked, because mask theatre is alien and 'arty' to most people today, whereas there was still a strong tradition of mask wearing for festival days in the time of historical Commedia.
>
> The problem with much of today's 'Commedia' is that it is a recreation or a museum piece instead of the living breathing street art that it was at the time. For any Commedia company to survive, they must evolve their process beyond re-creation and find what Commedia is today.[52]

TaskMaskers (1997–?)

This is a two-person company, working from Maryland in the United States, primarily performing at Renaissance Fairs, but also training others[53] in both mask theatre and *commedia dell'arte*. Their founder, Michelle Schultz, trained at the Dell'Arte School, and although maintaining a steady career outside the TaskMaskers, has been keeping the company going steadily since then, and has seen an increase in both the amount of weekends worked and of the training the company does for others.

As befits a Renaissance Fair-based company, the current two members are in character (Colombina and Pedrolino, a couple of not so honest Italian actors travelling in fifteenth-century England, or where/whenever the fair mythologically takes place) not just from the moment they arrive on stage, but from the moment the public arrive on site. They have several shows in repertoire at any one given time, and are constantly creating new pieces. The performance side of the company is called Teatro di Pecorino Romano, (the Roman sheep's cheese theatre), and even though they might perform for historically cheesy events, the company's aims are, at least on paper, certainly not. This is the company mission statement:

> TaskMaskers shares joy with others through mask theater. By creating,
> educating, and performing in mask, we seek to reach people and
> evolve them through laughter and pathos. We believe that mask
> theater is one of the most challenging and creative forms of
> performance and we strive to make mask theatre more acceptable and
> prevalent in today's theater community.

TaskMaskers' performance skills include mask, *commedia dell'arte*, some acrobatics and some magic. They make their own masks and run workshops with them. They are building a solid reputation on the Renaissance Fair circuit, as being good value and very worthwhile comedic performers, currently working nine weekends per year, but with more offers coming in from other fairs.

Other troupes

To close this section we cover some models of commedia dell'arte which, although falling outside the remit of 'professional performing company', nevertheless provide an insight into other ways of performing or exploring Commedia styles. Again we make no claim to inclusiveness – these troupes serve as exempla: the **Gobbi Players** complete the story of the **Unfortunati** and **Fortunati** – with an evidently better recipe for survival; **Desperate Men** are an example of an accidental Commedia company; **Fool's Paradise** are a commercial and corporate agency of all-round entertainers who amongst their many offerings include commedia dell'arte shows; **Le Mascheri di Gioia** illustrate the pitfalls of using Commedia as animation; **I Sebastiani** are a part-time company of amateurs whose aims mirror very closely those of many professional companies; **The Bubalaires** are a part-time, semi-professional company whose achievement is to invent comic performances based entirely on a grammelot of their own invention; the **Austin Commedia Society** are attempting an inclusive Commedia service and **Masquerade Productions** occupy a unique position as an immigrant culture educational service.

The Gobbi Players (1982–?)

What is now the Gobbi Theatre Company shares direct ancestry with the **Unfortunati**. The particular group of friends and acquaintances in the English Civil War Society created not one but two companies, the second of these, and by now the longer lived, was the Gobbi. The name comes from that given to deformed or dwarf court fools at the time of the Renaissance.

Initially its history is that of the **Unfortunati**. The company worked part-time and the numbers of participants varied. At one stage photographic evidence suggests that there were at least twelve people rehearsing and performing together. This loose dramatic alliance carried on until, in 1982 when a small faction decided to go professional. John and Angela Glennard, key players in the **Unfortunati,** an amateur troupe up till then, could not participate in this venture for family and career reasons. They decided to carry on regardless with whoever remained and became the two central figures of the new group, now called the Gobbi Players. The costumes, staging and masks of the company ensured, along with the vigorous and committed attitude of the performers, a visual and vigorous spectacle. John Glennard reckons that the company has since performed over 1,000 shows.

From 1982, although individual members still were part of the Civil War Society, they were performing less and less at battles and more and more at summer weekend festivals, and in the winter at period banquets. The cast stayed mainly the same until 1986, with professional musicians being drafted in for important engagements, when natural attrition and other commitments caused members to drift away.

From 1986 to 1991 another cast assembled itself, and stayed relatively stable, carrying on the same area of work in both a semi-professional and seasonal-professional manner. By 1993 John Glennard was the sole surviving member and was feeling the pressure of being both administrator and trainer. A third cast came into existence from 1991 to 1993, but then drifted apart. Glennard had nearly decided to fold the company when, almost by chance, a group of enthusiastic new members appeared from an entirely unexpected source.

The company had always run workshops as part of their programme, and favourable report had come to the notice of the local social and adult education services. Glennard was invited to run a series of workshops in a Manchester community centre. This was known as the Longsight Project. Its specific remit was to teach *commedia dell'arte* to local deprived youths, as a way of giving them experience of learning, rehearsing and performing theatre. The workshop sessions ran between October 1993 to April 1994. Although it was initially very hard to get anyone interested in participating, upwards of twenty regular members eventually materialised. This is not the only example of *commedia dell'arte* being used in social work, but certainly one which achieved some remarkable successes: several participants from this workshop joined the Gobbi Players company thus ensuring its survival. In 1994 a performing troupe of six or seven, including John Glennard as Pantalone, performed most weekends round the country. Some members of the Longsight project stayed in the company until 1996.

In 1996, although the company was still enjoying its semi-professional status and working regularly and profitably within its self-imposed guide-lines, personal difficulties emerged. The specific details are not important other than that they had direct parallels with a problem faced by the **Unfortunati**: if the company is a collective then should everyone have an equal say in its activities? The longest surviving member began to feel that the group was abandoning its roots and becoming more diffuse.

The eventual decision was that the company should abandon its semi-professional status and take itself more seriously, including paying people proper wages and applying for grants and the like. This resulted in John Glennard sacking certain people, Angela Glennard rejoining the company and numbers being fixed at a financially viable three. There seems to be a point when, having played *commedia dell'arte* for many years, the attitude develops that it should be done properly or not at all. Semi-professionalism or seasonal professionalism no longer suffices. This was a very similar situation to that which the **Unfortunati** faced, which resulted in the formation of the **Fortunati**, and also at the point when Les Fratelinis Bolognas branched off from the company run by **Jim Letchworth**.

It is hard to assess the theatrical achievement of this company as they performed out of the limelight of the press and the wider theatrical public, but they certainly kept bookings coming in and in 1987 were invited to perform at the dedication of the Globe Theatre site in London due to their 'period' authenticity and entertainment value. John Glennard proved an inventive scenario writer, able to rewrite or reinvent scenarios depending on circumstances or the availability of cast members. The company originated as a collective decision-making body and then moved into being run by John Glennard, much in the role of a traditional actor manager. His commitment to actor's theatre and to the ideal of *commedia dell'arte* prevented this role from being too intrusive into the stage life of each individual performer. He prefers to teach a new member a suitable Mask, and then let them develop it, rather than trying to keep control at all times. His experience of being on stage as the same Mask for such a period is certainly important. In terms of determining the Gobbi's success in performance, all members agree that 'the audience is a mirror of how well you're doing', not the director.[54] The company has evolved several formulae for performance over the years, including various acronyms such as ASA which defines the Commedia actor's direct relationship with an audience: Actor, Scenario, Audience. ASDA, on the other hand, signifies Actor, Scenario, Director, Audience, meaning that a third person's interpretation of the scenario can hinder the actor. The company has developed another equation which draws a direct correlation to how close the audience will come to the stage in relation to both audience numbers, and how well the show will go. It works.

Glennard is convinced that for any company to maximise its potential the scenario writer must be both performer and writer, so that she or he is able to write specifically for the Masks in the troupe. Only this way, he argues, can you capitalise on specific performance strengths and the sense of complicity between them. His attendant point is that if you take over existing scenarios there is always the difficulty of trying to adapt what has been written for the specific comic talents of others. In the truism of Pantalone, it is better to buy direct.

The Gobbis also feel that the Masks work best out of doors where their improvisational qualities are less curtailed. They take great delight in making the subject of their performances the foibles, hopes and hypocrisies of all, and not taking any specific party political line. All Masks get a chance to shine, and a chance to be shown up. In their own way they do try to make their shows a true mirror of the world, albeit framed by an antique form. Their present shows are less deliberately bawdy than before, with more of an emphasis on being able to entertain a family audience, parents and children equally, without gratuitous offence.

Desperate Men (1980–?)

Desperate Men were founded in Berlin by Ritchie Smith and Jon Beedell. They are primarily a street theatre company who make occasional forays into scripted indoor theatre, cabaret, community events, installations and site animation. There is always a strong surreal element to their shows, whether theatre or walkabout, and a deep commitment to both earning a living and to the art of the street performer. The company motto, as appearing on all letters and fliers during most of their existence, is 'We make mincemeat of flimsy reality'. We include analysis of their show *The Fountain* here because, although the company is rigidly autodidactic when creating new works, an examination of this particular show reveals very strong similarities to certain aspects of *commedia dell'arte*, particularly in the techniques developed to cope with pan-European audiences.

The creative process within Desperate Men is very strong, and by their own admission, is continually evolving. Part of their process is continually to challenge all the basic assumptions about each project until they are left with something concrete. From their beginnings as a duo they state they have 'great confidence in being mavericks'.[55] This process, which can appear 'opaque to the fainthearted observer',[56] gives the company the stated confidence constantly to reinvent itself, and to solve problems directly. In the present case this approach led to their reinvention of a fair proportion of the defining features of *commedia dell'arte*.

By 1993 the company had expanded to five members, and was looking for a new direction. The main objective was to produce an outdoor theatre show which could function equally well in England and Europe. This was seen as a company necessity at the time, and led the way to both stylistic and subjective exploration. The show was to be about boundaries as the political situation in Eastern Europe was becoming far more fluid than it had been when Moscow was exerting direct control. In rehearsal this idea was refined down to how borders separate people into haves and have-nots, and the image of the ownership of water as a concretisation of this was agreed. A fountain as a central object, surrounded by a circular border, became the chosen staging area, dividing those within the circle who had water, from those outside the circle who had none. This corresponded with their ideal street theatre set-up: the round. In performance, however, the circle surrounding the fountain did not always encourage the audience to entirely surround the performance area, and they often performed to an audience on three sides. The fountain itself also provided a central object to act as a focus to gather an audience.

Several other specific dramatic conventions were adopted during the creation of this piece following on from its need to be rooted generally, but not specifically, in a pan-European idiom: that all the characters would speak some form of grammelot (in Desperate Men, called 'Desperanto'), that the storyline would be driven by action rather than text, and that only easily recognisable character types would be used. The version of 'Desperanto' spoken in this show was character specific, in that all the actors adopted the rhythms of different European languages for their roles: Dutch, French, Portuguese, and Spanish for the Mayor, Gypsy Girl, Old Man and Servant respectively.

As the action, rather than words carried the storyline, the rehearsal process created two kinds of sections in the show: loose improvised passages whose length and emphasis depended on the audience's reaction there and then, and slick highly rehearsed islands of planned dialogue and action. There was also a strong musical element in the show, with a live sound-track provided by Shirley Pegner, who also directed the company's barbershop-style harmonic singing.

That the show was not primarily language based, as well as being firmly embedded within the company's own comic idiom, profoundly affected the choice of characters. They all had to be recognised in a very short period of time by the spectators, since there was little possibility of long verbal plot or character exposition if they wanted to hold a walk-past audience.[57] They developed characters which, on inspection, reveal very close similarities to the stock types of the *commedia dell'arte*. The Mayor could easily have been Il Magnifico or Pantalone, and his servant any of the *zannis*. The Gypsy Girl is directly comparable to a determined Colombina (or Molière's Zerbinetta), and her father is simply a stock foolish old man, e.g. Ubaldo. The body shape, rhythm and vocal quality of the portrayals of the characters supported such comparison.

That the shaman of the piece was a female is no surprise and represents some synchronicity with contemporary *commedia dell'arte* thinking. Carlo Boso's stated aim with *commedia dell'arte* is to bring it up to date, changing as few of its original precepts as was possible, whilst at the same time creating a pantheon of characters and masks that work for today. He decided that the one symbolic gap within the mask hierarchy was that of the woman of power. In workshop performances he has created some very strong mother figures, similar to *Mafiosi* matriarchs, and in TAG Teatro di Venezia's show *Il Falso Magnifico*, with the actress Laura Boato, he developed the character of Nera, the witch. She is the one Mask who symbolically accesses intuition and the healing powers of the earth as her power, and her direct opposite and antagonist is the male logic of the knowledge crazy Dottore. On a practical performance level her remit is fortune telling, magic potion manufacture and sale, and ultimately also to be a *deus ex machina* figure. Desperate Men and Woman created their character as a female figure of power, capable of taking on their Mayor/Magnifico and winning, and the method (linking into many traditional folk stories and myth cycles) of this victory was through magic, trickery and the occult.

Consequently the company had developed, or perhaps rediscovered, some of the essential ingredients of *commedia dell'arte* (and, arguably, all successful outdoor theatre): a central focus for the acting area; a storyline that survived by the deeds rather than the words of its characters, but nevertheless had a deeper resonance; a strong musical element; easily recognisable characters whose development for the audience is based on action rather than psychology, and also a collective decision-making structure. One appreciates, however, that the company might not be entirely delighted to be told after the event that they were performing a type of Commedia in *The Fountain*, as they are such dedicated iconoclasts and reinventors of the wheel of theatre.

The show was kept in repertoire for two years, and worked equally well both in Europe and in the United Kingdom. Although it is generally taken as read that continental audiences are more enthusiastic and appreciative than their island counterparts, a particular high spot for the company was the Traquair Fair in Scotland. The show succeeded in its objectives and gave the company a good reputation on the continent which has since stood them in good stead for future work.

Fool's Paradise

Fool's Paradise was originally formed in 1985 to provide visual interpretation, using traditional performance skills, as an integral part of a concert programme with the New London Consort, entitled 'A Medieval Extravaganza'. It was intended to recreate a Lenten gathering of jongleurs and performed at several major London concert halls as well as in Europe.

Rather than being a theatre or *commedia dell'arte* company in its own right Fool's Paradise is an agency or holding company run by John Ballanger, who assembles the necessary cast and entertainers for whatever the booker requires. The company works specifically in a historical mode and provides fools, jesters and period variety and theatrical events from anything to Roman, through Medieval, Tudor, Commedia, Georgian and so on, up to the present day. Generally they work on corporate events and historical theme venues, but have also worked extensively abroad. There is no fixed company as such, but those invited on board for the short-term events are always specialists in their area and have built up a working relationship with the company over several engagements. John Ballanger's earliest solo venture was as the juggling acrobat in the early incarnations of England's late lamented Medieval Players.

Fool's Paradise reputation was such that in 1995 he was invited to create a *commedia dell'arte* piece for inaugural concerts at La Cité de la Musique in Paris, in conjunction with the Gabrielli Consort and Players. This was performed over several nights with great success. The cast for this event was a mix of actors and skills performers (acrobats, jugglers, magicians, etc.) who developed a simple plot that showed off their strengths in the best and most entertaining light. Collective rehearsal was kept to a minimum.

The success of this model was due to two factors. The first being that the musicians and performers had a recognition of the strengths of the others' performance media and had experience at working with such a hybrid music/theatre/comedy/skills form, and secondly that the performers were themselves experienced and successful and stuck to what they knew worked.

In some respects this is exactly the same attitude to performance as when, in the *commedia dell'arte* paradigm, stock characters stick to a simple semi-improvised scenario and rely for the bulk of their material on their own individual back catalogue of gags and stage business. The difference is that Fool's Paradise performs for much shorter periods of time than the companies of yore. Despite being a successful businessman in the jestering trade, John Ballanger does go all misty eyed at the thought of being able to follow in the footsteps of Zan Ganassa, Martinelli and the Andreinis. In the field in which he works, however, he believes that there is not the money to sustain a company of the professionals of the standard he is used to working with, to recreate a Commedia for now.

Le Maschere di Gioia (1992)

Le Maschere di Gioia (the masks of joy) were formed to carry out a specific remit at the Bliss Hill industrial museum in Telford, Shropshire. Roberto Biffarni was invited to animate and interpret the museum's living history Victorian display, one of its main attractions. The company worked and trained for the project for six months and then dissolved.

As a company they have no great performance significance, but did use the social position of the archetypal Commedia servants in a paratheatrical and interpretative function, rather than solely as a performance art form. The Masks were kept alive by their continual interaction with members of the museum's public. They adopted late eighteenth-century versions of *commedia dell'arte zannis* as their stage personae, in keeping with historical aspects of Victorian Pantomime. Rather than present a set show in a conventional theatrical space, they decided to create their pieces as site specific, fitting in with the exhibits of the museum, such as a Victorian bank, circus tent and industrial pumping engines. They promenaded the whole museum in their *commedia dell'arte* masks, improvising with the public, then segueing into preplanned set pieces around the exhibits.

As well as setting out to entertain the public with the behaviour of the Masks themselves, they had an unspoken agenda: to depict the socio-economic and political effects of nineteenth-century industrialisation. The *zannis* ridiculed the developing class system whilst portraying the unpleasant and macabre conditions of the early industrial workers in an amusing and light-hearted way.

All the performers involved saw themselves as individual theatrical artists. The deeper approach to historical interpretation they evolved at the museum was their way of coping with the job of entertaining and informing the general public. Their residency was funded by the EU as part of the International Year of Culture initiative. Their work was much reported on, and favourably too, in Brussels, but they did not repeat the engagement.

In the never-ending quest for a thespian crust, many young actors find themselves in summer jobs animating in role otherwise inert displays. For anyone wishing to enter the arena of improvisation, the experience of continual interaction with members of the public can be invaluable, and certainly better than working a Disney or a Dalek. Exploiting the Masks of *commedia dell'arte* in this way, however, is no way to build a company, and probably a certain way to destroy one.

I Sebastiani (1991–?)

I Sebastiani are an American company that operates on a distinctly part-time basis. They are included here as an exception because their enthusiasm for their hobby puts them in an amateur category of their own. They say they want:

- to multiply the joy and mirth on this earthly orb;
- to understand the humour of sixteenth-century Italy;
- to know, first hand, how Commedia troupes operated, including what difficulties they faced plying their art through the fairs and market places of Italy and France;
- to develop the performing skills of the above;
- a steamer trunk full of tricks, bits, turns and tumbles that all have the musty aroma of the palace of the Doge;
- to entertain our audience without reminding them of more modern times.[58]

Their enthusiasm stems largely, but not exclusively, from their leader and founder Jeff Hatalsky, the Sebastian of the company name, but in the cast lists there is a fair degree of continuity and he is by no means the only scenario writer. The company has performed around thirty separate scenarios. This level of commitment is certainly not sustainable if it were one 'lone loon' trying to run it all without support. If one is thinking of performing *commedia dell'arte*, there is certainly a case for building up one's skills in a non-professional, non-livelihood threatening environment before embarking on a fully professional career, as with a few notable exceptions, the opportunities for in-depth Commedia training are few and far between. The model of the amateur set-up as a necessary step prior to risking earning one's comic crust from performance alone is beset with a particular problem though: the safer the performance environment is, in terms of earning a living, the less likely it will be that performers transcend it and develop truly professional skills.

The Bubalaires (1991–?)

The Bubalaires are an American company who, by a very roundabout route, reinvented one of the stocks in trade of the *comici dell'arte all'improvviso*: the use of *grammelot* as a performance language. This, combined with their uniquely developed company mythology, use of stock characters and strongly improvisational performance structure has given them a new approach to the creation of improvised plays. They are not a Commedia company as such, but are worthy of mention as one of the few companies who regard as their main strength such Commedia derived methodology.

The company's style evolved from combining the exploration of classical improvisation as part of the Theatre Antaeus[59] collective, training with John Achorn in Commedia performance techniques and mask work, and the desire to do something different with the improvisational skills thus acquired. Somebody brought into rehearsal an article about a Russian dance troupe, stranded in New England after the fall of the Soviet government. This troupe was adopted by the townsfolk, who eventually held sufficient bake sales and charity events to raise the air fares home for the dancers. This occurrence was tried out in the workshop by way of the improvisation game of 'translations', which involves speaking gibberish. The protocompany members did a gibberish press conference, playing the abandoned dance troupe, complete with translator. This was enjoyed so much by the company that they decided to try a gibberish show, posing as the 'Art Theatre Kollective of Czezno-Kocheski', a stranded classical theatre troupe forced to do a humiliating cabaret comedy to pay for their dingy hotel rooms.

The first show they performed was, in the words of their cofounder John Apicella, 'a real Commedia outing, with a fixed scenario and room for improvisation between the story beats or anywhere else we felt the urge.' It also included a 'magic scarf' which empowered the lucky wearer to be able to speak English, rather than gibberish. From the audience's reaction to the drama the performers realised that they preferred gibberish and dropped speaking English entirely. The chemical reaction between audience and the performers had produced a new form of *grammelot*.

The act has subsequently evolved into a slightly different structure in that it now entails a series of rehearsed opening numbers (sometimes one only, depending on the type of venue) and then audience based improv (in the American sense) in their Bubalarian *grammelot*, moving away from the Commedia tradition of a fixed scenario as a basis for improvisation and exploration. The thread that holds it all together, though, is that all the improv suggestions are both sought and performed by the troupe's stock characters.

The company as a whole[60] consider that what they do is definitely descended from classical *commedia dell'arte*, in that they use archetypal characters (usually from Czezno-Kocheski, but often Il Dottore and Il Capitano are included as well) and extensive *lazzi*. Taking a purely historical point of view, however, it could be argued that the entire improv movement is solely concerned with *lazzi*, rather than story-driven drama. The characters the company have evolved in their Bubalairian universe are: a bossy and fastidious Majordomo, the vain Leading Lady, the surly and cynical Seamstress and the dopey, ominverous, Janitor. These characters exist in a universe where they are eternally homesick for their native (possibly eastern European) country and are forced to sell substandard goods to survive, made by the evil Buba corporation which now runs Czezno-Kocheski.

The company itself is semi-professional,[61] with all of the members having careers outside their membership of the Bubalaires. All members appear committed to the company for as long as it can be arranged around their other commitments, but nevertheless have appeared at two separate San Francisco Fringe festivals, the Los Angeles NoHo Theatre and Arts Festival, as well as performing a Bubalairian version of the *Odyssey* for a six-week run.

That the troupe has achieved a comprehensible version of *grammelot* for a modern stage audience is undeniably their main achievement, but they have not yet risked all in going fully professional, and this indeed appears not to be their wish. This is a company with the potential for further development in specific areas of physical theatre and comedy. If they wish to go further they need to test their *grammelot* outside of their familiar cultural surroundings to see if they are capable of sustaining their version of Commedia beyond their one (undoubtedly good) joke, and to try it out internationally.[62] The company seems to have created a unique niche for themselves in their theatrical community, both in Los Angeles and San Francisco, and can be seen as an example of how utilising only three *commedia dell'arte* performance strands, stock characters, *grammelot* and improvisation on a theme or story, can create exciting theatre.

The Austin Commedia Society

The Austin Commedia Society is a grouping of Commedia enthusiasts, based in Austin, Texas. Although the professional performance wing of this loose confederation was set up on 15 March 1999 as a separate body, the various personnel had known each other and performed in various combinations for several years before that. We include them here as an example of a company, recently set up and still searching for their professional identity, both as a company and in the eyes of bookers and the paying public.

The society aims to carry out a wide range of *commedia dell'arte* based activities. At the time of writing these activities are in the early stage of development, and demonstrate great enthusiasm for the subject and an understanding of many of the levels on which Commedia can be approached. At the time of writing they are creating an online *commedia dell'arte* archive,[63] to become a free resource for other enthusiasts. It is to be hoped that this laudable activity does not distract them from developing an effective professional reputation. However enthusiastic one is for what may be, in all actuality, a Platonic model of popular theatre, and keen to share it with the whole world, both artistically and politically, financial support is an imperative. This is true especially as a company develops and performers acquire the responsibilities of long-term relationships, accommodation and family. They are also involved in creating an outreach training programme to be offered in Texas schools, at High School level, and running the performance company called I Megalomani. In 2001 they are planning, along with the local Tongue and Groove Theatre Company, to perform in and promote a *commedia dell'arte* festival. All of these should both raise the group's professional profile and create income.

The company was the inspiration of Aaron Johnson who, after performing for two seasons at the Texas Renaissance Festival as part of **I Arroganti** (the local Renaissance Fair Commedia troupe), decided to attempt a more expansive project in Austin. Spurred on and aided by Paul Joiner (who played Arlecchino in **I Arroganti**) and Beth McMillan, Aaron set about the process of building a company. The group is now sponsored by the Austin Circle of Theatres, and has a core membership of seven. There are several other grant applications pending at the time of writing, including an approved application for Austin City Funding. The fledgling company is currently being run out of Aaron Johnson and Beth McMillan's living room, whilst the company looks for permanent office and rehearsal space. Previously they have made do by rehearsing in a wide variety of spaces, including the Center Studio, run by local dancer/performance artist Ellen Bartell, thus evincing typical Commedia resourcefulness whilst in development. They have also involved themselves in various other operations to raise money for the company, including car boot sales, passing the hat, and of course, professional fees.

The company derive from a combination of academic drama and performance training,[64] all with a knowledge of history, together with a very large dose of performing in local theatre festivals and Renaissance Fairs.[65] They have had no formal *commedia dell'arte* training, as such, but have derived their style from watching others, improv training, and their own historical researches. As such they are very much in the tradition of independent actor-artists.

They have performed regularly at various establishments in Austin including Club Deville, The Austin Children's Museum, The Palmer Auditorium, the Austin Jazz and Arts Festival, Movements Gallery, the Frontera Long Fringe Festival and The Mind Over Money Theatrical Festival. They use traditional Masks, and are still in the process of finding out who in the collective is best at playing what. The rehearsal process is created round improvisations derived from a fixed scenario, with the dialogue and action becoming gradually more and more fixed. They still improvise dialogue in performance, though keep the physical *lazzi* and preplanned business the same in all shows. Thus the company can maintain both a degree of flexibility in performance, (derived from both the American style of improv, and from *commedia all'improvviso*), at the same time as carrying forward a strong storyline that appeals to a wide age range.

The company is organised as follows:

The Austin Commedia Society is a loosely structured company without official titles or offices. Each individual has certain administrative tasks that they perform well, but duties are assigned on a volunteer basis and who does what is usually based upon who is available and/or who can meet a particular deadline. Aaron is our leader and visionary and likes to have the final say in any artistic decision, but he leaves himself open to be overruled. That being said, we are not an organisation in chaos. We are dedicated individuals working for a common goal. This type of democracy suits our open creative process.[66]

It appears that, from a fortuitous set of circumstances, the Austin Commedia Society is indeed able to function organisationally and in performance very much in the perceived historical sense of democracy under a *capocomico*. They have a fair degree of support in their locale and a clear vision of what they want to do that is rooted both in past performance practice and modern circumstances. It will be interesting to see how the company grows as they develop professionally into a full-time organisation, and whether they can maintain their entrepreneurial idealism.

Masquerade Productions (1998-?)

Masquerade Productions, based in Melbourne, Australia, grew out of the company Melbourne Maskworks which ceased operations, according to Paul Bongiovanni, 'due to the artistic director falling in love and running away to live in Rome, never to be heard of again.' The original company was focused on masked theatre and comedy, so the progression to a specific form of mask theatre was in some ways a natural one.[67]

Masquerade is a Theatre in Education company, performing to both primary and secondary schools, with three core members at present – Paul Bongiovanni, Frank Lotito and Sam Acarito – and is organised along partially democratic lines. Paul Bongiovanni as artistic director decides on the direction the company is to take, and most decisions as to how to achieve that objective are made collectively. Currently the artistic policy is to create language-based shows for schools with the aim of exposing students to aspects of the culture and traditions of the foreign language they are studying, in this case Italian. The traditional culture they expose students to is, of course, *commedia dell'arte*.

> In so far as training is concerned, I have not done any formal training in *commedia dell'arte* at any institution as such. However, I do not believe that this has disadvantaged me in any way. I was first exposed to *commedia dell'arte* when I was at University doing a student theatre play that has as its basis the *commedia dell'arte*. I soon became aware that I was instinctively good at it, knowing where and how to place my energy to bring a masked character to life. I became very addicted to this style of theatre and further explored it at length. My experience thus came from performing *commedia dell'arte* shows. I attended several workshops by people who had had some formal training, and I managed to extract from them little bits of information and techniques that I was able to use. My opinion though is that *commedia dell'arte* needs to be performed and is not an art form that can be easily taught. I have spent months trying to train people to do some basic movements in the style and have always been dumbfounded when some actor who is a good performer generally would come along, put on a mask and take off.
>
> From this I quickly learnt that it is the high octane, adrenaline pumping action of a commedia character that will bring a performer to the right standard of *commedia dell'arte*. They can explore and inhabit the mask as much as they like, but when it comes to performing in this

style, it is a matter of jumping in head first and locking up your grandmother.

The company receives no funding revenue and depends completely on its performance income from professional fees, which are happily sufficient to pay the performer's wages, maintain an office and finance the continual running of the company and its current show.

In 1998 the company travelled to Adelaide and performed, as a favour to an Italian organisation based there, a first version of what was later to become their show *Carnevale Italiano*.[68] The results from this performance, as well as other performances in schools with Italian on the curriculum, convinced the nascent company that this was a viable source of income. The important discovery was made that teachers of Italian in schools were desperate for resources that would both inform and at the same time entertain their students.

A new script was then created, masks made and a whole new set was built, using company-based skills and help received in kind. A mail out to over 500 schools in Victoria with Italian on the syllabus, and the support of an Australian-based Italian community organisation[69], which organised a showcase performance and helped with a brochure, led to immediate bookings and an extensive tour, both in Victoria and in the rest of Australia. The show has been in continual performance all through 1999, since its première in February 1999, and has bookings into the year 2000. As part of this effective business plan the show was consciously devised so as to be able to appeal to both primary and secondary schools. Although a limited objective, Bongiovanni argues that it is a valuable one:

> Our current *commedia dell'arte* show so far has proved very successful.
> I do, however, know that this is because we are touring it to schools
> that teach Italian on their curriculum. Had I wanted to do a
> mainstream show based on the *commedia dell'arte* I would not have
> had anywhere near the success we are currently enjoying. Australia is
> very far away, and although there are many Italian migrants here,
> their children are becoming less and less familiar with their culture.
> This is one little way in which I can help keep the culture alive here.
> By doing a show that is based on such a fantastic theatre tradition,
> I can expose some of these children to their heritage, and also expose
> non-Italian children who are studying Italian at school to this
> wonderful theatre form.

Part Three

Forming, training and performing

Forming a company

Why you should want to form a *commedia dell'arte* company is entirely up to you, but we hope it has something to do with rejecting the primacy of television in favour of live interaction with an audience, a love of masks and physical comedy, and the desire to work within a collective, actor-centred structure. The touchstone of any organisational structure for a Commedia troupe is whether or not it gives the actors freedom to create 'within the scene', in the rehearsal room and on stage, rather than to recreate someone else's agenda, whether historical, political, or sellable. The specifics of Commedia style and content, as your troupe plays them, should have a major affect on the way your company is organised. The paradigm, of course, is as follows: a collective of actors all specialising in one Mask apiece, formed as an equal and mutual society with no one person, whether it be director or employer, assuming overall command in either artistic or financial matters. Whether that ever happened, even in the heyday of the big companies is certainly debatable, as we have seen earlier in this book. In the smaller, unpatronised troupes it seems to have been the norm, however, and what we attempt to address now is how something close to that ideal can be applied today as a viable working method.

The first thing one needs is a statement of artistic intent, then to develop a business organisation that supports it. No one is going to afford you a living for just being keen on Commedia: you have to go and make it your livelihood, and for that your passion must also become your business. So, although the spirit of collective creation may appear to preclude some form of written agreement, do try to commit some common aims and agreements to paper. These could be anything from legally binding articles signed by all members, to simply a discussion document or else a set of aims to be compared with achievements after a period of time.

As an improvising actor one should have artistic control over one's own words, mask and actions on stage. In most contemporary theatre practice that control has been ceded to the director as supposed agent of the author. The only comparable controlling roles within a Commedia company are those of scenario writer and *corago*, but their job is not to define but to enable the stage life of the Masks. Ideally then, actors need to play to their strengths and the company structure needs to reflect individual as well as collective independence. A new company needs, however, a certain amount of time to develop balance and direction: its structure must not disempower its improvisers from defining the product by the way they perform, rather than what they say in planning meetings.

Do not confuse training with rehearsal. At least some initial training is necessary for there to be a rehearsal process. That process may throw up the need for further training. That interaction, moderated by the experience of performing to different audiences in different milieus, is what we mean by 'balance'. Individual flair and panache can only exist within a collective and supportive performance framework. The star system, on the other hand, cannot exist within such a framework. Your company may have one or more stars in it – give them a pat on the back once in a while, but don't allow them to dominate the decision-making process. If you are the star, remember that historically the financial rewards were reflected in an equal division of moneys at the end of a tour or given period, with deductions made for costume, props, food, transport, accommodation – and for the company's future. A share system needs to inherit all of that.

How long?

Decide for how long, in the first instance, each person is going to commit her or himself to the company and to what extent. Also decide for how long you are, initially, going to run the company. In the first year of a company's existence people may have other commitments or need to earn a living from other sources. Try to be realistic and honest about what the commitments are or will be. Decide on when they might be reviewed.

Make a business plan

This may go against the grain of your sense of artistic flair, but you will get nowhere with banks, grant applications, etc., unless you undertake one. A three-year plan is best, replaceable towards the end of year two on a roll-over basis.

Company transport

Don't immediately be seduced by the need for owning permanent transport. Vans need maintenance and the older they are, the more they cost to run and repair. If one is only working for short periods of time and not carrying a lot of equipment, then short-term loans or hiring may be a better option. How much do you need to transport, where to and how often?

Rehearsal facilities

Rehearsal facilities can sometimes be needed all the year round, but are mainly just for short, predictable periods of time. If you're poor and just starting out, it is worth considering bartering shows or workshops as a viable way of paying for rehearsal premises. If you are going to perform out of doors most of the time, is it worth finding rehearsal premises that reflect this fact? Are there storage facilities at the rehearsal space that allow you to leave your equipment safely overnight?

Company base

At the outset the company base can easily be in someone's house, as long as separate phone, answer phone, fax, e-mail and a filing cabinet can be installed. If the administrator is also a performer, having a pay-as-you-go mobile phone may be handy, so he or she can be contacted when out of the office, whilst in rehearsal or on tour. If the company succeeds it will also start to generate a lot more office work and a greater volume of paper. It would, at this stage, generally be considered tactful to find larger premises than a corner of someone's room.

Specialised roles

The following are specific areas of responsibility that need to be addressed:

Mask maker or purchaser
Costume maker or purchaser
Prop maker or finder
Stage maker or purchaser

(All the above have maintenance implications as well.)

> Musical Director
> Booker
> Publicist
> Finance Officer

This list may sound banal, but it is important that there is a clear division of responsibility so there are no border disputes or duplication of work.

Finance

At some point the transfer of money between bookers and performers must be dealt with. This means that there has to be a bank account for the money to be paid into. What sort of account it is depends on the way the company is run. The following comments are based on English law.

The easiest way to start is to run everything through one person's bank account, and this works best if that person is already self-employed. The booker's cheque is paid into it and the performers' shares of the proceeds are invoiced separately to the holder of the bank account. All receipts and expenses are similarly deducted from the income and entered into this person's accounts. He or she is acting as a *de facto* employer.

If you open a bank account specifically for the company, after having decided that it is worth carrying on, then a joint account between all members is a good idea. The bank account should have the group's name and be called a 'trading as' account. Everyone invoices the company for their share of the proceeds, and all members are technically self-employed. Expenses and other deductions are made by way of standard bookkeeping methods. All the material possessions of the company are held to be in common possession of the signatories and at the end of each tax year a copy of the accounts, together with the value of the van, masks, stage, computer, answer phone and whatever else you have acquired must be submitted with you own tax return. It is a good idea to have an accountant to sort this out for you. Most good independent small-scale accountants will be prepared, for a one-off fee, to produce 'trading as' accounts that are acceptable to the Inland Revenue.

If the company carries on and wishes to become a limited company and or a charity, it is best to take as much professional advice as you can afford. The Independent Theatre Council in the United Kingdom can provide this advice, and produces information packs. Being a limited company can have its advantages, but will inevitably mean additional administration – which means extra costs.

New members

It is inevitable that company personnel will change over time. In a collective this has different ramifications than in a conventional theatre company and can be handled in many different ways, depending on the wishes and needs of the company.

Even if a company has been performing together for only half a year it will have developed its own idiosyncrasies and patterns of working. For any new performer or company member the first thing is to become acclimatised. He or she may be replacing an existing performer playing a specific role, or they may be part of a company expansion, but whichever is the case there should be an induction period whereby they are trained in the ways of the company before being assigned (or not) responsibilities within it.

There is always a clear choice: either they become a paid employee of the collective or they become part of the collective itself. The former is likeliest to happen if you are replacing a performer in an existing show at short notice, due to illness, injury or high dudgeon and defection on the part of the original performer. The latter may return (and so only needs to be temporarily replaced), or else the collective might decide that they don't want any new board members and are quite happy booking in talent. If a company, from inception, has existed for several years the induction process gets more complicated and potential performers might not want to take on administrative or other roles as well as performing ones.

Admitting people to the collective is preferable only if the person involved has a potential long-term interest. They may have previously been an employee of the collective, or be the lucky one after an audition; what is clear, from experience of several companies, is that they should not be included in the major decision-making process immediately since they are not yet familiar with company's administration, its business methodology or the idiosyncrasies of its performance style. The induction period during which they are trained in the company's method of performance, as well as in the various administrative tasks, enables both sides to assess each other for suitability.

Another thing to bear in mind, based on the certainty that at least half of your theatrical arguments will be about money, is whether new company members should, on acceptance into the collective, immediately achieve equal co-ownership and liabilities of the company properties. It might seem unfair to some that someone who has just joined has an equal share to those who have been in the company longer, but to some people running a company as a collective means just that.

The above is not intended as a definitive guide to forming a contemporary Commedia company, more of an indication. We have mentioned several of the more obvious traps, but no doubt there will be more that you will find yourself.

Training a company

Allocating the Masks

Ideally one would ask the Masks who they would like to be worn by. Enthusiasm (literally being possessed by the god of the Mask) is a basic criterion, perhaps more important than ability in the early stages. If you discover that everyone wants to play Arlecchino, use the impro cards which follow to set up an internal audition process. Sometimes the rest of the group will see a natural affinity in between you and a particular Mask that is not necessarily your first choice. Accept that not everyone has the stamina to play Arlecchino – or the mind set.

Training

Having decided who in your group is playing what Mask, you then have to train in *commedia dell'arte* together. The ultimate ideal is being able to improvise a scenario in front of an audience and to leave them feeling that they got more, not less, from the experience than from attending a conventional play.

We cannot emphasise enough that any exercise that builds trust and rapport between the performers, both as themselves and as the Masks they play, is worthy of inclusion in your training programme. Carlo Mazzone-Clementi recommends soccer, but any ball game which involves a sense of the presence of others in space and the quest for well-timed passing and receiving is valuable. Simple acrobatics involving two or more people are also excellent for building physical trust, but please seek out someone who is qualified to teach you them safely. Discoveries made in such sessions can often later be incorporated into performance, especially by the *zannis*. Impro cards, *canovacci* and even scenarios used for training, on the other hand, should not be used as group performance material. Such training materials are used to build up the skills necessary to perform in public. Developing entrances and exits, stage positioning, passing focus, listening to each other on stage, extemporising through the plot line, building a *repertorio* of personal *lazzi* and group *meccanismi*, trusting one's fellow actors not to drop the ball – all are vital skills for a Commedia performer, and are far easier to learn away from any spectators (except the rest of the group). Material used for such development will, however, have lost its edge before it gets to an audience.

Group improvisation

This is a form of improvisation that serves, either as a *lazzi grande* (big *lazzi*) to refocus the audience's attention after a disruption to the play, or else as an introduction to all the Masks to be used in a particular performance instead of a **prologue**. It involves, typically, the action starting with two Masks on stage, one, for example, doing violence to the other in some manner and escaping. Another Mask enters and the Mask who has just been injured takes their frustration out in a slightly more violent way on this new arrival, and then similarly escapes. A fourth Mask enters and is treated exactly the same, with a rising violence. This progression carries on until you are back with the original two Masks on stage, whereupon they simply carry on the story where they left off. As an alternative to violence, try a loaf of bread, a flower, etc. Another so-called 'chain' impro can be based on the idea of one Mask remaining on stage – A, A/B, A, A/C, A, etc., rather than A, A/B, B, B/C, C, etc. A famous example of this is to be found in the Flaminio Scala scenario *Il Cavadente* (the tooth puller). Pantalone bites Pedrolino and, in revenge the latter persuades the other Masks to join him in persuading Pantalone that his breath smells. One by one they encounter him with this fact until he is convinced and begs Pedrolino to find him a dentist – who turns out to be none other than Arlecchino in disguise, with a bag of carpenter's tools.

Impro cards

We have developed these for our own use in training: please feel free to photocopy them and cut them up for distribution – as we do.

Impro cards for two Masks

These are the building blocks of Commedia since, even when there are more than two people on stage, the action and dialogue should be structured to fit a focus pattern of 2 + 1, 2 + 2, etc.[1] This is because it is very difficult for a Mask to relate for long to more than one other Mask because of restricted vision. The situations are basic, not necessarily intended to be funny, and should be improvised with a minimum of entrances and exits. Allow only a few minutes preparation time so there is no question of 'rehearsing'. End with a freeze which should be held for at least one breath before lifting up the mask – you should always take time at the end of an improvisation to transform back into your social body so that no violence is done to the Mask, to your own spirit, or to the watchers' perception of what has just been done.

Remember that the Lovers, Il Dottore and Il Capitano, emanating as they do from a literary past, will eventually need written dialogue.

As your practice develops, you should write new cards for each other (but not for yourself: improvisation needs the charge that you get from being given something new).

Pantalone, Il Dottore

Pantalone fawns on **Il Dottore**'s every word, agreeing with everything he says on any subject, including the arrangement of marriage between **Il Dottore**'s son Flavio and his daughter Isabella. Then **Il Dottore** brings up the subject of a dowry and **Pantalone** begins disagreeing with everything he says.

Pantalone, Isabella

Isabella attempts to wheedle her father into allowing her to marry Lelio. **Pantalone** says *he's* the one that's going to get married – to Fiorinetta (the Courtesan). **Isabella** bursts into tears and **Pantalone** flies into a rage saying she ought to be grateful to get a new mother after all these years and goes off. Monologue from **Isabella** on her plight.

Pantalone, Valerio

Pantalone discourses to **Valerio** on the advantages of marriage. **Valerio** is all ears, hoping to find a moment to mention that he wishes to marry Flaminia. **Pantalone** then says that *he* intends to marry Flaminia and is glad that his son sees things his way. **Pantalone** goes off. Despair and disgust from **Valerio**.

Pantalone, Zanni

Pantalone repeatedly calls for **Zanni** who calls back a new reason each time for not coming on stage. **Pantalone** becomes angrier and angrier. **Zanni** appears behind **Pantalone** without him noticing and mimics his anger.

Pantalone, Brighella

Pantalone has a shady job for **Brighella** who repeatedly finds reasons for not doing it. Reluctantly **Pantalone** ups his price little by little, beginning with old clothes and ending with real money, painfully parted with.

Pantalone, Franceschina

Franceschina spurns **Pantalone**'s advances, reminding him of the inadequacies of old age. He promises her more and more extravagant gifts if she will only let him try one last time. She savours each one (in prospect) but still says no.

Il Dottore, Zanni (or Pedrolino)

Il Dottore has been to a restaurant and eaten a five-course meal which he describes in detail to **Zanni** who has not eaten for a long time. **Zanni** begins to fantasise that he too is eating the meal and **Il Dottore** joins in, helping him to imaginary delicacies, but eating most of them himself. When the 'meal' is over **Zanni** realises he hasn't eaten and **Il Dottore** discovers he too is now hungry.

Il Dottore, Florindo

Il Dottore tells his son that he has arranged the ideal match for him – Eularia. **Florindo** is mortified: it's the wrong woman – he's in love with Aurelia. **Il Dottore** tries to persuade him that it's for the good of the family (e.g. recites their family tree), but the more he talks, the more upset **Florindo** becomes.

Il Dottore, Il Capitano

Il Capitano boasts of his matchless courage. A mouse appears and he becomes petrified with fear. **Il Capitano** explains that the only thing in the world he is frightened of is mice. **Il Dottore** offers his patent cure for 'sourisophobia'. **Il Capitano** is cured, but then runs off when he hears a dog howling. Monologue from **Il Dottore** on 'lycanthrophobia'.

Il Dottore, Colombina

Colombina is sweeping the floor while **Il Dottore** discourses on the great lovers of history at the same time as trying to pinch her bottom. She uses her broom in a number of ways to evade him and eventually sweeps him off, still talking. Monologue from **Colombina** on the tiresomeness of old men and the winsomeness of her Arlecchino.

Cynthia, Colombina

Colombina is doing her mistress's hair in preparation for her first meeting with the beloved. She uses her opportunity to tell **Cynthia** what men are like and how she should handle herself, but **Cynthia** refuses to believe her.

Lavinia,
Colombina

It's Valentine's Day. **Lavina** is in despair because she hasn't received one. **Colombina** has had a card (probably from Il Dottore) – she quickly sums up the situation and pretends her card is addressed to her mistress. While **Lavinia** clutches it in raptures of speculation, **Colombina** tells the audience that she didn't really want the valentine anyway – Arlecchino's the only man for her, and he can't write!

Aurelio,
Ortensio

They try to outdo each other in describing the exquisiteness of their affection for a woman they have seen. Finally they realise that they are both talking about the same woman.

Flavio, Arlecchino

Arlecchino pretends to be Petunia, the object of his master's affections, so that **Flavio** can practise all the arts of courtship.

Florindo, Zanni

Florindo is completely smitten by his new acquaintance. He tries to explain to **Zanni** what love is, but **Zanni** does not understand. Eventually **Zanni** tries to dissuade **Florindo** from marrying the new Miss Right by listing all the previous disasters. **Florindo** is unmoved and goes off to meet his new love.

Fabrizio, Sylvia

Fabrizio has received his call-up papers. Little by little he breaks the news to **Sylvia** who thinks it is wonderful and imagines what he will look like in his uniform. Then she realises that they will be parted and despairs. Never mind, says **Fabrizio**, they can write every day – and they take turns to compose imaginary letters. Finally they part (with much sweet sorrow), then **Sylvia** realises that he might get killed and becomes distraught again.

Arlecchino, Colombina

Arlecchino has a letter. He tries to read it – but he can't read. **Colombina** tells him he is holding it upside down. He stands on his head and pretends to read it out. She tells him she knows he can't read and offers to read it for him. It is a love letter and he makes believe that she is addressing it to him as she reads it out.

Colombina, Arlecchino

Colombina says she's fed up – she never gets to go anywhere or do anything interesting. She sees **Arlecchino** and tells him she wants to go to the movies. He is broke, but pretends to take her anyway: when they get there he improvises the adverts, the movie, etc. She is so amused she forgives him for being a ne'er do well.

Colombina, Pedrolino

Colombina is sweeping the floor, dreaming of Arlecchino. **Pedrolino** watches for a while, then says he has a present for her. She is dismissive, but intrigued. He offers her a moonbeam that he has picked from the woods. She laughs and shoos him away. He says he will be back with another present. Alone she calls 'Arlecchino, I've got a present for you!'

Pedrolino, Zanni

They want to go to Disneyland, but can't afford it. Instead they create it for each other.

Il Capitano, Arlecchino

They are crossing the desert. **Il Capitano** boasts of his prowess as a desert warrior. **Arlecchino** is more concerned about being thirsty and keeps seeing mirages.

Arlecchino, Zanni

Arlecchino bemoans the fact that he is broke and it's Colombina's birthday. Enter **Zanni** with a piece of paper he has found. **Arlecchino** is certain that it is a lottery ticket. They both fantasize, separately, then together, about what they will do with the winnings.

Brighella, Franceschina

Brighella says he needs **Franceschina**'s help with a plot to catch Pantalone – wants her to entice him to her house. **Franceschina** replies that she needs **Brighella**'s help with her scheme to expose Il Capitano who has refused to pay her for services rendered. They both refuse, then both agree – for old times' sake.

Brighella, Zanni

Zanni is carrying his master's shopping home. He meets **Brighella** who tricks it off him, item-by-item.

Impro cards for three Masks

The question of entering and exiting now comes in to play (see below), but we suggest it is not yet time to use a backdrop since those 'off' stage still need to see as well as hear what is going on. They should watch with Masks 'up', then bring them down and enter at the appropriate moment. Make sure when all three Masks are on that there is a 2 + 1 split, never a 1 + 1 + 1. It is dynamic for the split to change (and usually funny!). At this stage we frequently send trios away to prepare for half an hour, then have a little festival of showing where the rest of the group can say what they have learnt from watching each other's 'performances'. In mask work you often learn more from watching than doing since time flashes by in the mask, leaving you exhausted at the end and either exhilarated or ruing lost opportunities.

By now female Masks should be working in rehearsal skirts. High heels, Pantalone's slippers and other specialist footwear need getting used to and cloaks, fans and other accessories should be available. Arlecchino should never be without his slapstick or Il Capitano his sword and other weapons should be available as necessary.

Il Magnifico, Zanni, Franceschina

Il Magnifico sends **Zanni** with a message vital to the safety of the state, and *exits*, threatening him with the direst consequences if he doesn't deliver on time. **Zanni** meets **Franceschina** carrying a tray of pies and forgets all the instructions in the amatory and gluttonous tussle that ensues. *Re-enter* **Il Magnifico**: he discovers that **Zanni** can't remember a word of the message correctly and is only prevented from hanging him by an intimate offer from **Franceschina**.

Pantalone, Pedrolino, Brighella

Pantalone tells **Pedrolino** to guard his house as there are thieves about. *Exit.* **Pedrolino** falls asleep and begins to dream. *Enter* **Brighella**. Seeing **Pedrolino** is sleepwalking, he gets him to rob the house and bring him the proceeds. He *leaves* and **Pantalone** *returns.* He discovers his loss and flies into a rage. **Pedrolino** wakes up and *runs away*.

Pantalone, Pedrolino, Flavio

Pantalone catches **Pedrolino** stealing and decides to hang him. He finds it difficult and **Pedrolino** helps him before pretending to die. *Enter* **Flavio**: he remonstrates with **Pantalone** who *storms off*. **Pedrolino** comes back to life and **Flavio** *runs off* terrified. **Pedrolino** pretends to be a ghost and scares **Pantalone**, who even gives him money to stop haunting him.

Two Dottores, Arlecchino

Arlecchino is on trial. One **Dottore** appears for the defence, one for the prosecution. Eventually **Arlecchino** silences them both and cross-questions himself, sums up, retires, comes back, finds himself guilty and sentences himself to death. (Additionally he can execute and bury himself as well.)

Il Dottore, Zanni, Brighella

Brighella convinces **Zanni** to play dead so that **Il Dottore** can experiment on his corpse – which he does.

Il Dottore, Colombina, Il Capitano

Colombina cleans the surgery, complaining of her lot. **Il Dottore** *enters* and attempts to molest her. She is saved by knocking and *lets in* **Il Capitano**. She *eavesdrops* while **Il Dottore** attempts to cure **Il Capitano**'s condition. *Exit* **Il Dottore**, *re-enter* **Colombina**. **Il Capitano** tries to seduce her but she now knows about his problem and taunts him accordingly.

Flavio, Il Capitano, Arlecchino

Il Capitano boasts to **Arlecchino** of his prowess with women. He makes him pretend to be Isabella and makes love to 'her'. *Exit.*
Enter **Flavio** with a message for **Arlecchino** to take to Isabella. **Arlecchino** says she won't want it – she's in love with Il Capitano now. **Flavio** won't believe it till **Arlecchino** demonstrates, then he bursts into tears.

Fabrizio, Vittoria, Zanni

The Lovers are having a row and refusing to speak to each other. They use **Zanni** as a go-between, but of course he gets the messages hopelessly garbled. Eventually they simply have to speak to each other in order to put matters right.

Il Capitano, Colombina, Pedrolino

Il Capitano makes up to **Colombina** who mocks him and *exits. Enter* **Pedrolino** – **Il Capitano** bullies him and is about to beat him when **Colombina** *returns* and scares him away. **Pedrolino** *is left* thinking she must be in love with him – he re-enacts the scene for his own delight.

Colombina, Franceschina, Il Capitano

Colombina complains about men as she does the washing – but she is looking for a husband. **Il Capitano** *enters*, boasts of his prowess, then tries to seduce **Colombina**, but he isn't the man for her. She *leaves* and **Franceschina** *enters*. She proves more than a match for **Il Capitano** and he finally *leaves* with his tail between his legs.

Isabella, Franceschina, Scapino (or Arlecchino)

Isabella and **Franceschina** argue over their respective attitudes to men. It turns into a cat fight and **Arlecchino** (who has been *eavesdropping*) comes on and attempts to mediate. Eventually they both turn on him and he is forced to scarper. They make it up and *exit together*.

Brighella, Arlecchino, Zanni

Brighella teaches **Arlecchino** how to pick pockets. *Exit. Enter* **Zanni**. **Arlecchino** teaches him how to pick pockets. *Exit. Re-enter* **Brighella**. **Zanni** offers to show him how to pick pockets. **Brighella** says what have you got? **Zanni** has an apple. He shows **Brighella** how to steal it from him – which he does.

Canovacci

A *canovaccio* is, in our definition, a short Commedia, designed to get the maximum amount of drama and comedy from a limited period of stage time; it is more of a slice of Commedia than the whole cake, so does not need to be as tightly structured as a scenario (which involves the whole range of Masks), or even to have a definite ending. We had previously assumed that the etymology of *canovaccio* stemmed from the notion that it was the plot summary pinned on the back of the canvas, i.e. the back curtain – thus indicating a shorter, probably outdoor performance – whereas the *scenario* was the same thing, but pinned on the scenery – thus implying a longer, indoor performance. However Thomas Heck has recently argued that the word is borrowed from embroidery where it means 'a piece of loosely woven cloth on which a line or pattern has been traced, upon which one embroiders, adding color and texture in the process.'[2] Whether this attribution is right or not, it is a valuable image for the performer to work from.

With more Masks on stage, more storyline is needed to bind the situations together. Stage positioning (see below) now becomes of paramount importance. Switches of focus can be achieved by one or more Masks freezing or going into slow motion whilst speaking *sotto voce*, in order to highlight the actions and dialogue of others. This is particularly important while asides are going on. The backdrop should be introduced and stage positions attended to. At this stage in a troupe's development, notes can be given after a first, internal, 'performance', then the piece can be reworked and re-presented. Notes should be given both between performers and by the rest of the group who have been watching. This will help to develop good rehearsal habits for the future when a piece is taken back into the rehearsal room after one or more public performances.

Poohpooh tartare

This first example of a canovaccio is really a modern *zannata* play inspired by the early antics of the zannis in tormenting Pantalone. Commedia at its most scatological.

IL DOTTORE
3 ZANNIS *his paramedic team*
PANTALONE
ARLECCHINO *his servant*

1. **The Doctor's surgery**. IL DOTTORE has a *visit from* PANTALONE who is worried about whether his equipment is in order since he has decided he must have a son and heir. IL DOTTORE says not to worry, men can have a child at any age. He gives him a bottle of blue pills to ensure that he has a boy. PANTALONE says put it on my account and *exits*. IL DOTTORE says there's no money in traditional medicine any more: he must modernise, then the insurance companies will pay. *Calls* ZANNIS and tells them they are going to become his mobile paramedic team. He trains them up – e.g. cardiac arrest, drowning, broken fingernails, etc. *Exeunt.*

2. **Pantalone's house**. *Enter* ARLECCHINO. *Lazzi* of being hungry.

3. *Enter* PANTALONE. He is intrigued by ARLECCHINO's contortions. ARLECCHINO tries to get PANTALONE to understand that he is hungry but only succeeds in making him hungry as well. PANTALONE sits down and demands the menu. ARLECCHINO starts to play waiter, takes his order then goes into an imaginary kitchen and becomes the chef. Behind PANTALONE's back he fills a plate with his own do-dos, sweepings from the floor, the odd fly etc. as PANTALONE calls impatiently for his food. ARLECCHINO serves it with style, turning himself into a table, complete with white cloth, so that PANTALONE can put his plate down. PANTALONE eats, finds it delicious but immediately feels ill. His stomach cramps get so bad that he has ARLECCHINO fetch IL DOTTORE.

4. Monologue from PANTALONE about how he doesn't want to die yet because he has no son and heir.

5. *Enter* IL DOTTORE, *followed by* ARLECCHINO. He takes PANTALONE's pulse, looks at his tongue, etc., and goes into conference with ARLECCHINO, explaining at great length that PANTALONE is pregnant. ARLECCHINO whispers in PANTALONE's ear. He is at first amazed, then delighted. He lies down and starts farting. IL DOTTORE gets on his mobile phone and calls up the ZANNIS. They *arrive immediately*, cover PANTALONE with the table cloth and rummage around underneath, coming up with a huge turd which they wrap in the cloth and hand to PANTALONE. 'It's a boy!' The proud father cradles it in his arms, making 'coochee-coochee' sounds. ARLECCHINO uses the cloth to disguise himself as a priest and conducts a mock christening (**Song**: – '*It's a boy!*'?). All peer at the 'baby' but are knocked back by the smell. *TABLEAU.*

The dual duel

Simple canovacci can be made from stitching impro cards together. This one is a little more sophisticated and shows how the arrival of Il Capitano requires the emergence of a plot. A useful training exercise would be to separate it out again into impro cards, then to run them as a sequence.

> PANTALONE
> ISABELLA *his daughter*
> FLORINDO *in love with Isabella*
> IL CAPITANO
> PEDROLINO *his servant*

1.   **Pantalone's house.** ISABELLA and FLORINDO play requited love – blighted only by the fact of Pantalone's disapproval. ISABELLA is promising to try once again to persuade her father to let them marry when they *hear* PANTALONE *coming* – FLORINDO *hides*. To her surprise, PANTALONE tells her if he can't find someone more suitable before dawn tomorrow he will finally allow her to marry Florindo since he has agreed to take her without a dowry. *Exit.* FLORINDO *emerges* and the lovers *exit together* joyfully.

2.   **The street.** *Enter* IL CAPITANO, just arrived in town, with PEDROLINO carrying his bags. He says he's heard the rich and beautiful Isabella lives here and boasts of how she will fall at his feet. *Sends* PEDROLINO to her with a letter of introduction.

3.   *Enter* FLORINDO, still in raptures. As IL CAPITANO boasts of his breeding, his military prowess, his immense wealth, his amatory conquests – FLORINDO progressively falls into despair. When IL CAPITANO announces his intentions *vis-à-vis* Isabella, his misery becomes total. *Exit.*

4.   *Enter* PANTALONE – IL CAPITANO makes his boasts again – with PANTALONE progressively becoming more and more ecstatic, saying he must meet his daughter. *Exeunt.*

5.   *Enter* ISABELLA counting the hours. *To her* PEDROLINO – gives IL CAPITANO's letter. ISABELLA refuses to read it, telling PEDROLINO that she is betrothed to another. PEDROLINO says good – the Capitano's a windbag and you're well shot of him.

6. *To them*, FLORINDO. ISABELLA tells him about IL CAPITANO and obliges him to challenge him to a duel. PEDROLINO *goes off* with FLORINDO's glove. *Exit* ISABELLA. Despairing monologue from FLORINDO. *Exit*, with great reluctance, to prepare himself.

7. *Enter* IL CAPITANO. PEDROLINO *returns* and slaps him with FLORINDO's glove. IL CAPITANO goes yellow-bellied, but PANTALONE *arrives* and he has to put a brave face on it. *Enter* ISABELLA disguised as a man. She outboasts IL CAPITANO and he *exits* with his tail between his legs. PANTALONE now proposes that 'he' is the man to marry his daughter. *Enter* FLORINDO relieved that IL CAPITANO has told him the duel is off. But ISABELLA picks up the glove saying she accepts the challenge instead. Pistols are decided on. *Exeunt* to prepare.

8. **Dawn. The duelling field.** PANTALONE acts as second for ISABELLA, PEDROLINO for FLORINDO. In the duel ISABELLA seems to shoot FLORINDO (who can't bring himself to pull the trigger). He faints. PANTALONE is delighted until ISABELLA lifts her mask, whereupon PANTALONE faints. ISABELLA explains the guns were loaded with blanks anyway. PEDROLINO revives FLORINDO and the lovers are reunited. PEDROLINO revives PANTALONE, who finally gives his consent. *TABLEAU.*

The sex change

Unless sexual ambiguity is intended, cross-gender casting of male lovers doesn't work. This canovacchio takes the possibility of a shortage of eligible young men into account.

PANTALONE
ANGELICA *his daughter*
ZANNI *his servant*
IL DOTTORE *a gynaecologist*
GEORGINA *his daughter*
ARLECCHINO *his lab assistant*
COLOMBINA
FRANCESCHINA

1. **The Doctor's surgery.** IL DOTTORE examines PANTALONE and tells him the operation has been successful – the fishbone implant is working

perfectly. PANTALONE and IL DOTTORE bemoan the fact that they both have only daughters. PANTALONE *leaves* for an assignation with FRANCESCHINA to try out his new weapon.

2. IL DOTTORE, *solus*, reveals he has been experimenting with ARLECCHINO by pouring hormones on his porridge. He *calls* ARLECCHINO who enters (and displays some very feminine tendencies). IL DOTTORE tells him he wants him to find a volunteer for his latest experiment – sex changing. ARLECCHINO says he'll do it. Yes, but I need a female subject too, says IL DOTTORE. *Exeunt.*

3. **The street.** *Enter* COLOMBINA. *To her,* ARLECCHINO, who says, how would you like to have a sex change? COLOMBINA says don't be silly, how would you still be able to love me? ARLECCHINO says he would have one too – they try it out. COLOMBINA says she prefers herself as she is – ARLECCHINO isn't so sure . . . *Exit* ARLECCHINO.

4. COLOMBINA, *sola*, says what fools men are, sex, sex and more sex. She longs for the finer things in life.

5. *To her* GEORGINA. She is sad because there is no man in her life. COLOMBINA tells her there are more important things. GEORGINA says sometimes she wishes she were a man – they have such freedom to do what they like, while she has to stay at home doing embroidery and waiting. COLOMBINA says in that case she has a plan, and they *exit together*.

6. **Pantalone's house.** PANTALONE sends ZANNI to arrange his assignation. *Exit* ZANNI.

7. PANTALONE now *calls* ANGELICA and tells her that soon she will have a little brother – Franceschina is sure to marry him now he is the man he always was. *Exit.*

8. ANGELICA, *sola.* She is disgusted – if only a suitable man would appear and take her away from all this sordidness. *Exit.*

9. **The street.** ZANNI *calls on* FRANCESCHINA, who *appears* at her window, then *takes him in*.

10. *Enter* ARLECCHINO, cross-dressed. Calls at Franceschina's door. ZANNI

comes out, exhausted. ARLECCHINO makes up to him. ZANNI says he couldn't manage another stroke and *leaves*. ARLECCHINO bursts into tears.

11. FRANCESCHINA *comes down* and says what's the matter. He says it's me, ARLECCHINO: I'm a woman and nobody wants me. FRANCESCHINA gives him some lessons in how to attract men. *Exit* FRANCESCHINA.

12. *Enter* GEORGINA, dressed as man. ARLECCHINO tries his new found skills on her with COLOMBINA *easvesdropping*. GEORGINA refuses ARLECCHINO's advances, saying she is a new man and doesn't go in for that sort of thing, and *exits*. ARLECCHINO is defused again. COLOMBINA comes into the scene and says there, you see, it isn't much fun being a woman. ARLECCHINO says it's because he's not a proper woman, but he knows a man who can fix that. *Exit, followed by* COLOMBINA, pleading with him not to be so silly.

13. ANGELICA falls in love with GEORGINA at first sight, but not vice-versa. Scene of unrequited love. *Exit* GEORGINA.

14. ANGELICA, *sola*, decides to commit suicide.

15. **The Doctor's surgery**. IL DOTTORE prepares to operate – rubber gloves and mask and a 'sprologuio' on his new technique.

16. *Enter* GEORGINA. She says it is pointless pretending to be a man, it's the whole hog for her. *Enter* ARLECCHINO. He says it is pointless pretending to be a woman, it's all or nothing for him. IL DOTTORE connects them together with tubes, wires, etc. ANGELICA *enters* next and begs him for sleeping pills. He gives her a bottle and she swallows the lot. He is about to begin operating again when ZANNI *arrives* clutching his privates – IL DOTTORE has a quick look and diagnoses syphillis. But I don't know anyone called Phyllis, moans ZANNI. IL DOTTORE is about to begin the operation again when PANTALONE and FRANCESCHINA *arrive*. PANTALONE is furious – after all the money he paid for the operation, FRANCESCHINA has a bone stuck in her throat, and is choking to death.

17. COLOMBINA appears above and blows a whistle, throws a firecracker, rattles a rattle, w.h.y. ALL *freeze* in various stages of dying or dementia. She apologises for the lack of a happy ending, saying that *commedia*

dell'arte has lost its way in the modern world, where the surgeon's knife is the new God. She knows it's old-fashioned, but if only we could accept ourselves as we are, then Arlecchino would love her again and the world would be a happier place. ALL come to their senses, looking thoroughly abashed. PANTALONE embraces his daughter, IL DOTTORE his. FRANCESCHINA spits out the bone, looks down ZANNI's trousers and say's 'It's only a pimple'. And, of course, ARLECCHINO takes off his dress and is reunited with COLOMBINA. *TABLEAU.*

Entrances and exits

Most entrances are made round or through the outside edges of the back curtain. If you have the choice, go through if you are coming out of a house, go round if coming from another part of town. If there are steps leading up to either side of the stage, these replace the 'town' entrances. With a back-drop entrance, remember that a western audience looks naturally from left to right as if reading a book. Entering from audience left therefore looks 'normal' (unless you do something about it) and from the right 'funny' – 'ha-ha' or peculiar according to circumstances. If appropriate, establish vocally from backstage the approach of your Mask before it appears in view – this sets up a sense of anticipation in the audience and also lets those on stage know that you haven't missed your cue! Immediately on entering, the Mask should adopt one of its basic stances, then look to both sides to estab-lish its 'gaze' before focusing on its on-stage intention. Particularly on first entering, the objective must be to be huge (have a 'Wow!' or 'Ahah!' cartoon image in mind), before adjusting to normal size to interact with other Masks. First entrance is also a good time to indulge in high-spirited acrobatics. Otherwise moving from the basic entrance position to the first on-stage posi-tion must be achieved by use of one of the Mask's basic walks – if you establish the Mask at its most typical, then more freedom is possible later.

Other possible entrances are through the centre overlap and 'above' (through use of a stepladder). The centre, as we shall see, is very strong and can only be used by high-, or would be high-, status Masks, such as Pantalone or Il Capitano. Having others open the flap for you can be helpful in increasing the impressiveness of the entrance. When entering 'above', come up as quickly as possible, commensurate with safety. Again freeze as if allowing the audience to take a snapshot, then establish both profiles of the mask before relating to the action. 'Above' positions should only be used by Lovers (particularly female), Franceschina, Colombina, and Pantalone when woken up in the middle of the night. Arlecchino is, as always, the exception to the rule and, as a *passe-partout*, can use all entrances, even, exceptionally, appearing under the drop.

Some curtains have slits in just below head height for eavesdropping: it takes a lot of practice to get the Mask through quickly, look left, look right, then establish a listening gaze without destroying the audience's attention to what is going on on-stage. Eavesdropping can also take place round the sides of the curtain or from above.

Exits should be even more powerful than entrances. Imagine thunderous applause, even if you don't get it. Part of what you are doing is to train an audience into showing their appreciation, this is not the same thing as playing for applause – on an exit you are offering them a punctuation mark between what you have just done and the following scene. This actually gives a lift to those left on stage, not a hole for them struggle out of.

Always exit *to* somewhere, not just off the stage. The world behind the drop should be made more real, more exciting, more enticing by the strength of intention of your exit than the visible world in front of it. Technically this is achieved by holding back part of your last line, pausing at the exit point and adopting a basic position (as on entering), then delivering the last part of the line before passing out of sight with redoubled energy. As with entrances, loud mumbling or other noises can continue once out of sight, thus increasing the illusion that there is another world that the Masks come from and return to.

Stage positions

The diagram below indicates where, traditionally, it was considered that specific kinds of action work best. If one thinks in terms of a painting, the lovers usually occupy the foreground, the front third of the stage, directly contacting the audience with their emotional overload; all deals, whether financial or marital (sometimes both together) are struck in the middle ground, the central third of the stage where actions such as the picking of pockets and the drinking of potions also take place; and in the background, in front of the backdrop, in the furthest third of the stage, is conducted all conniving, plotting and dark business. Sticking to these conventions quite quickly informs the audience as to how to read such a small and confined stage space.

The flowering of *commedia dell'arte* coincided with the burgeoning of the Mannerist movement. As a reaction to the balanced, classical proportions of Renaissance art, the Mannerist painters, poets and composers of madrigals,

AUDIENCE

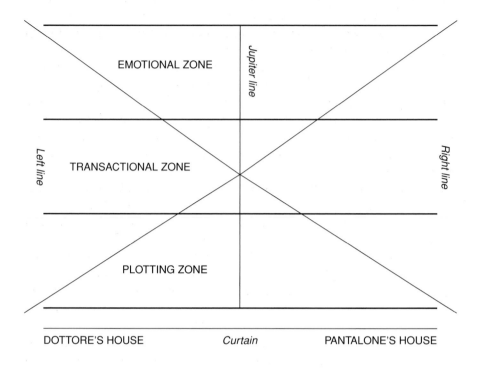

DOTTORE'S HOUSE   *Curtain*   PANTALONE'S HOUSE

BACKSTAGE

Figure 16 Diagram of stage positions.

deliberately ignored the previously accepted rules of composition and vied with each other in the daring use of space known as *discordia concors*, typified by the juxtaposition of seemingly irreconcilable elements. Simultaneously the improvised, professional *commedia dell'arte* was consciously separating itself from the text-based Renaissance *commedia erudita* of the amateur *dilettanti*, and the more refined of the early companies were eager, in order to evince their refinement, to embrace the artistically fashionable anti-renaissance stylistic devices of Mannerism. Typical Mannerist style in *commedia dell'arte* would have been the avoidance of harmony between on-stage elements until the 'happy' ending was due.[3]

The stage should never be left empty in Commedia, even for one second. On the contrary it should always, in the Mannerist sense, seem crowded. This is called *horror vacui*, another concept from Mannerist painting where the artist deliberately crowds the frame with objects and figures. The fewer Masks there are on stage, the harder they must work to achieve this effect, changing from zone to zone as the action develops – and this must be done without losing a sense of being in a picture, of offering the spectator a formal sense of composition by which to read the action. The ideal is always that, if a freeze frame were possible, each actor's physical shape and position, and the spatial relationship between all the Masks on the stage, should at all times give the audience all the information they need to understand the dramatic situation. For this to happen, the acting of the performers has to embody the reality of each line spoken, or dramatic statement made, with a precise physical equivalent which takes into account the contours being offered by the other Masks present within the stage 'frame'. The aim of the training should be that this working method becomes sublimated into the performer's stage presence. A simple exercise is for the whole group to sit in the audience, then for one Mask to step out and take up a position in the performing space. The next Mask to join it must complete a new stage picture, then the next, and so on. There will be nobody left to appreciate the final composition, but it should be held for long enough for all to sense its dynamics. In this way a company of performers, in much the same way as a painter, can formally compose the action on stage at chosen, prepre-pared, moments without resorting to a director.

Changes of relative position during a scene should not only be reflected by changes of zone, or of position within that zone, but should also be accomplished by use of the left, right, centre (or 'Jupiter') lines when coming forward and the diagonals when going back. Colombina has the right to occupy the central crossing point of these lines whenever she is on stage. At Sélavy we have them permanently marked on the floor in one of the studios.

Stock speeches

Since all the Masks embody an archetypal emotional position and are stereo-typical of a social class, they all end up in roughly the same types of dramatic situation whatever the scenario. Consequently the historical *commedia dell' arte* actors were able to memorise large amounts of stock speeches and or text, and use them seemingly 'off the cuff', in any number of performances. These were not improvised pieces of doggerel, but memorised well-written set pieces. Some were appropriated from classical and contemporary play-wrights, poets and authors, and some were written by members of the company. The details of a speech would be adapted in performance to the specific dramatic situation within each scenario. Tim Fitzpatrick has examined thoroughly the amount of actual improvisation that was entailed.[4] These speeches can either function independently of the plot, much in the same way as *lazzi* do, or as integral transactions or dramatic turning points within it. Below are lists of possibilities for two of the 'literary' Masks, intended as an indication of where to start to create your own speeches (or to begin the process of inspired plagiarism!).

Il Capitano

Threatening his rival in love
Excuses as to why he cannot fight today
Insulting his servant
Women he has known and made love to
Boasting of all his best qualities
Boasting of battles he has fought
Famous warriors he compares himself to
How much gold he has in his trunk (and where he got it from)
The genealogy of his name and of his famous ancestors (and what they did)
What he'll do to you if you disagree with him.
Begging his servant for a favour
Rational explanation as to why he is frightened of mice

Flaminia (the young female lover, who may use poems or songs as well as speeches)

Joy at seeing lover for first time
Despair at leaving lover for the first time
Despair at parent not letting her marry her lover
Despair at parent for making her marry an unsuitable partner
Fury with Colombina for taking too long over make-up/getting dressed, etc
Joy at recollecting words, actions, sighs of lover, having parted from him
Suicide speech when forced to leave lover and or marry unsuitable partner
Wheedling parent into letting lover (disguised as music or dance teacher/soothsayer, etc.) into the house
Petulant frustration that lover does not meet ridiculously high expectations

Horror and excitement at being disguised as Colombina as part of
    someone else's plan
Contempt directed at parent or servant who dares to suggest that *they*
    have fallen in love
'What is love?'

Isabella (the older female lover)

On the dignity of lovers
On the passions of hatred and love
On those who have died for love
On the fever of love
On how to fall out of love
On loving another more than oneself
On jealousy[5]

Song and dance

In the *repertorio* of any *commedia dell'arte* company, there should be an appropriate amount of songs, dances and musical decoration. Music is as vital a
part of a *commedia dell'arte* performance as **lazzi** or the Masks themselves.
Commedia dell'arte and opera, both comic and lyric, have the same historical
roots and still have something very major in common – the dramatic use of
music and song to extend moments of extreme human emotion.[6] The same
may also be said of many contemporary musicals. The companies included
in Part 1 of this book would all have excelled at madrigal singing since that
was the Mannerist new movement in music. We don't suggest getting into
Gesualdo or Monteverdi unless you already have the singing training
needed, but simple part singing is always enhancing of climactic moments.

In your company's repertory, you should aim to have pieces which
frame the drama, pieces which are integral to the drama and pieces which
accompany or complement the drama. Framing songs and dances have the
same function as a well-thought out picture frame: they allow the audience
to focus on the picture better, as they carefully define the edges of what
is to be looked at. One could, for example, use songs and dances to help
gather a crowd, to entertain a crowd before the show proper begins, to create
the right mood in a crowd so as they will appreciate the show more, to
allow the performers to check out the mood of the crowd before a show, to
provide a cheerful finale to the action, and to be an intermission entertainment. For the latter 'words and actions' songs, or songs with choreographed

movement seem to work well, if counterpointed with slower numbers. For the music and lyrics of the following suggestions, see Appendix F.

The Gobi Dance or the *Horses Branle* (up tempo rough and ready *zanni* dances), followed by a round, such as *Rose Rose*, may be a suitable opening, whilst *Pastime with Good Company*, sung as an up-tempo harmony piece has been used fairly often as a good finale.

For inclusion within the action, one has to look at the kinds of stock situations that the Masks find themselves in, and find suitable tunes to match. The pavan included can either be a formal dance within the action or else a framing number. For a general despair song we suggest *What if a Day*, which has a simple, but beautiful tune, and excellent words. For serenades the choice is limitless, though we have included the Shakespearean *O Mistress Mine*, as a cheerful upbeat example. On-stage, the singing (and mandolin or guitar playing) male lover should ideally be accompanied by a *zanni* band – who when the chips are down really can play, and make the serenade a proper musical number. It doesn't have to last long, because dramatically the climax can be an interruption by an irate parent or neighbour. If the lover does gain admittance to his true love's house as a result of a serenade, it is either the end of the drama, or else it was someone in disguise as his lover waiting for him. Pantalone should also have a good serenading voice, but be even less successful with it.

Incidental music, even simple drumming, can be supplied for chases, during love scenes, as support to *lazzi* or *meccanismi* and generally whenever there is a spare performer with enough time between scenes.

Instruments should adhere to the medieval, Renaissance and Baroque origins of the genre. All acoustic, percussive and folk instruments are appropriate; electric instruments are not because voices are not being amplified – and you don't want to die if it rains. It is also a question of 'feel' – sometimes, even a steel string guitar can look and sound incongruous. Similarly modern tunes do not really feel right within a traditionally masked and garbed Commedia. Period music and dance, as well as folk song and dance, if chosen and arranged carefully, do the job much better. The more the audience can be drawn into a never-never land of historical comedy, the more the satire, jibes about human frailty, hypocrisy and the like, can go to work. In our experience, as long as you persuade the audience that they are watching a piece of period drama, then you can get away with an awful lot that might otherwise seem shocking or too near the knuckle.

Rehearsing and performing

At a certain point in your training programme you should feel that if you don't perform you will burst. It's time to start rehearsing or the group will go off the boil – there's only so much that you can learn without an audience. Somebody has written a scenario: how to go about rehearsing it? At this point you need to forgive us for having used the word 'improvisation' rather imprecisely so far. There was not anything like as much improvisation in a traditional *commedia dell'arte* performance as the modern predilection for 'impro' might lead us to suppose. In *commedia dell'arte all' improvviso* nearly all the elements used were 'stock' and simply applied as needed to different scenarios. At its worst, this must have resulted in the deadliest of deadly theatre, the equivalent of painting by numbers. Part 1 of this book relates the stories of some of the best. Here is a short glossary of some of the *indici* (indications) that they might have used to mark up a scenario for performance, in the same way that '*allegro*', '*pizzicato*', etc. are written in a musical score.

ad libitum 'To the desired extent' – i.e. in performance to carry on in a particular mode for as long as is judged desirable rather than stopping at a predetermined point; not the same thing as to '*adlib*', i.e. to make impromptu remarks during an otherwise fixed sequence.

a parte 'Aside', but the Italian is better – literally the performer needs to be apart from the other Masks in order to make a direct comment to the audience. The convention of holding the back of the hand across the face cannot be used since the hand 'kills' the Mask if it comes that close. Therefore it is necessary to establish a separation – most often involving moving to one of the down stage corners.

a soggetto Sticking to the subject, accepting a basic premise and bombarding it from every angle.

bravura Usually used in the sense of '*bravura* technique' – a difficult skill accomplished with great panache.

bravure Exaggerated rhetorical phrases as delivered by Il Capitano.

burle Pranks or practical jokes at the expense of another Mask. From *burlare*, 'to ridicule' or 'make fun of', the derivation of 'burlesque'. Pedrolino's favourite pasttime.

capocomico The head actor, akin to the English 'actor/manager'.

capriccio A sudden start as made by a goat. Launching without warning into a poetical or fantastical outburst. A caprice employed by Pantalone in particular.

cascate Literally 'floods' – of obscene jokes or *lazzi*, usually scatological. Introduced when 'actors feel particularly sure of themselves or their audience'.[7]

chiusette Prearranged exit lines or 'tags' at the end of *uscite*, often a rhyming couplet (especially from the Lovers), sometimes even a quatrain.

choregos See *corago*.

concertare il soggetto The *corago*'s explanation to the company, not necessarily on stage, of the relationships between the Masks, the plan for exits, entrances, use of 'houses', *doti*, opportunities for *generici*, etc., in the scenario to be performed.

concetti Fanciful notions and far-fetched comparisons, beloved of the Lovers, Il Capitano and Il Dottore.

corago The nearest *commedia dell'arte* comes to having a director, often the *capocomico*, sometimes also known as *il guido maestro*.

doni The 'given' or traditional material for a Mask as kept in an actor's notebook.

doti The set pieces of a Commedia troupe, consisting of soliloquies, narratives, dissertations and studied passages of rhetoric. Some existed in manuscript form. Others were simply known by heart, and others were composed for some special occasion. *Doti* should be used at decisive points in the action, giving fixed points at which to aim and away from which to improvise afterwards. As in Japanese Kabuki, an audience may burst into applause when one is successfully carried off – in contrast to *generici*.

effeto meraviglioso The introduction of the marvellous via the use of a special effect, usually late in a scenario – typified in England by the transformation scene at the end of a pantomime.

generici Commonplaces – sententious maxims, descriptions, outpourings of emotion, diatribes, declamations of passion, love-laments, ravings, reproaches, declamatory outbursts, to be employed *ad libitum* in any appropriate situation. Other company members need to sense when they can be expected, lead up to and away from them without interrupting the flow. The audience's sense of the

style of performance must be continuous, as opposed to **caprice** or
doti.

imbroglio The complications which follow on after the exposition of a plot.
The tangle that ensues when the Masks try to cheat each other.

inganni Deceptions which move the plot along.

ingarbuglia What it sounds like – mumbling and bumbling, often between
Pantalone and Il Dottore, which results in a muddling of the situation.

lazzi There are two initial definitions of this contentious word: material
that is part of a performer's **repertorio** that can be called upon at short
notice whilst on stage to enliven the action, or a piece of business that
relates to character, rather than the plot. These definitions work if the
model of *commedia dell'arte* you use is that of *commedia improvviso* –
Masks improvising their way through a predetermined story line.
However, if your model for performance is that of rehearsed and 'set'
action and dialogue, the word *lazzi* takes on a more general
significance: another possible derivation of this disputed word to add
to those given in *Commedia dell'Arte, An Actor's Handbook* is 'azi', short
for 'azione', meaning simply 'actions', i.e. all comic business as opposed
to dialogue.

For present purposes we stay with the first two definitions. A *lazzi*
is typically used when a Mask is alone on stage to help create character
rapport with the audience, or else to rescue a scene that has gone off
the rails and is in need of the audience's attention being regained and
refocused. It is a piece of skill or *bravura*, done as a loop that returns
precisely to the point of departure.

In working up a piece for performance it is best simply to mark
places in the scenario where *lazzi* may possibly occur in performance.
To cast in stone where various Masks will perform their *lazzi* runs
counter to the flexibility in performance that *commedia dell'arte* thrives
on. *Commedia dell'arte* may be known for its *lazzi*, but it must never be
forgotten that all worthwhile scenarios and *canovacci* have a dramatic
story at their core, as with all conventional plays, and that is the reason
audiences stay to watch. They have (hopefully, if not you may as well
go home . . .) developed an emotional bond with the Masks and want
to know what will happen to them in the end. *Lazzi* may be one way of
providing entertainment during this journey, but they are certainly not
the whole trip. A *lazzi* is an embellishment, not the story itself, but a
commedia dell'arte story without *lazzi* would be a poor Commedia
indeed.

Good *lazzi* come from discoveries made in training which are then
developed as separate entities before being reintroduced in other

circumstances. Mel Gordon proposes the following categories: acrobatic and mimic, comic violence and sadistic behaviour, food, illogical, stage property based, sexual or scatalogical, social-class or rebellion, stage/life duality, stupidity or inappropriate behaviour, transformation, trickery, wordplay.[8]

meccanismi Whilst a *lazzi* occurs on the spur of a moment and generally concerns one or two Masks, a *meccanismo* is a prerehearsed and preplanned routine for several Masks. *Meccanismi* may be transferable between one show and another, if the storylines have a degree of similarity, but they are generally focused on providing a showcase for the company's talents, whilst at the same time maintaining dramatic tension. They are, at worst, a chance for the company to use all available skills to create *coups de théâtre*.

Examples: an acrobatic chase that ends up with a particular Mask in a particular set of circumstances, e.g. having escaped or been captured; a stage fight, whether with swords, slapsticks or kitchen implements, that has a particular outcome; a court dance in which everyone tries to dance with Isabella, but she always ends up escaping and dancing with her true love without missing a step; the servants trying to rescue someone out of a window with a tall ladder; the whole company creating with their bodies human scenery in which a scene is played by other Masks, e.g. the Rialto Bridge with people walking across it or even a haunted wood.

pazzia A speciality turn of impassioned madness, insanity or folly, usually associated with Isabella – but *fare piazze* means to act like a fool, meaning that the Lovers and Pantalone can indulge themselves as well.

repertorio The repertoire of a company or of an actor within that company, a catalogue of what is available.

sotto voce In an undertone.

sprezzatura 'The urge to continually outdo [one's] fellows in accomplishing difficult things gracefully.'[9] And also with nonchalance, and a certain disdain. Molière's Scapin is all *sprezzatura*.

squarci The opposite of *sotto voce* – the 'tearing apart' of a scene at full volume.

uscite A prearranged exit sequence, usually involving more than one Mask.

zibaldone The commonplace book where the *generici* of a Mask were written down. In English a commonplace book was originally a 'collection of passages or quotations appropriate to several cases, arranged under general headings, either alphabetically or some other classification'. [NED] Only later did the word come to mean 'hackneyed, platitude or truism'.

So, in order to perform a scenario, you need to decide whether you are ready to take the plunge and do it *all'improvviso*. If so, then someone, possibly the actor who wrote the scenario, needs to adopt the role of **corago** and take the company through the scenario, blocking entrances and exits and stage positions and giving indications of opportunities to use stock material as listed above. Then individuals, pairs, threes and fours know what they have to prepare but should stop well short of rehearsing it, with the exception perhaps of the ending – which will almost certainly involve all the Masks. Here is a short scenario, more like a long *canovaccio* except that it has sub-plots – the kind of thing you need to cut your teeth on before attempting anything in three acts.

La Guerra

PANTALONE
BELLICOSA *his daughter*
FLAVIO *a rich orphan*
PEDROLINO *his servant*
BRIGHELLA *a black marketeer*
FRANCESCHINA
IL CAPITANO
ZANNI *a private*

1. **The street**. IL CAPITANO drills ZANNI, watched in admiration *from above* by BELLICOSA. *Exeunt.*

2. *Enter* PANTALONE. BELLICOSA *comes down* and tells him that the longer the war goes on, the more she is in love with the Captain. PANTALONE says that doesn't matter – when the peace comes he's going to need another source of income other than the black market, so she will have to marry that rich young Flavio. BELLICOSA says he's a wimp and hasn't even volunteered for military duty. PANTALONE says good, you don't kill the goose that's going to lay the golden egg, whereas the Captain is unlikely to survive because he's trying to win the war too quickly. *Exit* BELLICOSA in despair.

3. BRIGHELLA arrives. PANTALONE fixes a contract with him for Il Capitano to have a little accident. *Exeunt* discussing their various black-market schemes.

4. FLAVIO *enters* full of the joys of spring. PEDROLINO *brings him* an envelope from Bellicosa containing a white feather. FLAVIO says it's beautiful, but what can it mean? PEDROLINO makes various suggestions – pen, backscratcher, etc.

5. *Enter* FRANCESCHINA. She makes advances to FLAVIO, saying there's a special offer on today to help the war effort, but he is adamant that there is only one love for him from now on – look his Bellicosa has sent him her token. FRANCESCHINA laughs – doesn't he know what that means? No. It means you are a coward! *Exit* FRANCESCHINA to look for Brighella.

6. FLAVIO to PEDROLINO: 'What does she mean – a coward?' PEDROLINO demonstrates by running away. Come back, says FLAVIO, and tell me what a coward is. PEDROLINO runs away again, etc. Finally FLAVIO *runs after* him.

7. BRIGHELLA *spots* ZANNI. 'Hey, come here, soldier, take this to your Captain.' He gives him a pineapple, with his compliments. Just to make sure he doesn't eat it himself, ZANNI is to pull out this little pin when he gives it to the Captain and bring it back. *Exit* BRIGHELLA.

8. ZANNI, *solus*, is fantasising about eating the pineapple when IL CAPITANO *enters*. He refuses the pineapple on the grounds that it must have come from the black market. He is on a mission from God and will live on bread and water until the enemy are defeated. *Exit*. ZANNI examines the pineapple again, removes the pin and *exits*. *LOUD EXPLOSION OFF.*

9. FRANCESCHINA *meets* BRIGHELLA. She complains that the war is ruining her man effort – too many men at the front, too many men at the back, not enough in the middle. Or to put it another way, too many men in hospital, too many in the ground, not enough in bed.

10. *Enter* ZANNI – broken arm, broken leg, etc. He salutes BRIGHELLA, presents him with the hand-grenade pin, falls over and *crawls off*.

11. 'See what I mean', says FRANCESCHINA, 'what sort of active duty is he going to be good for now?' BRIGHELLA is about to reply when IL CAPITANO *crosses the stage* singing 'Onward Christian Soldiers'.

'I've got a proposition for you', says BRIGHELLA to FRANCESCHINA.
It had better be a paying proposition, she says. *Exeunt* discussing *sotto voce*.

12. FLAVIO tells PEDROLINO he has finally understood the meaning of the
white feather: Bellicosa is trying to tell him that it is not enough to be
against the war, he must fight, but fight for peace! But how?
PEDROLINO makes several ridiculous suggestions before.

13. . . . ZANNI *crawls back on* with a begging bowl. FLAVIO gives him
money, but PEDROLINO takes it off him and returns it to FLAVIO.
This is repeated several times until FLAVIO finally understands what
PEDROLINO means: money is not the answer, Zanni must join the peace
movement now that he cannot fight any more. PEDROLINO puts a
flower in ZANNI's bowl.

14. PANTALONE *enters* and fawns on FLAVIO, saying how delighted he is
that his future son-in-law is safe and well and not risking mutilation
at the front from one of the fragmentation bombs he has just sold to
the enemy. No, no, says FLAVIO, he too must fight. *Exit, followed by*
PEDROLINO.

15. PANTALONE, dismayed, flies into a rage when ZANNI asks him for
money.

16. *Enter* IL CAPITANO. He tells PANTALONE that he has a battle plan: one
last push and the war is over. The armaments factories must be put on
double time. 'Our cause is just. We must prevail!' (He is clearly losing
his marbles.) BELLICOSA *eavesdrops. Exit* IL CAPITANO.

17. PANTALONE is in a quandry: he wants the profit from the armaments
factories, but he doesn't want to win the war. *Enter* FRANCESCHINA.
She tells PANTALONE that unless he settles his account he'll get no
more favours from her. PANTALONE says don't bother me now, I'm
trying to make a profit from loss – you'll get your money when I've
fiddled my winnings. (ZANNI tries to beg from him again as he *exits*).

18. FRANCESCHINA says she's got a heart of gold, but a purse full of
copper, but nevertheless she spares ZANNI a coin as she asks him
where the Captain is. Over there, says ZANNI and she *leaves*.

19. *Enter* IL CAPITANO. BELLICOSA *rushes down* to meet him. Scene of unrequited love: he cannot love her till the war is over. BRIGHELLA now *eavesdrops*. FRANCESCHINA *re-enters* and tells them she is from the local newspaper, come to interview the Captain. She has a list of his previous female conquests and he has to admit that each one is true. BELLICOSA is horrified and won't listen when IL CAPITANO says he is a changed man since he met her.

20. *Enter* FLAVIO and PEDROLINO carrying a placard '*MAKE PEACE, NOT WAR*', chanting, ringing bells and giving away flowers, especially to ZANNI. BRIGHELLA picks up a megaphone and says 'This is a public announcement! Enemy troops have arrived and are expected to occupy this area by tomorrow.' IL CAPITANO panics, then hurriedly joins the peace movement. Disgusted with him, BELLICOSA attaches herself to FLAVIO. PEDROLINO helps up ZANNI. FRANCESCHINA says 'If you can't beat 'em, join 'em', and the peace march circles the stage and demonstrates outside PANTALONE's house. PANTALONE *appears above* and says the war must go on – it is the only way to secure lasting peace. ALL stage a sit-in, as BRIGHELLA comes round selling marihuana. *TABLEAU.*

If, on the other hand, you feel that for your troupe going public *all'improvviso* is risky in the wrong kind of way here is an example of a short scenario which would be better rehearsed down to the point of fixing dialogue, etc. As a burlesque of a literary tradition, it is better suited to such an approach, and the inbuilt pace and lightness of style will keep it from seeming over-rehearsed in performance.

The storm (in a tea-cup)

After Shakespeare (long after).

UNFORTUNIO/FORTUNIO *twins (played by the same actor)*
PEDROLINO *servant to the exiled Unfortunio*
MELANDINA *in love with Unfortunio*
COLOMBINA *her maid*
CLARABELLA *in love with Fortunio*
IL CAPITANO *a pirate*
FRANCESCHINA *a female pirate*
ARLECCHINO

1. **An almost deserted island**. *Enter* PEDROLINO attempting to catch
   butterflies. He says 'This isle is full of noises, sounds, sweet airs and
   bits of Shakespeare . . . Sometimes a thousand twangling instruments
   will hum about mine ears and sometimes voices . . .'

   UNFORTUNIO (*off*) 'Pedrolino! Have you caught us anything to eat yet?'
   PEDROLINO mimes stalking a chicken. *Exit as if pouncing* as
   UNFORTUNIO *enters.* UNFORTUNIO keeps calling for him. A squawk
   offstage and feathers fly up behind the backdrop. Alas, says
   UNFORTUNIO, how unfortunate he is – exiled on this island with only
   Pedrolino for company, far from his beloved MELANDINA. PEDROLINO
   sticks his head through the drop and says 'grub up'. UNFORTUNIO *exits.*

2. **A pirate ship**. IL CAPITANO boasts of his plundering of the seven seas.
   He shouts *off* to splice the main jib and take a reef in the rollocker (etc.)
   and gives contradictory instructions to FRANCESCHINA who is at the
   helm. She meanwhile keeps leaving the wheel to harass him sexually,
   with disastrous results to the ship. He *exits* with his tail between his
   legs, saying he thinks he'd better go and look at the prisoners.
   Monologue from FRANCESCHINA on the frustrations of there being no
   real men on this man-o-war. *Exit.*

3. IL CAPITANO *re-enters* with the prisoners – FORTUNIO and CLARABELLA,
   both tied up. He says he will never let them go until her father
   Pantalone pays the ransom – a million euros. She says he never will, he
   keeps all his money under the mattress in old lire. FORTUNIO calls IL
   CAPITANO a dastard. IL CAPITANO laughs at him and begins boasting
   again.

4. FRANCESCHINA returns with ARLECCHINO, also tied up. I've found a
   stowaway, she says. I'm going to have some fun with him! Suddenly
   thunder is heard. IL CAPITANO panics because he is terrified of storms.
   The boat starts to rock and all are pitched from side to side. Howling
   gale. A jag of lightning jabs IL CAPITANO, who howls piteously.
   FRANCESCHINA says the rudder has broken and leaves the wheel. She
   unties the prisoners, saying they will be no ransom if they drown.
   A bucket of water is thrown over the backdrop and all '*swim*' off.

5. **Another part of the island**. *Enter* MELANDINA and COLOMBINA. 'Oh,
   how weary are my spirits', says MELANDINA. 'I care not for my spirits
   if my legs were not weary', says COLOMBINA. They have followed

UNFORTUNIO into exile and are searching the island for him. COLOMBINA says how much she is missing Arlecchino. *Exeunt* calling 'Unfortunio'. FORTUNIO rolls under the drop and lies still. The women *re-enter*, even more tired. No one told me it was such a big island, says MELANDINA. And that terrible storm last night that kept them both awake. Let's rest awhile on this beach. They fall asleep. COLOMBINA dreams of Arlecchino.

6. *DUMBSHOW*. ARLECCHINO *enters*, shows her all the money he has saved and they get married and live an idyllic life together. Meanwhile MELANDINA wakes and sees FORTUNIO and screams. ARLECCHINO *vanishes*.

7. COLOMBINA wakes and, more sensibly, administers the kiss of life to FORTUNIO. MELANDINA howls at her – leave him alone, he's mine! FORTUNIO comes to his senses. What does she mean – he's never seen her before in his life! He is betrothed to one who must be drowned, his beloved Clarabella. Would that he had drowned too – he goes into despair. MELANDINA goes into a fit of jealousy over Clarabella and *runs off*.

8. COLOMBINA asks FORTUNIO what his name is and he tells her. Not 'Unfortunio', she asks. No, he says, that's my twin brother – we were separated at birth because my parents could only afford to bring up one of us. Quick says, COLOMBINA, run after Melandina and explain. FORTUNIO *runs off*.

9. *Enter* PEDROLINO. He falls in love with COLOMBINA at first sight, but she thinks he is a monster and *runs away*.

10. *Enter* FRANCESCHINA – she falls in love with PEDROLINO at first sight but he is frightened by her sexual advances and also *runs away pursued by* FRANCESCHINA.

11. **Another part of the island**. UNFORTUNIO *discovers* CLARABELLA, also washed ashore from the storm. He wonders who she is and where she comes from. She wakes and mistakes him for FORTUNIO. He is bewildered and says he has never met her before. She assumes he is trying to break off their relationship and pleads with him not to reject her after all they have been through. He *runs off*.

12. CLARABELLA is contemplating suicide when *enter* FORTUNIO – he doesn't look at her, assumes she is Melandina, and says I'm sorry, you mistook me for my twin brother. Don't lie to me, says CLARABELLA, I know you're trying to get rid of me – she *storms off* with *him in pursuit* saying it's me, FORTUNIO.

13. *Enter immediately* UNFORTUNIO: he doesn't understand what's going on – there seem to be people all over the island. *To him*, PEDROLINO. UNFORTUNIO asks him what's going on – there seem to be people all over the island. PEDROLINO is about to answer when FRANCESCHINA *arrives* and he *runs off*. Seeing UNFORTUNIO she calls for IL CAPITANO who *arrives* and tries to treat UNFORTUNIO as if he were his prisoner. UNFORTUNIO draws his sword and threatens IL CAPITANO who *goes off* with his tail between his legs. FRANCESCHINA turns her attentions to UNFORTUNIO saying she didn't realise that he had so much fight in him.

14. *Enter* COLOMBINA. (ARLECCHINO *eavesdrops*, pretending to be a monkey.) COLOMBINA sees UNFORTUNIO and says which one are you? 'What do you mean, which one am I?' She explains to him that he has a twin brother who is also on the island. He is (understandably) amazed. And what are you doing on the island, he asks. COLOMBINA explains she has come with Melandina to be with him in exile. 'Who's Melandina', says FRANCESCHINA. UNFORTUNIO goes into paroxysms. 'His fiancée', explains COLOMBINA. Oh, no, says FRANCESCHINA, just when I thought I'd found a real man.

15. FRANCESCHINA calls for IL CAPITANO who *re-enters* tentatively. It's all right, says FRANCESCHINA, I give in, come here, you'll have to do. COLOMBINA announces that it is time for the first happy ending: she calls her mistress. MELANDINA *enters* and, before she can say anything, COLOMBINA whispers in her ear. She melts and accepts UNFORTUNIO. *TABLEAU* of two couples. COLOMBINA says 'Your revels now are ended. You are such stuff as dreams are made on.' She claps her hands and they *vanish*.

16. 'Time for the second happy ending', says COLOMBINA. She claps her hands again and FORTUNIO and CLARABELLA *enter from opposite sides*. She whispers in both their ears and they are reconciled. And now, says COLOMBINA, I expect you would like to meet your brother Unfortunio and here he is. She claps her hands but *enter* PEDROLINO with a written

invitation which he hands to FORTUNIO who reads it: Unfortunio is preparing a banquet for them with all the fresh fruits and viands of the island and will they please come at once. *Exeunt* the LOVERS.

17. COLOMBINA announces that it is now time for the unhappy ending: she no longer thinks Pedrolino is a monster, but neither can she love him since she has left her heart on the mainland with Arlecchino and it is now she who is in exile. *MUSIC*. She day dreams. *Enter* ARLECCHINO – they dance together as PEDROLINO watches. ARLECCHINO tries to fondle her breasts. She screams 'Arlecchino!', realising that it really is him. The OTHERS *all return*, singing and playing. *DANCE*.

The prologue

Traditionally the prologue is delivered by either Colombina or Il Dottore, though there may be reasons to do with the argument of a particular scenario for that to change. It may also have to do with who in your troupe makes the best instant rapport with an audience. Whoever you choose should not be left to their own devices: they need a script, preferably written by somebody else so they don't feel too lonely out there, and also a sense of the support of the whole company. The best way for this to be offered is for them to actually introduce the Masks via some pretext or other which has nothing to do with the show, but a lot to do with the company. This is particularly valuable when your audience knows nothing at all about *commedia dell'arte*. Such a prologue is a *meccanismo* and needs rehearsing as such. Within it each Mask should give a brief *lazzi* or other speciality.

The traditional indication that the performance is about to begin (given that there were no house lights that were dimmable and no front curtain to raise) was three quick knocks, followed by three slow. On the sixth knock something *must* happen. An overture with musicians either visible or not is also a good idea.

Singing and music

A troupe needs a musical director, either internal or external. Let them arrange the dances and tunes, work out who sings which part and train them to do it. Sing as a group and keep this as an ongoing skill, developing and expanding a repertoire. If you buy musical instruments, don't buy cheap, and buy ones that will survive both indoors and outdoors without going out of tune – and buy hard carrying cases for them. Hurdy-gurdies, for example are very nice instruments, but can go quite badly out of tune very quickly if left in the sun. Whether owned personally or collectively, insure them – even if that's the only insurance you can afford!

In performance try to build in a beat to catch your breath before singing, especially if you have just undergone a great deal of exertion. Any song (especially a part song) will fare badly with a breathless beginning. Similarly with a part song, unless the whole group has perfect pitch, time needs to be created for someone to give the starting note. Place all musical instruments in a safe place so they don't get trodden on by enthusiastic *zannis* bouncing on or offstage, or filched by children from the front row.

Curtain calls

Couch potatoes have forgotten how to applaud – you need to remind them for both your sakes. Again because there is no blackout and no curtain to fall (and even if there is don't use it!) you need a non-technological method:

1 Freeze in a tableau until applause starts.
2 Move then freeze again on an agreed beat. This acts as a punctuation mark: they know it's over but not quite. The new tableau should have an ironic comment built into it.
3 Rule of three: repeat (2).
4 Move into a line, but keep the masks on and don't bow.
5 Remove the masks and stand holding them against your chest so the audience can compare your face with the mask's and admire the craft of the mask maker.
6 Walk off stage, splitting from the middle left and right.
7 Run round the drop and back on from the opposite side without the masks.
8 Bow traditionally, taking the lead from the centre, as yourselves.
9 Applaud the audience (and anyone else who deserves it).

Outdoor performances

Some guidelines to bear in mind:

1 The audience should get a clear view of the stage from a place where they will not block other entertainments, vehicles, people or

tradespeople using the space, and consequently get moved on during a show.

2 Ensure there are unimpeded entrances and exits for the performers.

3 Set up in a good acoustic environment. Open fields may be good in theory, but a solid wall at some distance behind the audience will both limit the background noise coming in, and allow the actors' voices to be bounced back.

4 Background noise: one should either schedule one's performances by negotiation with other noise makers, or try and avoid being placed near generators or canned music. It is worth being nice to people around your performing space, so that they agree to turn down what they're doing during your performance. This is especially important if you are busking a show. If you are a paid act, noise should be dealt with by the bookers, though do not assume they will do so unless prompted. It is always worth putting something in the contract to this effect. A booker who sees you fail in an impossible situation will not always realise that it isn't your fault, and a little effort before the show can ensure you are not put in this position.

5 Have emergency plans in case of rain, such as waterproofs to cover the stage, costume rail, musical instruments and anything else of value – and an indoor venue to switch to if at all possible.

6 Plan for access of vehicles to site, so that you don't end up carrying your costumes and stage materials absolutely further than is necessary. Carrying things to and from the van is one of those jobs that just has to be done, and can cause quite a lot of bad feeling if not done in an equitable manner.

7 Make up a list of responsibilities and tasks for specific people to carry out when you arrive on site and when you leave, e.g. contact the booker/stage manager, decide or confirm performance space and times, who carries the stage, and who sets out masks, costumes and props, is responsible for making sure the site is clean after the get-out, etc.

8 Have a secure place to put all valuables during a show, either in the van or with the site or venue stage manager. This will include performer's wallets and watches, and also masks and props of value. Try and develop a system to cordon off the backstage area so that the public can't wander round backstage during a show.

9 Position the stage so that the audience, not the stage, is in the shade, and the sun is in the actors' eyes (and not the audience's). An audience that is too hot will always wander off to buy ice-creams or go to sleep, and an audience blinded by the sun can't see the action and will go

away because they are fed up with squinting. As a performer you may be blinded by the sun, but at least you are well lit. Bear in mind that the sun will have moved round during the time between set-up and performance.

10   Position the stage, if possible, out of the prevailing wind, for the benefit of both performers and audience.

11   Carry a well-painted and decorated 'A' board with you, upon which you can chalk in large friendly letters the times of the next performances.

12   Have a clear distinction between a busked show out of doors (short and to the point, typically a *canovaccio* and some *meccanismi* or *grande lazzi*), and a booked and prepublicised out-of-doors show (typically a *scenario* and a warm-up). If you are busking shows do not attempt a full-length *scenario*. With a busked show you want the audience to be there at the finish, so you can either take the hat around or else use the moment to publicise another performance.

13   Carry with you a large bag of wooden wedges and planks to stabilise the trestles underneath the stage. There is no such thing as a level surface to put a stage upon, not even the *Piazza San Marco*.

14   Have some wooden benches for the actors to sit upon between shows, and at least a couple of duck boards to lay on the ground in case it rains, so you don't run up onto the stage with wet shoes.

15   Always do a full warm-up if possible, even if the audience are gathering. In fact a company doing a warm-up will often begin to attract a crowd.

16   Parades are to let potential audiences know that the show is happening later. Don't parade immediately before a show – it's a tiring thing to do and messes up your make-up. The Masks should not be seen before their first entrance, anyway, so a change of image for parading is recommended.

Appendices

Appendix A

Writing a scenario

A scenario is, by our definition, a more complex dramatic structure than a *canovaccio*. A scenario takes longer to perform, typically conforms to a three-act pattern, and has multiple-strand plot development and more plot-based humour. Usually there is a prologue to explain the particular circumstances that the audience must comprehend if all the story is to be followed, though each individual scene within it must also be treated as an individual entity that can be enjoyed on its own.

The following information is primarily aimed at the scenario writer within the group, though recommended reading for all performers, so that they know what kind of stage information to prioritise when as they are performing. There is a particular order of events to constructing a three-act scenario which we list below. Unless one is attempting a Commedia adaptation of an existing text, do not aim to follow a predetermined storyline, rather aim to put the Masks in the best possible situations with each other, in the context of the three-act structure, and seeing what develops, scene by scene: you're on an adventure and only the Masks can advise you as to where they want to go next.

Background information

1 Choose a contrasting range of Masks from within the company, playing to the strengths of the performers, ensuring at least one potential love interest, at least one strong master to get the plot started, and at least two servants to act as go-betweens, plus one outsider (usually Il Capitano) to complicate matters. This argues for a company of at least six: any fewer and you should stick to *canovacci*.

2 At the earliest possible stage decide what songs and dances the company will need to learn for the proposed scenario: these have to be practised

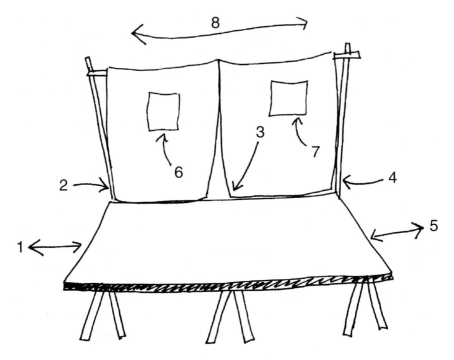

Figure 17 Typical 'houses' and entrances of a trestle stage.

1   To and from the country
2   Entrance to Il Dottore's house
3   Entrance to Pantalone's house
4   Entrance to Brighella's inn
5   To and from the rest of Venice
6   Window to Il Dottore's house
7   Window to Brighella's inn
8   Balcony of Pantalone's house

regularly over a period of time, whereas the scenes would go cold with such an amount of rehearsal.

3 Choose, if possible, a general theme for your show. The combination of Masks that you have will very often suggest one, e.g. more than one Capitano leads almost inevitably to a war scenario, but which war? Again, be guided by improvisations that you have seen the Masks do, rather than forcing them to go to a part of the world where they may not 'live' because it suits your polemics rather than theirs.

4 In relation to the theme, choose a location for the action. If you choose the basic street with its traditional houses, then fine, but if you choose a different location, make sure that it has enough entrances and exits to ensure the potential for exciting action. Outdoors is generally better than indoors, unless the indoor space has plural exits and entrances (hotel lobby, palace antechamber, etc.). You need to be much more *locus* specific than in a *canovaccio*, although the scene can change if the shift is pointed up clearly enough.

5 Choose a motivation for each Mask that relates to the other Masks or to their relationship within the scenario's dramatic location. Note that each motivation or need is to be treated as the equivalent of a Stanislavsky super-objective: it is what the character *wants above all other things*. In our workshops we call it the 'Gimme', as in 'Gimme sex', 'Gimme money' or 'Gimme food'. In a scenario these basic drives need to become more specific and must have the potential for action, rather than contemplation. They are the springboard for each Mask's plot line through the scenario, and must be directly related to both its traditional needs and also the strengths of the performer currently interpreting it.

Carlo Boso considers that fear, and the attempts by the individual to escape from it and find happiness, lies at the core of a Mask's motivation. Antonio Fava (quoted in the programme to *Love is a Drug*) puts it even more strongly:

> The pleasure we derive from comedy corresponds to the fulfilment of a basic need – the need to overcome fear, even if only for a moment. Fear of all kinds: terror, superstition, vertigo, our fear of dying, our fear of the unknown, of our leap into the abyss – all the fears which stalk us. Our greatest fear is the fear of Death – an enduring and central feature in the comic tradition.

All chosen motivations or needs should, on one hand be clear enough to the audience to open a direct emotional channel between them and the performer, and on the other hand be consistent with the Mask's known behaviour. This implies that every time a Mask is on stage it is either actively trying to gain something, or else escape from something. These actions must appeal to the audience on an emotional and visceral level, not an intellectual level. Ideally a Mask is always on the journey between the complete joy of getting what it needs, and the total fear of losing something it holds most dear.

6 Perhaps ask the company to do some initial improvisations to check whether each Mask has an opposition to their want or need. A Mask with no other opposing force is useless on stage. Each Mask must go through the following process:

> need realised and stated – opposition or series of oppositions to need – conclusion.

Keep in mind that oppositions can come from the Masks themselves, other Masks, or the constraints of society in general. Do not try and be too original or creative at this stage: the existing Commedia hierarchy works for, not against you. Try to create in each scene that initially comes to mind the maximum emotional possible 'stretch' for each Mask.

Envisioning a three-act structure

Now begin the process of ordering all the information developed above. It may help to write out a table, listing, for example Pantalone and his household on one side and Il Dottore and his on the other, with any 'lone rangers' such as Il Capitano, Brighella or Franceschina in the centre, but further down. Get a set of coloured pens and draw lines of connection between Masks. Do this for all three acts.

Typically each Mask needs a scene in which its need is made known to the audience, then a series of attempts to overcome the opposition to that desire, and finally a conclusion. For the Lovers, and sometimes their servants, this is typically a happy ending and marriage – and for the enemies of love – repentance, defeat and confusion. Let the audience know what the Mask's need is as early as possible in the scenario, sometimes even in the prologue. Next come a series of confusions as the opposing forces to each Mask's happiness come into play and finally the resolution or finale. There are specific kinds of information relating to each of these three sections.

The beginning section, or Act I, is the briefest when, in order to get the plot moving, the audience and Masks need to get the information across in as brief and comedic a manner as possible. If the plot information a Mask needs to impart is fairly 'dry' in nature then it is appropriate to dress this up with improvised or preplanned business so the audience don't go to sleep, get bored or go away. Molière is recommended reading.

The middle section, or Act II, is where the chaos starts, as all the information the audience needs to understand the comedy has already been put in place. In this section the only special instructions needed are to keep the pace up, and don't solve any of your Masks' problems, unless only seemingly. Try to save all the resolutions up for the end. If one Mask does inevitably end up getting what it wants at this point, perhaps due to the needs of the other Masks in writing the scenario, simply put another opposition in place, or have satisfaction interrupted at the last possible moment by a chase, fight, conscription into the armed forces, earthquake or other random earth-shattering event.

The final section, or Act III, should take place on a high plateau of fantasticality which can only be reached by means of the previous two acts. This may be an imagined place, e.g. Pantalone has been taken to the moon, or an actual one, e.g., the gardens at night. The process of Commedia is from the physical to the metaphysical and this is the time to get metaphysical. All the Masks' difficulties must be re-presented, and a positive resolution provided for as many of them as possible, in this order: first the Lovers, second the servants, third the old men and Il Capitano. Do this as quickly as possible so the audience is left reeling with the skill, bravado and sheer unlikeliness of this happy surprise. They need to appreciate the wonder, satisfaction and sheer joy of a simple ending after encountering such difficulties in the plot. It is often necessary to build in a *deus ex machina* device at this stage to keep the pace up and to wrap up all the surviving plot strands. However the audience is also generally aware that this kind of luck doesn't generally happen in real life. The happy ending in itself is an ironic joke. If it has any message it is that love will triumph if we let it, and that this generally doesn't happen in the real world. The speed of the resolution should, however, be backed by a celebratory carnival ending: a song and a dance in a suitably upbeat and joyful manner.

Procedure and mechanics

Act I

Remember that generally, for reasons noted in Part 3 of this book, scenes are played between two Masks. Use 'French' scene numbering, i.e. use a fresh number every time a new Mask enters. The simplest exposition structure is the 'chain' system already outlined for group improvisation:

Scene 1:   A and B play a scene which lets the audience know their motivations. A leaves.

Scene 2:   C enters. B and C play a scene in which C's motivation is introduced. B or C leave.

Scene 3:   D enters, etc.

This is, however, simplistic and won't carry an audience for very long. Here are a few suggestions for adding dramatic value to entrances:

- One Mask, having revealed all to the audience or to another Mask, is about to act upon their desire or need, but is prevented from carrying on by the entrance of another Mask. e.g., Flaminia and Lelio are expressing their love to one another and are about to elope, when Pantalone, Flaminia's father enters. Interruptions such as these are worthwhile also in the sense that they allow the generation of further material, such as the excuses Flaminia has to give her father for being caught in the company of the banned Lelio.
- Have a Mask make an entrance in the middle of an action, e.g. Il Capitano sharpening his sword, Pantalone counting his money or Franceschina blowing kisses to an offstage lover.
- A Mask calls for help and another, happening to be there, joins them on stage.

And to exits:

- A later meeting is arranged between the Masks on stage, which allows one to exit to make preparations.
- A master or mistress gets rid of their servant by a direct order.
- A servant gets rid of their master or mistress by a direct lie.
- A Mask on stage is called for by one off stage.
- A Mask on stage is threatened by the impending arrival of one off stage.

Remember a Mask does not just appear on stage. It needs to come from somewhere with sufficient reason for the actor playing the Mask to make a strong, energetic entrance. If you can't find a plot justification for such an entrance, a 'McGuffin' will do. McGuffins were invented by Orson Welles, and have been developed by David Mamet in his book *On Directing Film*. A McGuffin is a plot device to get characters into the arena of action for reasons that have nothing to do with the action so far. They are involved in something else when we first meet them, but that something gets dropped as soon as the major plot motivation comes into play. For example, in Tag Teatro di Venezia's version of Scala's *The Madness of Isabella*, Isabella's motivation is to regain Orazio's love at all costs. The McGuffin that gets her into the action is that she has just escaped from the Turks where she has been imprisoned since she last saw him.

A Mask, then, may enter in Act I driven either by a McGuffin or by its primary motivation, but from then it must both leave and re-enter the performance area only in order to develop that motivation. By the end of Act I, all the Masks' motivations should be known to the audience, but not all to each other. Once the needs, fears and problems are all out in the open, the audience should see the Masks as an interlocking variety of alliances, disagreements and conflicts. Generally the higher status masks dictate the course of the action from then on, and the order of the scenes, or at least attempt to do so. The servants try to fulfil their own objectives, whilst at the same time at least pretending to help or fulfil those of their masters.

Note that it is very rare that one bases a scenario entirely around one Mask, or the adventures of one Mask (with the exception of Pulchinella). Commedia scenarios, historically at least, give all Masks equal stage time and equal prominence during that time.

Act II

Generally speaking Act II is composed of the first meetings, first arguments, first defeats, first confusions, and the first confrontations between Masks who have not met in Act I, either because they should meet but have not yet found the means of doing so, or because they really should not meet, but the encounter has proved impossible to prevent. As already mentioned, it is important not to solve the Masks' problems at this point, but to complicate them further. If you do give a Mask what it wants, take it away again with extra conditions or hardships added.

Any Mask that makes an exit with a specific motivation in Act I must always enter again with that motivation or need, e.g. Zanni has been sent with a message to Isabella: he must turn up in Act II still with the message, still looking for Isabella. We may have got involved in any number of subplots by this stage, but he must still be trying to fulfil his prime objective.

In Act II the plot is looking to explode into action, and you will find out at this stage whether you have given the characters good enough motivations to create action and consequent *imbroglio*. If you find it tricky to get the Masks to interact in this way, then you should question whether the motivations you gave them in Act I are strong enough to carry them into action, and not only action but interaction with the other Masks.

If, however, everything is going well at this stage, three options on plot line for each Mask should become apparent:

1   Pursuit of own objective: what it wants; proceeding with and enlisting aid for its plan, and combating its opponents.

2   Reaction to others' chosen objectives: helping friend or loved one. Voluntary delaying of own objective.
3   Reaction to surrounding circumstances: getting caught up in other's plots, disasters, etc., the involuntary delaying of own objective.

These three forms of plot are all valid, and choosing which is appropriate for each Mask depends on the following: (a) the action must get more complicated, not simpler and (b) it must lead to further needs, problems, and consequent new actions, as characters form alliances, oppose and misuse each other.

The pattern of entrances and exits remains very similar to that of Act I. However pairs of allies or a master and servant can be treated as one unit. This is because they are moving in the same direction of the plot as each other, albeit temporarily, e.g. Oratio and Pedrolino disguised as Hungarian jewel merchants in Act II of Flaminio Scala's *The Fake Madwoman*.

All the Masks should be seen either simultaneously or in quick succession at the end of the act. This gives the effect of an emotional, plot-based climax to the action so far. It also becomes the point when all problems already out in the open become far worse. The audience needs to be left cliff-hanging: how can all this possibly be resolved in Act III?

Act III

The overall pattern of Act III is that of building to a *scène à faire* which brings all the Masks together at its conclusion, followed by the untying of the Gordian knot, with each individual Mask having a final confrontation with their nemesis or getting their desire fulfilled.

The pattern of entrances and exits remains the same, as far as is possible, but with even more groups of Masks moving round as units, e.g. Capitanos and their kidnap victims, masters and servants, pairs of eloping Lovers, schemers and their victims, Masks in disguise associating with the wrong partner.

There is a much greater likelihood of group chases, fights, escapes, etc., in this act as the actions of the individual Masks begin to have final impact upon the others. These should be treated as prerehearsed set pieces or *meccanismi*, e.g. masters chasing servants, heroes chasing cowards, duels, multiple disguised people all rendezvousing at the same place as if by accident, tavern brawls, everyone chasing Arlecchino, or Pantalone, the Turks attacking, etc. You may also want to build in an *effeto meraviglioso*, as described in the glossary in Part 3 of this book. This is because sometimes there is simply nothing more the Masks can do: you have exhausted their repertoire and something technical, beyond their normal capabilities, is necessary to cap the action, e.g. a fireworks display.

The *dénouement* follows the *scène à faire*. There are then two possible model endings: a comedy where everyone who deserves to, or nearly deserves to, gets married – and a tragicomedy (*tragicommedia ridiculosa*) where everyone dies, albeit mainly by mistake.

In case there aren't any convenient ways of tying up all the plot strands once you have got all your Masks on stage together (and there often won't be!), remember to have a *deus ex-machina* device ready. Typically this job is to announce swiftly further unexpected revelations just at the point when everyone is about to stab each other in the back and the chances of a happy resolution, in the eyes of the audience, are looking pretty slim. These revelations need not make sense in the light of the main plot, but should merely serve to allow everyone a happy ending. It is a device that should be powerful enough to conquer the previous animosity or antipathy the Masks feel towards each other. Examples:

- Two characters see similar birthmarks on each other and realise they must be long lost relations and therefore cannot possibly fight.
- A letter or message that someone has been trying to unsuccessfully deliver during the whole course of the action is finally opened and found to say that someone or other is now an heir or heiress and can marry whoever they want.
- A promise made in a rash moment of desperation is called in, typically allowing Arlecchino to marry Colombina.
- One character has a change of heart and reveals all their evil schemings.
- One character, previously not thought to be in disguise, takes off their disguise and reveals themselves to be a woman, long-lost son, rich prince, etc.
- An object that all the masks had been searching turns up and has an unexpected effect.
- Any combination of the above, though sometimes a revelation has to be linked to one specific Mask.

As previously mentioned, this happy end is an ironic joke, but it must be performed as if it is for real. The holy purpose of comedy is to reaffirm life and hope. In a *commedia dell'arte* scenario the odds of a happy resolution must seem so remote at one point that to conjure a happy ending out of all the chaos can seem nothing short of a joyful miracle for the audience. This expresses the hope for the audience that out of chaos can come love and some measure of order. The fears that the Masks work with and against during the three acts have been laid to rest and the possibility of joy and future happiness for the human race is restored. We, of course, all safely watching as members of the audience, realise that this happy ending could never happen in the real world, but that is part of its magic: we are shown that it *could* be possible and that no one in the scenario is without the possibility of redemption.

Appendix B

Mask making

Instructions as to how to make a half-mask out of leather are given in the Appendix to *Commedia dell'Arte: An Actor's Handbook*. Your ultimate ambition should be to use leather and if you have money, rather than time and craft skills at your disposal, you should write to one of the mask makers listed at the end of this appendix.

How to make masks out of materials other than leather

As well as fulfilling its theatrical function, a mask needs to fit its wearer and be comfortable for him or her to wear for a period of time. Making a mask for a specific person means taking into account the shape of their face and the relative positions of forehead, eye holes and lip line, etc. One can either design the mask in clay first and use callipers or dividers to check that the measurements on the buck correspond exactly with those of the wearer's face, or else take a plaster cast of the actor's face and build up the mask features on that directly. Once you have the full-sized design of the mask, either in clay or plaster and clay, then you have to choose the medium of the mask itself.

Making a maquette

A maquette is a small version, rough or trial run for the mask proper you are going to make. Using clay or plasticine, and a variety of tools, experiment with the proportion and design until you have got a small-scale version of what you want. Look at the maquette from different angles and see if it changes expression or stays the same. Make sure that it is a genuine three-dimensional object, rather than a flat one which will only be able to project forward, and hence limit the actor's expressiveness. It is much easier to experiment and try out ideas on a small scale, rather than on a fully-sized facial buck.

You should have a very good idea of the role or character that the mask is to portray, and also what kind of auditorium or performance space the mask will be used for. For example the masks designed by Antonio Fava tend to be full of character and detail, as well as bold sculptural lines, and appear to work best for close-up and middle-range performances, as at a distance the more intricate details of the mask tend to get lost, whilst Stephano Perocco's masks are less finely detailed, but allow the actor a wider range of movement and mask interpretation as they tend towards larger bolder shapes, suitable for larger auditoriums and out of doors.

Building in clay

Building a mask form in clay should simply be a matter of scaling up your maquette to the size of an actor's face. One can always measure the most significant distances on the surface of the maquette and then proportionally increase them, or one can do it by eye. If you do the former an indispensable tool is either a pair of measuring callipers, or an old school drawing compass.

It is important to have in mind the edges of the mask at all times, so as not to hinder any later casting one might do from this block, and also so that the mask maker can get a good all-round look. Always place your clay block on a board strong enough to bear its weight and give a margin of around 4 inches (5 centimetres) around the edge, to take into account any later additions of plaster cast or similar, as well as having the back edge of the mask raised at least a couple of inches from the board. You may find it helpful to set wires into the buck and through the board so that you can stand it up later in order to look at the contours of the mask as it will be worn, rather than from an aerial perspective.

One can either construct the whole buck out of clay (using an armature or similar support if required), or else build up the features of the mask on a plaster likeness of the actor's face, the 'living death mask' described in the appendix to *Commedia dell'arte: An Actor's Handbook*. If you are spending a few days creating your mask buck in clay, then do not forget to dampen the clay every night with a little water and wrap it in a waterproof bag. Otherwise the clay will dry out and become very hard to work. The waterproof bag should be light enough not to crush the wet features of the mask block overnight.

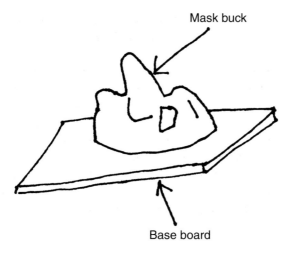

Mask buck

Base board

Figure 18 Mask making

Assemble a variety of tools, either bought or found, that will enable you to both shape and texture the surface of the clay you are working. Bits of bent wire are generally useful, as are teaspoons and chopsticks. Art shops will sell you similar tools at a far greater expense. Once you have this life-size sculpture of the mask you wish to create, the next step is to create some form of laminate to go over the top of it, which then can be removed to form the eventual mask. Depending on time, resources or artistic skill there are now various options open to you, which are described below.

Plaster bandage

This comes under the brand name of Mod-Roc in the United Kingdom and is available from most modelling shops, as it is a staple material for the manufacture of scenery for scale-model railways. It can also be obtained from medical suppliers as plaster cast bandage. In some ways it is the most unsatisfactory material to use, as when finished the material is quite thick and heavy for the actor to wear, and not that durable, but it does have the advantage that it is fairly easy to use for a beginner, and results can be obtained fairly quickly.

Starting with your sculpted block, one first has to put a barrier of Vaseline, petroleum jelly or cream aqueous between the block and the mask laminate one will later remove. This is to protect the block so that when you remove the mask from it, the laminate does not stick to it and consequently damage the buck so it cannot be used again. The use of such a barrier cream also makes the laminate slide off the block much more easily. Cover the buck, and supporting board around the edges of the buck, with a thin film, smoothing out lumps with your fingers making sure that all nooks and crannies are covered.

Next assemble a bowl of water, a pair of sharp scissors and the plaster bandage. Start by cutting the plaster bandage up into lots of different sized shapes, making sure that you have a series of long strips. These long strips will then be used to strengthen the edges of the mask, perhaps the weakest part of it. The shapes cut should correspond roughly with the surfaces and planes on the mask, allowing overlaps on the angles and features. Before applying the bandage to the block, position the bowl of water between the supply of ready cut bandage and the buck. This will stop you spilling drops of water on the unused bandage and rendering it unusable. Once you have put the plaster bandage in water it must be applied immediately, otherwise it will dry out, and once dried out is useless.

Having assembled your ingredients, piece by piece, dip the bandage in water and apply it to your Vaselined buck. Push it gently onto the form with your finger and smooth the surface, also gently, working the plaster in the bandage into a smooth finish. Make sure each piece overlaps the adjacent pieces for strength. When you have covered the entire mask with one layer, add the long strips all around the edge of the mask.

It will be necessary to put three or four layers of bandage on to achieve a reasonable strength. These should all be done in one session, rather than having to wait for one layer to dry before applying another, as with papier mâché. One should be methodical about layering the bandage on, so that the thickness and strength of the resulting mask will be uniform. It may become quite hard to remember which layer you are on sometimes, so it is often a good idea to put a dash of colouring pigment, such as poster paint, in the water between layers. That way each layer you put on will be a different colour and much easier to notice.

Note that plaster bandage is inherently quite thick, so that as you apply it to a male buck the intricate details you have sculpted may become obscured, and any sharpness of overall shape may be blurred. It may be necessary to recreate these details in the plaster bandage as you apply each layer. The material is quite forgiving for this kind of activity, but do not try for too fine detail since when dry plaster bandage is fairly brittle, and sharp edges and narrow details will swiftly degrade with use.

For the final layer take special care to smooth out the plaster with your fingers to achieve as good a surface as possible. After you have applied the final layer you must leave the whole structure to dry in a warm place. Clear up your tools and place your remaining plaster bandage in a waterproof bag for later. It is a good idea to empty the bowl outside since small particles of plaster, over a period of time, will most certainly block up most internal plumbing U-bends. A sculptor or model maker who works with plaster on a regular basis will very likely have a plaster trap built into their plumbing to avoid such blockages.

When the plaster is completely dry, then you can remove it from the block. You do this by the following method. Gently insert a narrow knife blade between the buck and the plaster bandage to a depth of half a centimetre, and gently move the blade all the way round the block, loosening as you go. When you have completed this, applying firm but gentle pressure, take the buck in one hand and the mask in the other and pull apart. Hopefully with a little gentle persuasion the two will come apart.

Several things could go wrong at this stage. The mask may not want to come apart from the buck. This may be because the plaster has not dried sufficiently, and so leaving it alone to dry for a bit longer may be the answer, or it may be because you need to loosen it a bit more with a blade, in which case do so. A major difficulty also might be if there is an amount of undercutting on the buck, so the actual shape of the buck is preventing the mask from sliding off. This is generally the case with large hooked noses. The way round this is to gently slide a narrow blade under the edge of the mask and try and cut through the clay or plasticine, so the mask will come off with the clay of the nose, or whatever undercut it was, still attached to it. Once this has been done, there are two more tasks. You must use a small spatula to clean out the residual clay from inside the mask, and to repair the buck if you want to take another cast off it.

Repairing the buck is fairly easy if you have your maquette still to hand, as it is simply a matter of redoing the sculpting. If you take this path, or even if you are storing the clay for another day, you must remove all the petroleum jelly or aqueous cream from the surface of the buck. If you do not, it will after a few uses degrade your clay severely. This is easiest to do with the blade of a blunt knife. Throw away this resulting sludge as there is no further use for it. Clay must be stored in a waterproof and airtight bag between uses.

When you have taken the plaster mask off the buck, the inside of it needs to dry out, so leave it in a warm place until the inside is touch dry. When it is, first using an old spoon, and then an old toothbrush for the smaller bits, clean out all traces of the petroleum jelly from the inside of the mask. Then take a sharp pair of scissors and trim any loose edges off the mask all the way round. When this process has been completed you are ready to cut the eye holes.

This task is the most risky one in making a mask, as a mistake here will ruin the mask completely, so great care must be taken at all times. One should decide on the shape and size of the eye holes first and then draw them to scale on a piece of paper. You cut these out and keep them. Meanwhile go to the person who is due to wear the mask, and measure the distance between their pupils. Mark this distance on the inside of the mask with a pencil, corresponding with the design of the mask, and then place the paper templates over them, centring them on the marks. Draw round these with a very sharp pencil and then remove them. It may help to keep them in place whilst you draw round them, so use a dab of water or Vaseline to hold them there.

To cut the eye holes out use a very sharp modelling knife, and cut in the following manner. Do not attempt to cut through the plaster in one, but first of all score a line gently in the desired shape. This will be a guideline for any further cuts. Next score around the eyeholes again, still gently, following the score made by the previous cut. Carry on this process until the eyeholes are cut. Resist the temptation to increase the pressure of the cut at any point, especially as you begin to get to the other side, as any slip here will result in a large cut that will ruin the shape of the eye. Once the eye holes have been cut, trim any loose bits of material that may be round the eye hole and put it on, and look at yourself in a mirror. You may want to make an adjustment and alter the shape or size of the cut at this stage.

To paint or decorate the mask it is suggested that you use dark organic colours at first, and copy other mask colour schemes to get the idea as to how it is done, before embarking on any radical new colour scheme. Use matt colours at first, and note that a few layers may need to be applied as plaster is fairly absorbent. Once you have painted it to your satisfaction, then varnish it inside and out to seal the mask. A partial gloss varnish is best as it catches the light and adds sparkle and life to the mask.

Once the mask is painted then you can add any decorations, animal fur hair, eyebrows or moustaches by gluing them on. The last thing left to do is to decide on how the mask is to be attached to the wearer. The most usual way for a mask of this kind is to use a haberdashery tool, which will punch a small hole in the edge of the mask and put a circular holed rivet in it, which elastic can then be passed through. The tension and length of the elastic is different for each person, so adjust the elastic on the person who is due to wear it. It is best to pass elastic through both the holes and then tie the two ends together to form a loop. This way there is a double strand of elastic holding the mask onto the wearer's head.

Vacuum forming

Vacuum forming is a technique, which if you have access to it, provides a source of identical cheap masks. The downside is that they are made of plastic and can be quite brittle. You need your clay buck to start off with, and need to make sure that there are no undercuts at all on it, as vacuum forming as a method cannot deal with them.

Most modelling or art departments in colleges, and often schools, will have a vacuum forming machine, and sometimes small packaging firms will have one as well. It functions by heating up a sheet of plastic and then forcing this sheet of plastic down over the buck or mould, forcing the plastic to take the shape of the mould. The thicker the sheet of plastic that the particular machine can handle the more durable the mask will be.

The mask can then either be used on its own, having carefully cut eye holes and elasticated it as above, or used as a wearable template to sculpt further upon, by adding papier mâché, putty, or some other bulking product. This is often a good way of checking how a particular design is going, by sculpting one version in clay and then vacuum forming a mask off it, and seeing how it works on an actor. That way you will know whether more modifications are needed.

The plastic sheets needed for vacuum forming come in various colours, which could give you the base colour for your mask.

Papier mâché

Papier mâché itself can either be a pulp made of water, glue and paper waste, or else a laminate of paper strips, water and glue. When dry it is light, durable and has, depending on the kind of glue used, varying degrees of rigidity. It is a longer process than working with plaster bandage, but the results are better as the mask is thinner, lighter and potentially capable of allowing greater detail. It is also capable of being finished so it can look like leather if you so wish, and this treatment provides an excellent finish.

The initial process, as regards creating a clay buck and then putting a barrier layer of Vaseline or similar, has been described in the section on plaster bandage. You should then decide on the kind of glue you are going to use to bind the papier mâché together. A conventional paper glue, such as Gloy, works well and has the following properties when finished: a rigid lightweight mask that has a fair degree of porosity so the skin of the actor beneath the mask can breathe. This makes for a slightly more comfortable wear, though the downside is that, being fairly rigid, the mask is also brittle, so will not survive being dropped very often. When painting, to maintain porosity, poster paints and inks, rather than acrylics or oils should be used.

If you need to create a more robust mask, that is more likely to withstand the rigours of performance, then you need a mask that has a certain degree of both flexibility and rigidity. For this end a wood glue such as Evostick or other PVA-based brand glue is recommended. This adhesive is slightly stronger than ordinary paper glue, and when dry has a slight spring to it that makes it more forgiving on the face and more durable. It is, however, not porous, so the actor's face breathes round it, rather than through it. This means that there will be build ups of perspiration behind the mask during performance which may be awkward, as getting an eyeful of salty water in the middle of a show is distracting and painful for the performer. This can be countered by putting in thin foam pads behind the mask to absorb sweat from the actor's face, but this really depends on the mask and the actor.

This mask can be painted with most materials as there is no need to maintain porosity. But since the mask is flexible, and not completely rigid, it is necessary to mix a small amount of Evostick or PVA in with the paint you choose. This will ensure that the layer of paint that you apply also has a degree of flexibility. If the paint does not have these properties, it will flake or chip off.

To start you will need a bowl of water once again, and this time lots of torn pieces of newspaper about an inch square. It is important that you tear the newspaper, rather than cut it, so the fibres in the newspaper are exposed at the edges. Pour PVA into the water at a ratio of 4:1 or even 3:1 of water to glue. Mix thoroughly till it achieves a uniform texture and fluidity.

Then take a single piece of newspaper, dip it in the fluid, until it is soaked through, and apply it to the buck. Repeat this process, smoothing each piece of glue-soaked paper down with your fingers on to the exact contours of the buck, so that each piece overlaps its neighbour slightly. Carry on until the entire surface area of the buck has been covered. You must repeat this process at least four times, until the buck has had four layers of glue-soaked paper put upon it. As with the plaster bandage method, an extra few strips round the known weak points in the mask, such as the bridge of the nose and where you will attach the elastic, are necessary. To keep track of how many layers you have put on, add small amounts of colour to the water, so that each layer is a slightly different colour, or use pink newspaper for alternate layers. For instructions as to how to remove the mask from the block, and to cut the eye holes, see the section on plaster bandage.

If you are in a hurry to produce your mask, then it is possible to use blotting paper, instead of newsprint, which is thicker, more absorbent and is slightly more malleable before it dries. It is, however, considerably more expensive than old newspapers, which are free.

Other materials

There are two other substances worth mentioning when creating a mask on a buck. The first is a substance not generally available in the United Kingdom any more called Celastic, and the second is a mixture of starch and scrim.

Celastic is an industrially produced substance similar to blotting paper, which comes in sheets, and can be cut up and treated like papier mâché. The problem with it is that it needs to be dipped in acetone, a powerful and very unpleasant chemical solvent, to activate it. This means that protective gloves must be worn, the making must be done outdoors or in a well-ventilated room, and all safety and storage instructions must be strictly kept to. It dries very quickly however, and is both strong and flexible, which does make it at least quick to work with, and often only two layers are needed. It is often used to make puppets, so ask your local puppeteer for a source of supply.

It is also possible to use a mixture of scrim (thin bandage-like gauze, or any other very thin material) that has been soaked in a strong starch solution. The resulting masks are very strong, but drying times are uncertain as they will depend on the strength of your starch solution and how many layers of scrim you are using. You should be aiming for a layer at least four millimetres (an eighth of an inch) thick.

Female plaster moulds

All the above techniques are concerned with creating a mask layer on the outside of your model, which is called a male mould, but when you are more sure of your designs a much better finish is obtained by using a female mould. A female mould is when the mask template is hollow and the inside of it becomes the outside of the mask. Consequently you are able to transfer all the details of your design onto your mask, and not just a proportional approximation of your original clay design. Papier mâché and Celastic are ideally suited for this technique, though plaster bandage and starch and scrim are not.

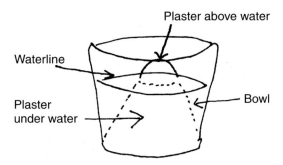

Figure 19 Mask making, mixing bowl filled with plaster

Having made your clay buck, and given it the best finish you can, you must then mount it on a piece of solid board or wood, which is proud of the buck by at least twelve centimetres (six inches) all round. Then put a layer of Vaseline or cream aqueous all over the buck, being careful not to damage the sculpture, and round the edge of the buck, as well as half way to the edge of the board as well. You then need to mix up your plaster of Paris. Flexible mixing bowls are best to use as they are easiest to clean afterwards. Fill two thirds with water and then pour the plaster in until it leaves a mound just sticking out of the water. Then mix the plaster up with a circular motion until it achieves a uniform creamy texture. Take a little of this mixture in your fingers, whilst still wet, and dribble it over the buck fairly quickly, letting the liquid plaster adhere to the buck. If you get the texture of the plaster right this will ensure a very detailed surface to the mask.

Wait a few moments until the plaster in the bowl begins to get warm (a sign that it is beginning to go off) and then take a handful of the by now slightly firmer substance and drop it on to the buck from a height of a few inches. Carry on this procedure until the buck is completely covered. The idea is that dropping the plaster onto the buck from a low height will both ensure that the plaster takes the form of the clay and that it will do so without damaging it or changing the original shape of your buck in any way. Ideally the buck should be at least 4 to 5 centimetres (2 inches) thick all over.

Leave overnight to dry, and clear up your tools, again making sure that any excess plaster is not washed down the sink. When you are sure that the plaster is completely dry, you first remove the base board, and when this has been removed, you carefully dig out the clay infill. The closer you get to the edge of the clay, the more careful you must be, so as not to damage the inside of the mould. Sometimes slabs of clay will come off very

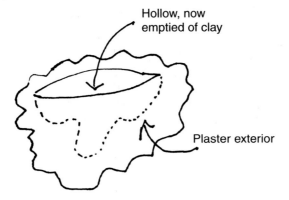

Figure 20 Mask making, female mould

easily, but sometimes you will have to apply gentle force with a thin blunt object to remove particles in deep lying areas. Once you have removed the majority of the clay, leave the inside of the mould overnight to dry again, and clean out, with a little detergent, all the remnants of Vaseline and clay. Once you have done this you are free to use your female mould much the same way as you would the male mould: apply a barrier layer to stop the papier mâché from sticking to the plaster, and then a few layers of your chosen laminate. The problem of getting the mask out once it is dry is overcome by extending the edge of the mask right up to the edge of the mould and loosening the mask with a blade in these areas only. These areas can be trimmed once the mask is out of the mould.

Leather mask makers

United Kingdom

Mike Chase
The Mask Studio
Ruskin Mill
Nailsworth
Gloucestershire GL6 OLA
e-mail: mask.studio@virgin.net
web page: www.mask-studio.co.uk

Ninian Kinnear-Wilson
32 Moscow Drive
Liverpool 13 7DH

Italy

Antonio Fava
Teatro del Vicolo
CP 404 Reggio Emilia

Stefano Perrocco
Via Avogrado 1
30035 Mirano (Venezia)

Donato Sartori
Centro Maschere e Strutture Gestuali
via Cesare Battisti 191
35031 Abano Terme (PD)
Padua

Denmark

Stephan Vernier
e-mail: zanni@vip.cybercity.dk

Australia

Jennifer Stannards
P O Box 754
Byron Bay
NSW 2481

USA

Newman
Commedia Mask Company
PO Box 1874
Takilma, Oregon 9735
e-mail: newnfool@cdsnet.net

Jim Letchworth
Commedia Tutti Frutti
e-mail: Zani4@aol.com

John Apicella
Bubulaires
e-mail: Bubalaires@hotmail.com

Appendix C

The stage

The most important features of a *commedia dell'arte* stage are that it should it be portable, be able to support a backdrop, be of sufficient height for the actors to be seen, and of sufficient size for the actors to be able to act upon. It should also have enough safe entrances and exits so that the pace of the action can be maintained, and be constructed of materials that fit with the style of theatre being played on it. It is possible to perform *commedia dell'arte* on a stage made of aluminium tubing and decking, but generally wood and organic materials are best. If your stage is made of aluminium scaffolding you will also have to tour materials to dress it with, so you might as well make honest use of wood in the first place.

Portable stages come in two varieties, those designed to be taken to bits to be transported and reassembled at the site of performance, and those designed to be transported in one piece. The former are more adaptable and, as the size of a *commedia dell'arte* stage doesn't vary very much, the next question is how large the individual sections of which it is composed should be. When deciding this it is paramount that you consider the size of van, trailer or whatever transport you will be using. By the way, old farm carts do look terrific to perform on, but are generally not roadworthy, and hence have to be towed on a large trailer as the axles and wheels are not designed for metalled roads and the rigours of touring. There is also the problem that the wheels get in the way of the sight lines.

A platform stage for Commedia is, roughly, 5 metres by 3 metres (plus backstage area if required). As an amount of rough and tumble will take place on it, the sections of which it is made up have to be fairly sturdy. If your van is of sufficient size then one can construct either three pieces of staging 3 metres by 1.67 metres, which lie side by side, or else four pieces in a box formation, each 2.5 metres by 1.5 metres.

Construct each individual deck section out of thick tongue and groove planking, so the weight of each plank supports the next. Secure the tongue and groove decking to the bearers with lost-head nails. Don't bother with

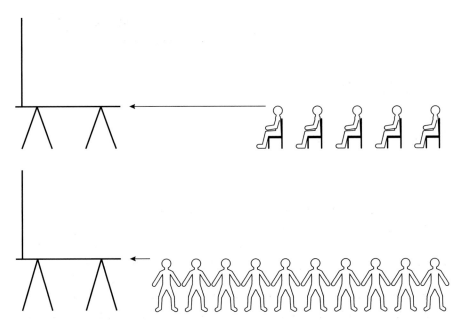

Figure 21 Overhead sightlines: (a) The eyeline of the seated audience should be roughly level with the height of the stage, therefore making all action on the stage visible to all seated audience. (b) Here the eyeline of the standing audience is level with the stage, making it possible for all people, whether audience or not to see the action. This allows casual passers-by to see the action, hopefully understand the action from the masks' physicality, and then come closer and become audience proper.

secret nailing through the tongues, but use a punch to drive the nails below the surface of the stage. Support each section with three struts going the length of the platform as the main load bearers, ideally with a 10-centimetre (4-inch) section. Run similar supports along both ends as well, so that you can bolt through them into adjoining sections. Use coach bolts (which are not threaded their entire length) with washers either end and wing nuts.

The height of the stage is also crucial, and will be reflected in the size of the trestles you build to mount your stage on. If your audience is generally sitting down, then your trestles only need to be one metre high, or the height of a seated person, but if the audience are standing then the trestles need to be the same height as the average person.

Theoretically it should be possible to build trestles that do both, as their height can be changed by how wide their legs are spread, but for building a first stage this practice isn't recommended. The trestles should be sturdy enough to support the weight of the stage platforms and the entire cast at

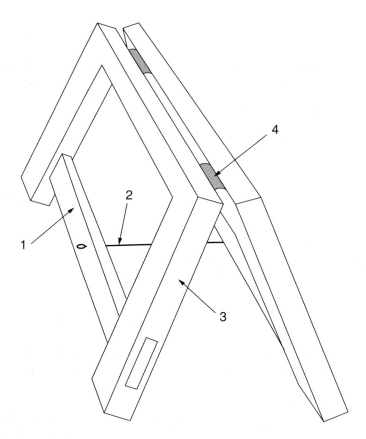

Figure 22 Stage construction

Trestle Diagrams Key (see also Figure 23)

1   Trestle cross piece
2   Rope at correct length for optimum trestle width
3   Trestle upright with jointed corners
4   Hinge placed on inside of trestle uprights
5   Trestle upright with jointed corners
6   Stage platform
7   Threaded bolt from top of stage to below hinge point on trestle uprights
8   Top of 7 countersunk in stage to provide level performing surface
9   Tie bar, through which 7 passes, and is of sufficient width to be proud of both sides of the trestle
10 Wing-nut, finger-tight, securing tie bar to 7, and hence to top side of stage platform
11 Guides into which trestle tops fit
12 Tie off point for rope or bungey, anchoring trestle top into guide grooves
13 Bungey or rope tied on underside of trestle top cross piece anchoring them in position in guide grooves
14 Pair of large gate hinges linking two halves of each trestle, secured to inside of trestle uprights.

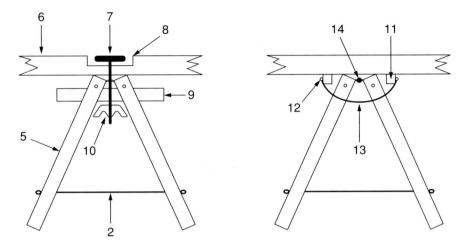

Figure 23 Stage construction (see Figure 22 for key)

once, ideally jumping up and down. The right angles of the trestle frames should be properly tenon-jointed by a carpenter, not plated. The simplest way of ensuring that the trestle legs stay the correct distance apart is by using a knotted piece of strong rope, and passing it through a predrilled hole in the trestle itself.

Two basic ways are suggested of attaching the trestle to the stage, the first being to attach guides to the underside of the stage platform for the trestles to slide into. These are then secured with rope (though gravity does most of the work). The second method is to drop bolts through the stage, passing through the gap in the trestles before being secured by washers and wing-nuts to a tie bar.

These descriptions are only intended as guidelines as to how to proceed, with some solutions offered as to specific often-encountered problems. It is always necessary to start with an exact scale drawing, access to the correct tools and skills, and a fair idea as to how much all the wood and iron-mongery will cost. Everybody usually wants a trap door as well – our advice is not to have one at first since they are a nuisance when not required. When a scenario does require one, have a separate section made up which is only toured for that show.

Access is another issue: you need a minimum of a get-off ladder or treads behind the drop, possibly access steps on either side at the front. The simplest form of these are 'open string', fitted to the edge of the stage with pelmet clips, but even then they will need to be made by a carpenter in order to get the treads and risers right in relation to your stage height.

If there is no room for stepladders back stage you will also need to consider one or two Jacob's ladders bolted to the back of the stage for entrances 'above'. It is usually best to have these welded in mild steel.

Appendix D

The backdrop

Having built your stage, next you need to provide it with a backdrop. The reasons for using a backdrop are quite straightforward. It provides a concealed place to make entrances from and exits to, as well as defining set theatrical areas such as Pantalone's house, Il Dottore's house, or Brighella's inn. Ideally one backdrop should serve most of the shows you ever do, though there may be some variations depending on the specific requirements of some scenarios. A backdrop is not a brick wall, nor should it simulate one. It has a living presence for the spectator because it is rarely still (especially when Brighella and Franceschina are having sex behind it).

As a design object it should serve as a neutral canvas against which the colourfully dressed Masks can be seen clearly: it should not, therefore, be too brightly adorned or too intricate in design. If you are performing out of doors, forget the Renaissance perspective sets, and settle for something non-representational. A backdrop is functional, not representational; its functionality has to do with the number of entrances required through it, the number of windows required within it, and the calculation that it is higher than the tallest performer fully costumed, given the overhead sight lines from the audience.

The colour should be generally uniform, but nevertheless not completely neutral and dull. Generally deep rich organic colours, rather than drab neutrals, make the stage and backdrop together a more interesting visual ground for the highlights of the costumes. On the other hand white (providing you can keep it white) can have an emphatic effect.

When creating design sketches for the backdrop and frame, it is a good idea to design specifically for one from one or another of the following options, as extensive sewing and carpentry in mid tour can be annoying: a stand-alone backdrop that needs no stage and can rest on the ground, a backdrop that is an integral part of the stage construction, and a hybrid that can fit both on to your stage and on the ground in its own right. Whatever you build and however many variations you wish to carry with you on tour do take note of the two most embarrassing (and yet infrequently mentioned) design parameters: don't make anything in a workshop that won't fit through the smallest venue door and make sure that, when disassembled, the longest item still fits in the van comfortably. When the Unfortunati stage was designed and built, it was created around what would fit inside a long wheel-base Ford Transit. The stage itself, divided into three, fitted in through the back doors. These three board sections rested on the six trestles which went on the van floor, and in the gaps between the trestles went the costume trunks. The stage ladders and the uprights went down the sides as packing, and three gym mats went over the top of the staging, providing a comfortable surface for actors to rest upon whilst 'in transit'.

Stand-alone backdrop

This must be able to go up both out of doors and indoors, and on a variety of surfaces. Therefore we can gratefully discount the idea of using guy ropes and tent-style pegs as a support mechanism for the uprights. Not only would theatre and tarmac car park owners feel badly towards you if you banged stakes into their sacred surface, but you would also be creating a series of potentially lethal obstacles to trip over whilst performing. A stand alone backdrop must be free standing.

Figure 24 presents a diagram of a free standing frame – designed by John Rudlin for various Commedia touring projects, and currently being used by *La Compagnie des Trois Oranges*. It has a firm base to sit upon, so is relatively stable, and this can be further stabilised indoors with stage weights or sandbags. Although there is an obstruction either side of the backstage area due to the triangular support braces, the performers can easily get used to not colliding with them, as this is the performing area which they will always be using.

It is built out of copper plumbing tubing (which is relatively easy to cut, either with a hacksaw or a rotary cutter), is relatively strong and is also easily available from most builders' merchants. Ideally if there are two diameters of pipe available, you make the main lengths out of the smaller diameter tubing, and buy the connecting 'T' pieces out of the slightly larger diameter tubing, so they will slide off and on with ease. If you only have one diameter of pipe available, connectors can be made out of the same diameter tubing, by making a saw cut along the length of the connector tube (see 7 in the diagram below) and expanding the width of the resulting cut pipe with a screwdriver.

Something you might consider is cutting the long pipes in half for ease of transport, and using a larger diameter (or saw-cut) sheath to link them

Backdrop exploded view

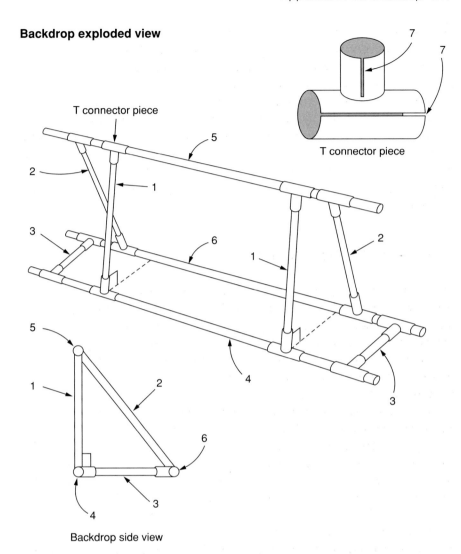

T connector piece

Backdrop side view

Figure 24 Backdrop frame design:

1   Pipes 1 metre long
2   Pipes 2 metres long
3   Pipes 2.25 metres long
4, 5, 6   Pipes 3 metres long
7   Cuts made in pipe sleeve, to allow same diameter pipe to be inserted either in or through

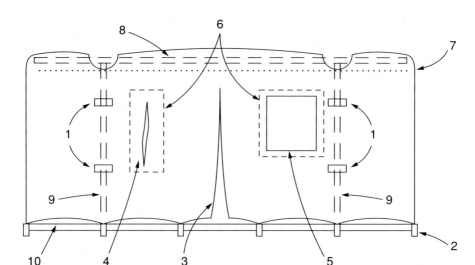

Figure 25 Front view of curtain showing construction details

1   Ties on the back of the curtain to connect it with the frame uprights
2   Ties on the bottom of the curtain to connect it with the ground-tube
3   Slit in curtain as middle entrance
4   Slit version of window
5   Square version of window
6   Shape of flaps needed for behind window slits, sewn to curtain at the top of flap only
7   Amount of curtain material needed to fold over and create a tube, so as the curtain can be suspended from the top tube
8   Position of top tube
9   Position of upright support
10 Position of Ground tube

together when you erect the stage. If you do this, insert a length of steel pipe or wooden doweling inside the pipe ends to take the strain: copper does bend if unsupported. Similar inserts can also be used at the offstage ends to extend the curtain bearing pipe and overcome the obstruction caused by the supporting triangles.

Calculating the exact lengths of tubing to buy is easy with a little bit of reference to Pythagoras, but a general principal is to have three long pieces the same width as your performance area, twelve 'T' piece connectors (not including spares, please note), two pieces to connect the front ground tube to the back ground tube, two pieces to connect the back ground tube to top tube, and two pieces to attach the top tube to the front ground tube.

With a stage width of around 6 metres, and an actor wearing a hat being just below two metres, try the following dimensions: three lengths of pipe 6 metres long (4, 5, 6), two lengths of pipe 2 metres long (1), two lengths of pipe 1 metre long (3), and two lengths of pipe 2.25 metres long. (2).

Once you have assembled your backdrop frame for the first time it is imperative, with the aid of different colour electrician's tape or similar, to mark all the ends of pipes that go to the same joint in the same way. As long as the tape or marking does not easily come off this will save an awful lot of time erecting the backdrop frame, and make the job of setting up for a show far easier. Instead of being a three-dimensional jigsaw puzzle of fear-some complexity, it becomes simply a matter of connecting up all the bits with the same colour.

Having constructed your frame, the next thing to do is to hang a back-drop on it. By far the easiest way to do this is to build the curtain with sleeves in it for the backdrop to slide through it. Ties should be sewed on at the bottom of the backdrop and also on the uprights to ensure that the curtain does not billow too much. All windows cut in this kind of backdrop should not simply be open holes, but be hemmed and have drapes behind them attached to the main curtain, so that they still mask actors backstage.

Fully attached backdrops

The main difficulty with backdrop frames attached to outdoor stages and their curtains is what to do about the wind. There are three solutions, all of which depend on the wind speed and strength. The first is to provide something of sufficient strength so that the wind does not blow it over; the second is to provide something that the wind blows round, and the third is to provide something that the wind blows through. The difficulty lies in making something that actors can hide behind and make entrances round or through, that doesn't flap alarmingly, dangerously or noisily, or in a worst case scenario become a sail and try to fly away. The solution to each of these problems will also depend on the practical and artistic choices made by the company. Some possible solutions are:

1   A backdrop gantry fully attached to stage by secured uprights (bolted at a secure point) with the curtain attached by a continual rope tie at the bottom.
2   A backdrop gantry fully attached to the stage by secured uprights (i.e. bolted at a strong point) and a curtain weighted down by moving weights, ideally a heavy chain. The aim being that if the wind does get up above what is expected, its pull on the curtain will lift the weights up, rather than rip the curtain or lift up the stage.

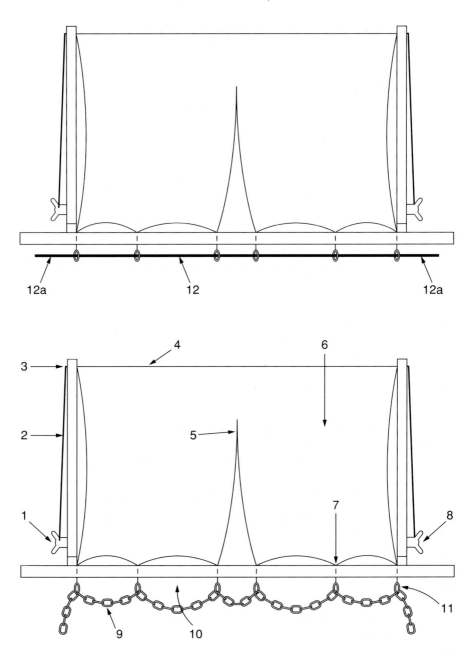

Figure 26 Backdrop gantry design (*continued opposite*)

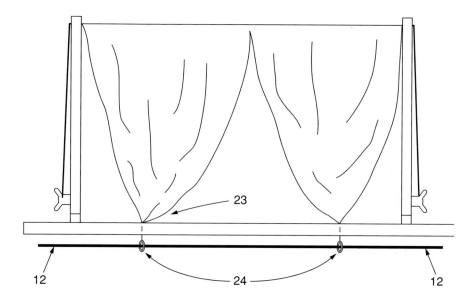

Figure 26 Backdrop gantry design

1   Stage right backdrop rope tie off point
2   Rope supporting curtain
3   Hole through gantry upright for curtain rope
4   Seam sewed in curtain for rope to pass through
5   Central entrance slit in curtain
6   Curtain
7   Curtain flush with stage at attachment point of cloth loop
8   Stage left backdrop rope tie off point
9   Weighted chain passed through, or otherwise attached to cloth loops
10   Stage underside
11   Cloth loop protruding through stage floor with chain passed through
12   Cloth loop protruding through stage floor with taut rope passed through
12a   leading to rope tie off point, possibly a cleat on underside of the stage
13   Depth of stage behind curtain
14   Backdrop gantry upright
15   Gantry support
16   Bolt holes to secure backdrop gantry to stage
17   Gauze or muslin curtain
18   Stage trestles, approximate positions
19   Gap between curtain and ladder up which actors must enter
20   Tie off point for backdrop to uprights
21   Stage uprights
22   Hinge and pin attachment for upright to back of stage
22a Hinge and pin attachment for upright to back of back trestle
23   Curtain bunched at bottom, flush with stage
24   All curtain loops passed through same hole in stage, held in place either by taut rope or
     chain

3   A backdrop gantry fully attached to the stage by secured uprights (as above) and the curtain gathered into artistic bunches, so as to allow the wind to blow through. These bunches can either be tied directly to the stage, or weighted. With this device one keeps the clear 'houses' and entrances and exits clear, although it becomes impossible to have a genuine surprise entrance for the audience. It is possible to design a backdrop and curtain that can do 1, 2 and 3.

4   A backdrop gantry that hangs at an angle over the back of the stage with a curtain made of netting or muslin so that the wind blows through it. The material has to be sufficiently light so as not to pose a danger for actors if it flaps about. Such a curtain can be dyed or decorated, but has to be of sufficient height that an actor, coming up from backstage, entering up steps or a ladder between the stage and the curtain, misses the curtain with his or her head. A problem for Capitanos with tall plumes! This method is applicable to quite high stages, with a good backstage area.

Appendix E

Costume

Commedia dell'arte costumes are extensions of the persona of the Mask, and should be treated as such when designing them. Whether your show is a 'make' or a 'find' (or a mixture of the two) keep in mind that the historical designs, and their associated colours, are what have worked best with the Mask up till now, and for good reasons. It is possible to create modern versions of the archetypes, but it is still advisable to keep to the outlines of the original or the Mask may refuse to 'live'. Remember that against a plain backdrop all colour on stage will come from the costumes. Obtain an offcut of your backdrop material and lay your colour swatch on it, both for each Mask, and then together with each other Mask normally encountered. Adjust as necessary, then compare them all together for the finale.

Fabrics should be made of natural fibre, not only from a historical point of view, but also because costumes made from them will 'breathe' better outdoors – and they will clean easier as well. When designing, take into account any particular movement characteristics or special abilities of the wearer, for example high kicks and acrobatics, or secret pockets that the scenario might demand. Have in mind, however, that costumes designed for a Northern European climate may be cause for medical concern when performing in Southern Europe in the summer. Thick wool and worsted are to be avoided.

The masked characters are the easiest to research, as their basic forms are well known, but to provide period character dress for the unmasked characters, (the Lovers, Colombina, Franceschina) you will need to start drawing. Since fashion is an important consideration, rather than the time-lessness of the masked characters, you can choose a period – any time from the sixteenth century to the present day, so long as the company are happy with the image and the movement implications. If drawing is not your forte, simple outlines will do, then glue or staple the fabric samples on.

Pattern cutting comes next. If you haven't done it before, this is not the time to start. If someone is going to do it for you they will supply you with

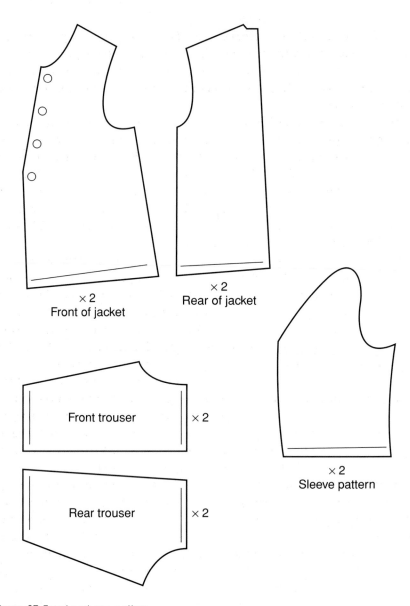

Figure 27 Zanni costume pattern

a chart for taking actors' measurements. Scale the pattern up on pattern paper, or even newspaper, then pin the pieces on to the hapless actor and adjust to fit. Lay the pattern on the fabric, taking the warp and weft into account, chalk round with tailor's chalk (don't forget to allow for seams and hems) and cut out.

Figure 27 shows a basic shape upon which the basic Zanni, Arlecchino and Brighella costumes can all be constructed. For Zanni, the costume stays white; for an early period Arlecchino sturdy patches of multicoloured cloth are sewn on; and for Brighella the green stripes of livery are added. The material should be strong, off-white and of a natural fibre with some weight to it. The earliest *zanni* clothes were made of flour sacks which had to be closely woven; judo suit material is today's nearest equivalent and has the same advantage of taking some of the pain out of tumbling.

Once sewn together using a suitable cotton, all these costumes require leather belts, as well as the relevant hats. Adapting finds from jumble sales and charity shops is recommended. Additional feathers are generally a must for the servants' hats, as historically they were both decorative and free. Not peacock or ostrich plumes, though, as these would be worn by the Lovers who had money to spare for such ostentation. The exception is Arlecchino who sports a rabbit scut. All also require money bags or pouches. Zanni should have had no buttons, Arlecchino simple wooden ones, and Brighella shiny metal ones. It is important that, although these characters are servants, their costumes must look beautiful on stage in their own right, stylised representations of dirty bedraggled and poor peasants, rather than actually being poor and bedraggled. All characters must wear either long white socks or stockings, the material of which should depend on social class.

Shoes are often thought about too late – actors need them early enough to get used to walking in them, but not so early that they start to ruin them. They must be right because in a lot of cases they are directly in the audience's eye line. If we don't believe in the shoes, why should we believe in the Mask? For this reason bare feet are out, even for the low-lifes, as they belong to the actor, not to the Mask. For the servants the important thing is that we don't notice their feet – and if the shoes aren't right we will. Il Capitano's performance, on the other hand, can be 'made' by the right boots, i.e. ones that we can't help noticing.

Appendix F

Songs and dances

The Gobi Dance
(rustic dance tune)

The Horse's Branle

(another rustic dance tune)

Rose, Rose

(a simple round)

Rose, Rose, Rose Red
Shall I ever see thee wed?
Aye, marry, that thou wilt
When I am dead

Pastime with Good Company

(probably composed by Henry VIII)

Pastime with good company
I love and shall until I die,
Grudge who will, but none deny,
So God be pleased, this life will I.
for my pastance,
Hunt, sing and dance;
my heart is set,
all goodly sport,
To my comfort,
who shall let me?

Youth will needs have dalliance
Of good and ill some pastance
Company me thinketh best
All thoughts and fancies to digest.
For idleness
is chief mistress

of vices all;
then who can say
But pass the day
Is best of all?

Company with honesty
Is virtue; and vice to flee
Company is good or ill,
But every man hath his free will.
the best I sue,
The worst eschew,
My mind shall be
Virtue to use,
Vice to refuse,
I shall use me

What If A Day
(Thomas Campion)

Melancholic ballad

What if a day, or a month or a year,
Crown thy delights with a thousand sweet contentings,
a thousand sweet contentings.
May not the change of a night or an hour
rob thy delight with as many sad tormentings,
as many sad tormentings?
Fortune, honour, beauty, youth,
are but blossoms dying.
Wanton pleasures, doting love,
Are but shadows flying.
All our joys, are but toys
Idle thoughts deceiving,
None hath power, of an hour
of his life's bereaving.

Th' earth's but a point of the world and a man
is but a point of the earth's compared centre,
the earth's compared centre.
Shall then the point of a point be so vain
As to triumph in a silly point's adventure,
a silly point's adventure.
All is hazard that we have
Here is nothing biding
Days of pleasure are but streams
Through fair meadows gliding.
Weal or woe, time doth go,
time hath no returning.
Secret fates guide our states
Both in mirth and mourning.

What if a smile or a beck or a look
Feed they fond thoughts with many vain conceivings,
many vain conceivings?
May not that smile or that beck or that look,
tell thee as well they are all but false deceivings,
all but false deceivings?
Why should beauty be so good
In things of no surmounting?
All her wealth is but a shroud,
nothing of accounting.
Then in this there's no bliss,
which is vain and idle,
Beauty's flowers have their hours,
Time doth hold the bridle.

What if a world, with a lure of its wealth,
Raise they degree to a place of high advancing,
A place of high advancing?
May not the world by a check of that wealth,
Bring thee again to a low despised changing,
a low despised changing?
While the sun of wealth doth shine
Thou shalt have friends plenty;
but come want, they repine,
not one abides of twenty!
Wealth and friends holds and ends
As they fortune rise and fall,
Up and down, smile and frown,
Certain is no state at all.

Pavane: Belle qui tiens ma vie

(slow, courtly dance and/or part song
from Orseographie, *Thoinot Arbeau, 1589)*

Last two lines repeated on each verse

Belle qui tiens ma vie
Captive dans tes yeux
Qui m'as l'ame ravie
D'un soube-riz gracieux
Viens tot me secourir
Ou me faudra mourir

Approche donc ma belle
Approche toy ma belle
Ne me sois plus rebelle
Puisque mon coeur est tien
Pour mon mal appaiser
Donne moy un baiser

Pourquoi suis tu, mignarde
Si je suis pres de toy?
Quand tes yeux je regarde
Je me perde dedans moy
Car tes perfections
Chanent mes actions

Je meurs mon Angette
Je meurs en te baisant
Ta bouche tant-doucette
Va mon bien rauissant
A ce coup mes espris
Sont tous d'amour aspris

Tes beautez et la grace
Et tes divins propos
Ont echauffe la glace
Qui me geloit les os
Et ont remply mon coeur
D'une amoureuse ardeur

Plustot on verra l'onde
Contre mont reculer
Et plustot l'oeil du monde
Cessera de bruler
Que l'amour qui m'epoinet
Decroisse d'un seal poinet.

Mon ame souloit
Libre de passions
Mais amour s'est faiset maitre
De mes affections
Et a mis sous sa loy
Et mon couer et ma foy

O Mistress Mine

(Composer anon.)

from Twelfth Night *by William Shakespeare*

O mistress mine, where are you roaming?
O mistress mine, where are you roaming?
O stay and hear your true love's coming
That can sing both high and low
Trip no further, pretty sweeting;
Journey's end in lover's meeting
Every wise man's son doth know.

What is Jove? 'tis not hereafter
What is Jove? 'tis not hereafter
Present mirth has present laughter
What's to come is still unsure
In delay there lies no plenty
Then come and kiss me, sweet and twenty,
Youth's a stuff will not endure.

Other sources to consult

Any edition of Playford's *The Dancing Master*.

Any edition of Thoinot's *Orseographie*.

Mabel Dolmetsch, *Dances of England and France 1450–1600*, Routledge and Kegan Paul, 1949.

S. A. J. Bradley, *Sixty Ribald Songs from Pills to Purge Melancholy*, Andre Deutsch, 1968.

Cecil J. Sharp, *Country Dance Tunes*, Novello and Company.

Notes

Part I

1   *Hallam's Introduction to the Literature of Europe*, London, 1901, vol. 2, p.502.

2   Paul C. Castagno, *The Early Commedia Dell'Arte, 1550–1621, The Mannerist Context*, American University Studies, Series XXVI, Theatre Arts, vol. 13, New York, Peter Lang, 1994, p.66 (quotation wrongly attributed by Castagno).

3   Kenneth Richards and Laura Richards, *The Commedia dell'Arte, a documentary history*, Oxford, Blackwell, 1990, p.45.

4   Hugo Albert Rennert, *The Spanish Stage in the Time of Lope de Vega*, New York, Dover, 1963, p.129.

5   Ibid. p.140.

6   E. Rigal, *Entremeses*, ed. Rosell, Paris, n.d., vol. 2, p.214.

7   *La Piazza Universale*, Venice, 1585.

8   Bartoli, *Notizie istoriche*, 1782, quoted Richards and Richards, op. cit., p.220.

9   1655, vol. 2, p.37.

10   The normal charge was two *sols*.

11   Virginia Scott, *The Commedia dell'arte in Paris 1664–1697*, University of Virginia,1990, p.16.

12   Brotherhoods who (unlike the Parisian *Confrèrie de la Passion* who pocketed their profits) used their funds to run hospitals for the poor.

13   N. D. Shergold, 'Ganassa and the Commedia dell'arte', *The Modern Language Review*, LI, 1956, p.360.

14   Ibid.

15   *Epistolario*, ed. A. G. de Amezua, Madrid, 1943, vol. 4, p.18.

16   Richards and Richards, op. cit., p. 219.

17   Shergold, op. cit., p. 361.

18   Also, for example, in 1581 *Los Italianos Nuevos* (also called *Los Corteses*) toured Spain. This seems to have a company led by Massimiano Milanino and Marc Antoine Scotivelli,

since the latter and his wife, Maria Imperia, appeared as executors for another actor who is known to have been killed in a brawl in Madrid on 19 October 1592.

19   According to Castagno, op. cit., p.69, the allusions are even more complex: 'fêr' means 'forge', but could refer to férie, 'festival', or 'holiday', or even to fare, 'to make'.

20   A satire on the burghers of Piombino in Florence. Salimbeni invented the role which was later taken up by Gaultier Garguille in France.

21   The Calendar of State Papers, quoted by Allardyce Nicoll, The World of Harlequin, Cambridge, 1963, p.166.

22   Winifred Smith, The Commedia dell'arte, New York, 1912, p.148, no source given.

23   Henri, the third son of Henri II and Catherine de' Medici was 'elected' to the throne of Poland in 1573, largely due to his mother's influence. He went there reluctantly and, on death of his brother, Charles IX, escaped from his Polish subjects (who attempted to retain him by force) and returned to France, but not before first dallying awhile in Italy.

24   Porcacchi, 1574, quoted Cesare Molinari, La commedia dell'arte, Mondadori, Milan, 1985, p.114.

25   H. A. L. Fisher, The History of Europe, Eyre & Spottiswood, London, 1935, vol. 2, p.576.

26   Pierre de L'Estoile, 1577, quoted Ferdinando Taviani, Le Secret de la Commedia dell'arte, Buffoneries, Paris, 1984, p.255.

27   Ibid.

28   Ibid.

29   There was one comédienne de profession in the sixteenth century, Marie Fairet, the wife of Michel Fasset. Otherwise ' . . . women appeared occasionally in Paris theatres, but always representing the Queen – the parts of soubrette, nurse, and old women's roles being always played by men.' E. Rigal, Le Théatre Français avant le Période classique, Paris, 1901, p. 55.

30   Smith, op. cit., p.150.

31   Ibid., p.151, no source given.

32   This occasion is celebrated in a poem in G. Borgogni's Rime di diversi celebri poeti dell'etá nostra, Bergamo, 1587, p.310, but there is no mention of when it took place.

33   Luigi Rasi, I Comici, quoted Richards and Richards, op. cit., p.76.

34   Ibid.

35   Smith, op. cit., p.175.

36   Lea, op. cit., p.265.

37   Lea, op. cit., p.272.

38   G. B. Rosetti, Dello scalco, Ferrara, 1584, quoted Allardyce Nicoll, Masks, Mimes and Miracles, reprinted Cooper Square, New York, 1963, pp.310–11.

39   Cited in Armand Baschet, *Les Comédiens italiens à la Cour de France*, Paris, 1882, p.244.

40   Pierre Louis Duchartre, *The Italian Comedy*, Harrap, London, 1926, p.96.

41   Lea, op. cit., p.269.

42   Molinari, op. cit., p.144.

43   Lea, op. cit., p.199.

44   Quoted Richards and Richards, op. cit., p.222.

45   Rennert, op. cit., p.142.

46   Lea, op. cit., p.294.

47   Ibid., p.293.

48   Letter from G. Z. Hondedei, quoted Lea, op. cit., p.295.

49   Quoted in Allardyce Nicoll, *Masks, Mimes and Miracles*, reprinted Cooper Square, New York, 1963, p.317.

50   Rasi, quoted Lea, op. cit., p.297.

51   Ibid.

52   Ibid.

53   Castagno, op. cit., p.68.

54   Ibid.

55   Scott, op. cit., p.20.

56   Tallémant des Réaux, quoted Enid Welsford, *The Fool*, Faber and Faber, London, 5, p.292.

57   Lea, op. cit., p.280.

58   Allardyce Nicoll, *The World of Harlequin*, Cambridge, 1963, p.175.

59   Duchartre, op. cit., p.94.

60   Ibid.

Part II

1   Interview with Olly Crick, 3/12/98.

2   Interview with Olly Crick, 16/11/98.

3   Ninian Kinnear-Wilson, John Broadbent, Eric Atkinson and Diane Dodd.

4   Mr Punch, dissatisfied with his lot in life, plans a burglary with his friend, which is then completed with the obligatory householder murdered. He then murders his accomplice and tries to molest the late friend's wife. He is captured by the police, kills the policeman and arresting magistrate, and finally manages to evade St Peter and the Devil who both try to claim his soul.

5   The plague is raging. Dr Burymore has patented a cure which Pantalone adulterates and sells at great profit. Unknown to them Brighella further adulterates the medicine and the plague victims' suffering increases. A young divinity student and Pantalone's daughter try to put things right but it takes the Doctor's mad sister to finally recover her marbles for a happy ending for all to be achieved.

6   See explanation under **Desperate Men**.

7   Didi Hopkins, interview with Olly Crick, 28/1/2000.

8   Ibid.

9   Fully entitled *Mr Jeromeo's Illustrious Tragedians Perform Tonight the Farce of 'The Flying Doctor' for HM the Queen and her Court.*

10   Sally Brookes, Sophie Matthias, Nina Peterson. Belinda Sykes also joined the group on occasion as an off-stage musician during this year.

11   Translated extract from a review of the Fortunati's *Beyond the Mirror* at the ASTRA theatre in Vicenza by Antonio Stefani, *Il Giornale di Vicenza*, Tuesday 15 November 1988.

12   This company, under artistic director Mike Alfreds, had recently completed an adaptation of several of Il Ruzzante's plays entitled *Comedy without a Title*, first performed on 17 May 1983 at the Theatre Belgrade in Coventry. The following is extracted from Alfreds' programme notes:

> Although he has the reputation of being a precursor of *commedia dell'arte*, Ruzzante wrote essentially realistic plays, comic in tone, but disturbing and moving in their content. His Commedia reputation probably rests on the character he created for himself to play, the quintessentially self-deceiving coward who exploits every situation to his best advantage and then attempts to justify his behaviour in terms of idealism. The basic theme is, after all, survival at all costs in the face of famine, war, harsh elements and infidelity.

13   Stratford-upon-Avon, Henley-upon-Thames, Cambridge and the Edinburgh Fringe.

14   Letter to Olly Crick, 30/9/1999.

15   The complete **Moving Picture Mime Show** play list is as follows: *The Seven Samurai, Creatures from the Swamp, The Examination, City Limits, Handle with Care, Intimate Hopes and Terrors, The Compleat Berk* (directed by Ken Campbell), *Passionate Leave* and *The Generalissimo*.

16   The half-masks used in this production were all made by the cast, based upon *commedia dell'arte originals*, but all given names of Italian cars, such as Maserati, Bugatti, Fiat except of course, the very repressed and very English, Morris Minor.

17   The cast was as follows: Tony Haase, from Cliffhanger Theatre, Tamsin Heatley, from Lumière and Son, Richard Hawley, from the Impact Theatre collective, Peta Lily from Three Women Mime and Toby Sedgewick.

18 Mask maker and artistic director of Geese Theatre Company, specialising in theatre work in prisons. Also collaborated with the **Unfortunati** and occasionally performed with the **Fortunati**, when Sarah Nixon was unavailable.

19 Also present in the workshop and performance were David Gaines, ex-**Moving Picture Mime Show**, and Ben Keaton.

20 Antonio Fava from the programme of *Love is a Drug*, collated by Renata Allen, the show's dramaturg.

21 Isabella feigns death to avoid an unsuitable husband chosen by her father. Her real lover searches for her body in the cemetery at midnight, with his servant Pedrolino, but she is nowhere to be found. Both she and her lover go mad, but which one is feigning? As the story gets more and more comic, the actors backstage argue over which is the greatest form of drama, comedy or tragedy.

22 Interview with Olly Crick, 27/11/1998.

23 Geoff Beale and Howard Gayton, 'The Use of Language in Commedia dell'Arte', *Theatre Research International*, vol. 23, no. 2, Summer 1998.

24 Pantalone is searching for the philosopher's stone. He is aided by his servant Pedro Muscadet, who persuades Pantalone that the only kind of experiment worth doing is the kind that involves Pedro being given money to go and buy expensive ingredients. Meanwhile Pantalone's son, Octavio, falls in love with Isabella. As part of Pedro's plan to totally fleece Pantalone, he convinces Pantalone to marry the first person who comes along. Pedro plans to be in drag, however Isabella arrives to see Octavio before Pedro has time to disguise himself. Pantalone imprisons her and banishes his son, as a rival. Mr Spavento and second Zanni, Molly, have to sort out the situation. Everyone ends up in disguise except Pantalone, who ends up marrying Isabella's servant Claudia. Isabella and Octavio marry and another happy ending is achieved.

25 Interview with Olly Crick, 16/3/1999.

26 E-mail to Olly Crick, 16/1/1999.

27 Peter Lathan – *your About.com Guide to: British Theatre*.

28 Review by James Williams.

29 E-mail to Olly Crick, op. cit.

30 Il Dottore (the *Vétérinaire Extraordinaire*) was first played by John Gribbin, then by Marc-Olivier Girard; Arlecchino by Jane Sutcliffe, then Juliano Periera; Colombina, Claire Bullet; Pantalone, Alex Sarbeni; Zanni, Dave Rogers; Lovers, Alban Hall and Amanda Speed; Petit Pierre (Pedrolino), Fraggle.

31 From *Commedia dell'arte and the Actor* by Mazzone-Clementi, from *Mimes and Miming* ed. Bari Rolfe, 1980, Panjandarum Books, Los Angeles, California.

32 From 'The Redwood Curtain', a booklet produced by the company.

33   Ibid.

34   Currently there are Renaissance Fairs happening in the following states, most of whom have their own websites, which generally, if not always, will give details of performing troupes. The number in brackets refers to the number of fairs in that state. Alaska (1), Alabama (1), Arkansas (1), Arizona (2), California (24), Connecticut (2), Florida (13), Georgia (1), Iowa (7), Idaho (1), Illinois (3), Indiana (2), Kansas (2), Louisiana (1), Massachusetts (4), Maryland (1), Maine (1), Michigan (1), Minnesota (1), Missouri (1), Montana (1), North Carolina (2), New Jersey (2), New Mexico (4), Nevada (3), New York (5),Ohio (5), Oklahoma (3), Oregon (2), Pennsylvania (2), Tennessee (2), Texas (8), Utah (1), Vermont (1), Virginia (1), Washington (6) and Wisconsin (1). There is also one in Ontario, Canada.

35   Members of both troupes have been Ernesto Maldonaldo, Donna Yarborough, Paul Joiner and Aaron Johnson.

36   Letter from Ernesto Maldonaldo to Olly Crick, 7/2/2000.

37   In the Spring and in the Fall, there are fairs in Southern and Northern California, in San Bernadino and Novato respectively. These, the Renaissance Pleasure Faires are the largest and oldest of the re-enactment/craft fairs in the United States, started in 1963. They were the brainchild of Phyllis Patterson and the non-profit organization Living History Center (LHC).

38   As well as both Drew and Jim Letchworth, their third brother Lee joined the company as a juggler, with his juggling partner Lee Grodsky. In this show, Drew played Pulchinella, the two Lees played the Baker and his nameless assistant respectively. Barbara Reinertson played Colombina. Jim played Pantalone, current San Francisco Mime troupe member Ed Holmes played Arlecchino, and long-term and current collaborator, Paul Harkness played *Il Dottore*.

39   The company now also included three male film and television actors, Jack Tate, John X. Heart and Richard Dupell, and two actresses, Marilyn Prince (who had previously worked with John Achorn in Theatre of Marvells), and Judith Harding, who hadn't, but was the partner of Arlecchino, Ed Holmes.

40   All the men from this disbanded company, except Jim, went on to appear in the film, *The Right Stuff* as I Fratelli Bologna (the Bologna Brothers).

41   With Jim Bohlin, Stu White and Bruce Parry.

42   Larry Williams, stand-up comic and member of improv group, Loose Change, as Leandro, Nito Wilson as Il Dottore, Joreth Torpov as Arlecchino, Megan Kenyon as Circe, Marilyn as Colombina, Jim as Brighella, Paul Tracy as Prospero, Barbara Tracy as Miranda/Isabella, together with Avis Minger and Dave Miles on accompanying fiddle and percussion respectively.

43   With members of the company, doubling and tripling roles to make this happen.

44   This new version featured Letchworth as Arlecchino, Joreth as Brighella (a straight role swap, so Letchworth could kiss his wife on stage), Marilyn Prince as Colombina, Jeff Hixon as Leandro, Teresa Mariani as Isabella, Jeanne Thomas as Circe, Bob Taxin as Prospero, Paul Harkness as Il Dottore. Nito Williams moved to percussion and the late 'Stripes' played mandolin.

45   Larry Williams and wife Kim Williams as Leandro and Isabella or Franceschina, Letchworth and Prince as Arlecchino and Colombina, Jim Bohlin as Il Dottore and Joe Mueller as Pantalone and Pulchinella.

46   New musician, Jody Veahman, was also added on mandolin.

47   Larry Williams as Leandro, Paul Harkness as Il Dottore, Judy Severns as Isabella, Paul Scherman as Pantalone/Punchinella, Guy Tartaro as Il Capitano and Jody Veahman and Misha Segal on mandolin and guitar respectively.

48   From a letter to Olly Crick, 26/10/1999.

49   Ibid.

50   Ibid.

51   Ibid.

52   Ibid.

53   The company has taught classes and/or coached such groups as the Cleveland Signstage Theater, the Harlequin Players, the National Conservatory of Dramatic Arts, the Maryland Renaissance Festival's Young Actors Ensemble, and the Colorado Renaissance Festival.

54   John Glennard, interview with Olly Crick, 26/1/1999.

55   Ritchie Smith, interview by Olly Crick, 16/2/1999.

56   Ibid.

57   The Mayor owns a fountain of clean drinking water. Rather than share this vital commodity he decides to claim it for himself and instructs his servant to charge money to people who need the water. The old peasant is refused water, and his daughter tries to sort out the situation, falling in love with the Mayor's servant. The well suddenly dries up and the Mayor blames his servant for the catastrophe. The by-now thirsty Mayor buys bottled water from a wandering medicine woman to survive, and a spring on the edge of performance area suddenly comes to life. As this occurs the bottled water he has bought turns to dust in his mouth. The Gypsy, Old Man and Disgraced Servant all drink from this new spring as the Mayor advances on them with a gun. There is a fight and the Gypsy is shot. The Mayor scares them away, drinks from their water cup and exits, leaving the dead body behind.

58   I Sebastiani mission statement, as laid out on their web page.

59   A classically-trained actor's collective with the desire to become Los Angeles' resident theatre company. Visit their website for more details: www:antaeus.org

60   John Apicella, Rob Watzke, Helen Slater, Laurie Kilpatrick and Alice Vaughan. John Apicella also makes the leather *commedia dell'arte* masks which the company occasionally uses.

61   Two out of the company, however, John Apicella and Helen Slater, name their primary source of income as being professional actor.

62   'The challenge is a fair and tempting one.' The company reaction to this comment in a draft version of this article sent to the company.

63   http://www.to/commedia/

64   The University of Houston, the University of Texas, Columbia University, South West Texas University and the South Western University.

65   The Texas Renaissance Festival, the Sterling Renaissance Festival, Scarborough Fayre. Extract from letter to Olly Crick, 20/12/99.

67   Melbourne Maskworks was incorporated in 1992. Its artistic director and associated artists were engaged in the design, making, performing, teaching and promotion of masks until December 1998. Melbourne Maskworks' theatre productions used mask versions of classics by Molière, Voltaire and Shakespeare, as well as well-known fairy tales to create highly energetic, usually comic, physical theatre.

68   It is Carnival time in Venice and Pantalone is preparing a huge feast to celebrate. He has invited Capitano Spavento, not only to partake of the festivities, but also to consider marrying his daughter Isabella. Isabella discovers this and is mortified. Arlecchino and Brighella comfort her, but they do nothing to help her plight. Instead they spend their time playing tricks on each other and Pantalone because it is carnival. When Il Capitano arrives he enlists Arlecchino's help to woo Isabella. Therefore Arlecchino disguised as the evil criminal Los Banditos del la Mancha comes to challenge Il Capitano to a duel. They fight. The Capitano wins. Isabella however, discovers it is Arlecchino and leaves in a huff. Meanwhile the real Los Banditos (Brighella) comes into the picture. A chase ensues, with Arlecchino finally defeating the criminal.

69   CO.AS.IT: *Comitato Assistenza agli Italiani,* or The Italian Assistance Committee

Part III

1   See the scene analysis in Tim Fitzpatrick, *Commedia dell'arte and Performance: the Scenarios of Flaminio La Scala,* Renaissance Drama Newsletter Supplement 5, Graduate School of Renaissance Studies, University of Warwick, Autumn 1985.

2 'The use of Music in *Commedia* performance' (in *Theatre Symposium. A Journal of the Southeastern Theatre Conference*, vol. 1, 1993, pp.7–12).

3 See Paul C. Castagno, *The Early Commedia Dell'Arte*, Peter Lang, New York, 1994, *passim*.

4 *The Relationship of Oral and Literate Performance Processes in the Commedia Dell'Arte*, Edwin Mellen Press, 1995.

5 Isabella Andreini, 'Fragmenti di alcune scriture . . .' (Turin, 1621), quoted Richard Andrews, *Scripts and Scenarios, the Performance of Comedy in Renaissance Italy*, Cambridge, 1993, p.191.

6 Orazio Vecchi's *Amphiparnaso,* a typical Commedia scenario set to music with duets, trios and quartets, was performed at the Bavarian court of William V in 1597. Adriano Banchieri's *La Pazzia Senile*, a similar work, was first published in 1598 and reprinted the following year – which gives some indication of the vogue for the elision of the two forms.

7 Pierre Louis Duchartre, *The Italian Comedy*, Harrap, London, 1926, p.73.

8 *Lazzi*, Performing Arts Journal, New York, 1983. (You will search this book in vain, however, for useable *lazzi*. The historical examples given are for the most part better used as impro cards. Watch Laurel and Hardy instead.)

9 John Greenwood, quoted Castagno, op. cit., p.147.

Index

Bold italicised page numbers refer to illustrations